THE SIEGE PERILOUS

MITHRA SLAYING THE BULL
(from the Heddernheim bas-relief)
see Chapter VI

The Siege Perilous

ESSAYS IN BIBLICAL ANTHROPOLOGY

AND KINDRED SUBJECTS

S. H. HOOKE

S C M PRESS LTD
56 BLOOMSBURY STREET
LONDON

First published 1956

Printed in Great Britain by
Robert Cunningham and Sons Ltd.
Longbank Works, Alva, Scotland

Contents

The reproduction of 'Mithra Slaying the Bull' is by permission of the Curator of Sammlung Nassauischer Altertümer, Wiesbaden.

To

W. R. MATTHEWS

with gratitude and affection

from

S. H. HOOKE

Introduction

To anyone who rashly adventures upon the reading of this book it may seem to be a curious assortment of unrelated essays. As a *captatio benevolentiae*, and to some extent an explanation, I venture to offer a fragment of autobiography. In 1930 I appeared before a selection committee of the University of London as a candidate for the position of Samuel Davidson Professor of Old Testament Studies. The chairman of the committee was the late Bishop Gore. Looking benignant and apostolic he gently asked me what I intended to do with the professorship if I should be appointed. I replied, somewhat optimistically, that I wished to try and build a bridge between the three disciplines of Anthropology, Archaeology, and Biblical studies. In spite of such presumption I was appointed to the chair, and during my twelve years' tenure and since my retirement I have endeavoured to carry out, however inadequately, that purpose. The papers here collected, in their diversity, represent the results of my attempt, and it is the purpose underlying the attempt which gives to the book any unity it may possess. Some of the papers represent tentative and exploratory positions which I no longer occupy, and which belong to the beginnings of what has come to be called 'patternism'. I remember when the paper entitled 'Some Parallels with the Gilgamesh Story' appeared in *Folk-Lore* in 1934, the late Vernon Bartlet of Mansfield College, Oxford, wrote to me a passionate appeal not to go on doing this kind of thing. In the long period of twenty-five years which have passed since the appointment mentioned above, I have made many friends, some no longer living, but many still here, with whom I have shared the adventures and explorations which these papers faintly recall. Among them there is one dear friend whose help and encouragement never failed from the first, then Dean of King's College, London, and now Dean of St Paul's, Dr

[7]

W. R. Matthews, to whom I dedicate this book in all gratitude and affection.

I have to acknowledge gratefully the kind permission of the S.P.C.K., the Sheldon Press, the Folk-Lore Society, the Society for Old Testament Studies, the editors of *Antiquity*, *Vetus Testamentum*, *Sobornost*, and *The Modern Churchman*, to reprint the various papers which make up this book. I have also to thank Mr Ronald Gregor Smith and the Board of the Student Christian Movement Press for their enterprise in giving this undistinguished book a place among their distinguished publications.

S. H. HOOKE

Twickenham, April 1955

CHAPTER ONE

The Siege Perilous[1]

IN Malory's *Morte d'Arthur* we read of that famous chair made by Merlin, called the 'Siege Perilous', in which none might sit save Galahad, on pain of being destroyed.

Having committed myself to the perilous adventure of occupying this presidential chair whose cyclopean proportions are better suited to the massive learning so lightly carried by my distinguished predecessor than to my own very slender pretensions to scholarship, I feel in danger of the fate of the frog whose ill-starred efforts to make good his natural deficiencies still serve to point a moral and adorn a cautionary tale.

It is surely the duty of anyone who represents the Folk-Lore Society to be respectful of tradition, and I have observed that tradition prescribes that a presidential address should bear something of an oracular character. There is comfort, however, in the reflection that not only from the Dodonian oak might an oracle go forth, but even from the lowly reed; and there is further encouragement in remembering that there was an annual occasion, in those ampler days when the ritual pattern dominated men's lives more completely than in these more amorphous times, wherein a person of no account might find himself elevated for a brief space to the heady eminence of a king, if only a festival one. For a short time he could with impunity indulge in the luxury of saying what he thought about his betters. It is true that he came to a bad end, being despoiled of his brief dignity and slain, presumably for the good of the crops. But he probably thought it was worth it.

The perilous seat, however, to which reference has been made, is not this presidential chair to which I have jestingly compared it. It is a metaphor for that 'bad eminence' occupied

[1] Presidential Address to the Folk-Lore Society, 1936. First published in *Folk-Lore*.

[9]

by what has been called the 'historical school' of anthropologists. It is an exposed position, much subject to bombardment from long-range heavy artillery, and it is not without some hesitation that I devote this paper to a defence of the historical approach to the studies of which the science of folklore forms a branch of considerable importance. It is not without justification that the British school of anthropologists, with its tendency to the *via media* and its preference for the rare virtue of common sense, has directed its criticism against certain extravagant claims on the part of the historical school.

In his review of Professor Rose's admirable Frazer Lecture on *Parallels*, Dr Marett playfully describes the historical school, so-called, as professing to clothe the naked and provide with histories those poor folk who have none of their own. There is truth in his not unkindly satire. But it is encouraging to observe that my predecessor in his two presidential addresses, and that eminent archaeologist, Professor Gordon Childe, in his presidential address to the Prehistoric Society last year, both show the way to the proper use of the historical method in the study of human behaviour. The latter address demonstrates most admirably the interdependence of the functional and the historical methods of dealing with cultural phenomena, and it is unfortunate that they should ever have been regarded as antagonistic.

If I may draw an analogy from the kindred science of Archaeology, the functional method followed by most anthropologists to-day may be compared with the surface method of excavation, which consists of removing the whole of a definite habitational layer from a given site and considering its evidence as constituting a picture of human life as it was lived at the particular period represented by that excavational layer. But no modern archaeologist would dream of considering the evidence of a single excavational layer apart from its relation to other habitational layers above and below it.

The time element in the problem of reconstructing a complete picture of human life in any given site can only be determined by the stratigraphical method of excavation. A trench cut through an ancient inhabited site will lay bare the successive layers of habitation and expose to the eye of the observer the sequence of time changes through which the culture of that particular site has passed.

Analogies are always dangerous, but in this case there is a valid comparison between the stratigraphical method of excavation and the historical approach to anthropology. The historical approach implies the recognition of the time aspect of the study of human behaviour. To say that the present is organically bound up with the past is to utter the most obvious of platitudes, and yet a number of causes have operated to prevent the practical recognition of the fact in the field of anthropology.

In the first place, one might say almost by the accident of birth, the science of anthropology, although defined by such an eminent anthropologist as Dr Marett as the whole study of man, has been practically confined to the study of existing 'primitive' peoples, the 'poor folk who have no histories of their own'. How far this last assumption is correct is a question which may be dealt with later, but taking it as true in the literal sense that such peoples have no documentary histories wherewith to clothe their nakedness, the result has been a general tendency to deny to history, in the broader sense, any part or lot in anthropological studies.

This tendency has been strengthened by another accident, the existence of the Empire. By a most natural and laudable development imperial legislators have recognized the practical value of anthropology as a means by which they may arrive at an understanding of the mental processes of the native races for whose well-being they have undertaken the responsibility. But this happy alliance between proconsuls, *in esse* or *in posse*, and professors, while it has stimulated anthropological studies and increased the well-being of native peoples, has still further served to relegate poor Clio to the position of a useless anachronism.

A third factor in this situation was the revival, ten years ago, of the historical approach to Anthropology, under the leadership of Sir Grafton Elliot Smith and Dr W. J. Perry.

The natural tendency in a new movement to over-emphasize certain aspects of its position exposed it to a severe and not always fair attack, and still further enhanced the tendency to discredit the application of historical methods to anthropological studies. But now that the dust of the controversy has subsided, the main achievement of the movement referred to stands out clearly, namely, the establishment of the importance for anthropology of the study of the ancient civilizations of the Near East.

It is perhaps only natural that anthropologists who have lived for long periods among primitive peoples; who have learnt to speak their languages, and studied their customs, religion, and social structure as the expressions of a living culture, should doubt whether a knowledge of the ancient civilizations of the Near East derived from the labours of archaeologists and historians could ever have a value comparable with the results of their own first-hand knowledge of a still living culture.

But there is something to be said on the other side. With the ever increasing tendency to specialization in the various departments of human studies, it is difficult for students in one branch of research to realize what advances are being made in another branch, and what bearing such advances may have on their own studies.

No one who is not actually engaged in the field of Oriental studies, and of the archaeology of the ancient East in particular, can possibly realize how great are the advances which have been made in recent years in our knowledge of the details of the daily life of, let us say, a Babylonian citizen in the second millennium B.C.

The field anthropologist can give us a vivid account of the making of a sacred drum, of the materials employed, of the ritual connected with its making, and the uses to which it is put when it is made.

The Mesopotamian archaeologist, on his side, can give us from the original sources the method of making and covering the sacred *lilissu*-drum, the materials employed, the ritual and the very words of the spells used in consecrating it, and can describe the magical use of the drum on such an occasion as an eclipse.

Or again, the field anthropologist can describe with great wealth of detail the ritual that hedges about a pregnant woman, and all the various magical devices employed to avert every kind of evil influence from her at a time when she is specially vulnerable.

Similarly, the student of Babylonian ritual can give in almost equal detail the ritual means employed by a pregnant woman to protect her from hostile demonic influences during her period of pregnancy. We know exactly what she did each day and each month, what spells and incantations she uttered, what ritual actions she performed, until the birth of her child. Some of the details, such as the tieing of various sacred knots containing magical objects, offer interesting parallels with savage customs.

It would be possible to go through all the various occasions of public and private life in ancient Mesopotamia and present illustrations of detailed knowledge which is surely no less worthy of the attention of the anthropologist than the material derived from the study of still living culture-patterns among savage peoples. One need only mention Ebeling's *Tod und Leben, u.s.w.*, or his little monograph, *Aus dem Tagewerk eines assyrischen Zauberpriesters*, as examples of the kind of material that calls for the serious study of anthropologists, although hitherto it has only engaged the attention of philologists and archaeologists.

But this is not by any means the most important aspect of the subject. A recognition of the facts enumerated above would be merely an extension of the comparative use already made by Sir James Frazer and others, of material from both classical and ancient Oriental sources. That there is nothing new in such a point of view may be shown by a quotation from Dr Marett's valuable little book, *Anthropology*, published years ago in the Home University Library series. In this he says: 'It remains to add that, hitherto, anthropology has devoted most of its attention to the peoples of rude— that is to say, of simple—culture; who are vulgarly known to us as "savages". The main reason for this, I suppose, is that nobody much minds so long as the darwinizing kind of history confines itself to outsiders. Only when it is applied to self and friends is it resented as an impertinence. But although it has always up to now pursued the line of least resistance, anthropology does not abate one jot or tittle of its claim to be the whole science, in the sense of the whole history, of man. As regards the word, call it science or history, or anthropology, or anything else—what does it matter? As regards the thing, however, there can be no compromise. We anthropologists are out to secure this: that there shall not be one kind of history for savages and another kind for ourselves, but the same kind of history, with the same evolutionary principle running right through it, for all men, civilized and savage, present and past.'

This is admirable, both in intention and expression, and it is only necessary to remark that, on the one hand, anthropology has continued to pursue the line of least resistance since this was written, and, on the other, that the concept of Darwinian evolution applied to human history seems to require some modification.

But more than this is involved in the historical approach to anthropological studies. If we may for a moment invoke Hardy's Time Spirit as our guide, and take an aerial view of the course of civilization from its beginnings, that course seems to assume a certain schematic pattern, although some parts of the pattern are still in shadow. The combined spatial and temporal aspects of the course of civilization assume the form of three concentric circles. The innermost circle is surrounded by a nimbus of the faint beginnings of culture, indeterminate at the edges, and growing sharper towards the boundary of the circle. This nimbus represents our knowledge of the palaeolithic and early neolithic cultures derived from archaeology and pre-history. The innermost circle contains the group of those ancient civilizations comprising Crete, Egypt, Anatolia, Mesopotamia, Palestine and Elam, with the Indus valley beginning to emerge from the shadow as a possible element in the picture. In spite of sharp differences in the individual cultures of these various regions, there is a striking resemblance in the material and spiritual aspects of the cultures which constitute this inner circle. The material resemblance in such matters as pottery, artefacts and architecture, has often been pointed out by archaeologists, but the resemblance in such matters as concepts and ritual practices is only just beginning to be considered. The work of such students as Perry and Hocart has done much to direct attention to this side of the question.

The importance of this inner circle for the temporal or chronological aspect of the history of civilization may be illustrated by a quotation from Mr Crawford's *Man and his Past*, a book which is indispensable to all students of human history. These are Mr Crawford's words: 'Absolute age in archaeology is rare, and for periods earlier than about 600 B.C. rests ultimately all the world over upon Egypt and Mesopotamia. A system of relative chronology can be established by excavation in any country that has been long inhabited, but it is left hanging in the air until linked up with Egypt, whether directly or indirectly through a third region. It is like a trigonometrical network set up in the heart of a newly discovered country. It is complete and perfect in itself, but unless it be connected up with some other system, or unless an astronomical reading is taken, we cannot place the network upon the map of the world. A single link is sufficient to make connexion with the chain of organized knowledge.'

The second of these concentric circles contains a group of civilizations of which the western area lies in a more brilliant illumination than the eastern region. This circle comprises the Hellenic civilization, whose clear light has somewhat eclipsed the importance of the inner circle; the Etruscan and Italic cultures; the intermingled spheres of Celtic and Teutonic cultures; the more shadowed area of Slavonic culture; the twilight region of the Caucasus whence come the still untested theories of Iapetic culture; the great Persian and Byzantine civilizations; and their successor, the great Arab civilization of the Middle Ages; thence eastward into the area of the civilizations of India, China, and Japan, still only imperfectly illuminated by the results of archaeological and anthropological study.

By contrast with the inner circle this second circle presents a far less homogeneous aspect, whether we consider it spatially or temporally, in breadth or in depth. That is to say, we find a far greater degree of variation as we pass from one area to another, or from one historical period to another. Hitherto the attention of the students of civilization has been concentrated rather on the differences than on the resemblances observable within the various areas and time-periods of this circle, but there is a growing tendency to look for such resemblances as may be found here, and to consider their significance. It may be added that the outstanding feature of this group in its time aspect is the pervasive influence of Hellenic culture, not only in the West but also in the East.

The third and outermost circle comprises the great ring of so-called primitive cultures lying like a coral-reef round the circle of what we may call, from the historical point of view, the secondary cultures of the West and of the East. Here we find the primitive cultures of Australasia, Melanesia, Polynesia, and Indonesia; the African tribes in all their vast variety; the rapidly vanishing remains of the culture of the North American Indians in their reserves; the traces of the once brilliant civilization of the Maya and the Aztecs, and the survivals of the culture of the food-gathering peoples of South America; and finally the Arctic cultures of the Esquimaux and the Siberian tribes.

As we have already seen, it is this third circle which, for various reasons, has hitherto been the chief field of anthropological investigation. Conquerors, explorers, travellers, traders, missionaries, and finally trained anthropological fieldworkers, have furnished a vast body of material, of unequal value, which still remains to a great extent unsifted and unrelated. But the general impression, in contrast to that derived from the consideration of the second circle, is of a greater degree of simplicity and homogeneity, in the midst of an immense variety of individual differences. There is a striking similarity everywhere in such concepts as those of *mana* and *tabu,* and their practical application; in cosmological and origin-myths; in initiation ceremonies, and in kinship systems. It may also be added, since the point is of significance for our enquiry, that this circle presents hardly any depth, at least on a *prima facie* view. The temporal aspect is missing; these are the poor peoples who have no histories of their own.

When we consider these three circles it is apparent that there is first of all a temporal relationship between them. The great civilizations of the central circle are the oldest fully organized civilizations of which we have any knowledge. They are roughly speaking contemporaneous, they rise together and decay together, but they contain the seeds of all the vital characteristics of the second great group of civilizations comprised in the second circle. A great, yet almost unobserved change has taken place during the last quarter of a century in our knowledge of the relation between these two circles. In his presidential address already referred to, Professor Gordon Childe says: 'Since the war many intermediate links between North-western Europe and the Near East have come to light in the Balkans, in Russia and in the West Mediterranean. At the same time unsuspected Oriental parallels to North European types have been recognized as specialists on the local material have become familiar with relics from Egypt and Sumer. During the last ten years the definition of channels for diffusion and the identification of a multitude of traits that might have been diffused have rehabilitated the doctrine of *Ex Oriente Lux.*'

It is this clear establishment of definite lines of communication between the inner circle of ancient Oriental civilizations and the second circle of secondary cultures that constitutes the most significant advance of recent times. But there is also an ever increasing body of evidence to show that many of the most important elements of this ancient culture passed along these channels and helped to shape the pattern of the younger cultures which grew up around the area of the inner circle. It is impossible, within the limits of this paper, to do more than illustrate the point by a few examples.

One of the most vital elements in the civilization of the

ancient East was the invention of writing. All the ancient scripts known to us in this area, the Minoan, Egyptian, Sumerian and Hittite, were originally pictographic, and there is a remarkable similarity between the early pictographs of these various systems, although it is impossible in the present state of knowledge to claim the origin of this invention for any one of these early cultures. It would be foolish to rule out the possibility of independent invention. But about the fourteenth century or even earlier, we find that the need for a simpler mode of writing than the cumbrous syllabaries of Egypt and Mesopotamia brought into existence at least two rival forms of alphabetic script, the Phœnician alphabet and the cuneiform alphabet of Ras Shamra. The greater simplicity of the Phœnician script caused its rapid spread, first over Syria and Palestine, then westward and southward, until, as is well known, it became the parent, not only of Arabic script, but of all the western alphabets. The historical, that is, the genetic, relation between these various forms of derived scripts is, in its main outlines, too well established to be questioned.

But the passage of such a vital element of culture along well-recognized channels from the inner to the second circle could hardly fail to involve the carrying with it of other elements of culture. Individual letters of the alphabet do not go off on independent argonautic journeys. An alphabet is carried from one culture area to another in some kind of literary form, commercial letters, contracts, treaties, votive inscriptions, fragments of literature, and all these contain seeds of culture. Some of the seeds fell upon stony ground, no doubt, and died, but some bore fruit abundantly. Furthermore, the question of script is bound up with that of language. It is possible for a particular script to be taken over and adapted to the needs of a people speaking a different language from that of the people whose script they have borrowed, as we see in the case of the adaptation of the Sumerian script to the entirely different Semitic speech of the later settlers in Mesopotamia, or again, in the case of the adaptation of the Phœnician script to the language of the Greek-speaking peoples of the Mediterranean.

But, in general, the script and the language go together, the one is the vehicle of the other. In the first half of the second millennium we find that the general use of cuneiform script throughout the greater part of our central circle is accompanied by the use of Akkadian as the general language of international communication, a fact which is established by the evidence of the Tell el-Amarna Letters. Similarly, the prevalence of the Phœnician script a thousand years later is accompanied by the very widespread use of Aramaic as a medium of international intercourse. During both these periods marked by the use of a common script and language, we find that myths and stories, representing the original forms of many of the commonest motives in folklore to-day, were being carried far beyond the boundaries of our inner circle. Dr Halliday, in his extremely interesting book, *Indo-European Folk-Lore and Greek Legend*, has referred to one well-known case of this kind, the *Story of Ahiqar*, and, incidentally, has brilliantly illustrated the true application of the historical method to this part of the material with which we are concerned. Mr Sayce, in his paper on *The Origins and Development of the Belief in Fairies* given before this society recently, refers in passing to another ancient story, the Egyptian tale of *The Two Brothers*, which has also travelled far from its original home. Mr Sayce's 'Conclusions', at the end of his paper, afford an admirable example of the application of historical method to the special field in which this Society is interested. I cannot refrain from quoting one particularly apposite passage: 'It should be emphasized that the movements out of the general North African cradle-land were several, and may have taken place scattered through long periods of time. The cultural contributions of the different waves might therefore vary, partly because the waves started from different regions, and partly because the beliefs of the homeland itself may have changed during the time between the successive waves. The amount of this possible change should, however, not be overestimated. It is possible for a culture that has attained an equilibrium with its environment to be static over very long periods. Dr Frankfort has discussed several material survivals and has shown that the peculiar arm-clamps still worn by the Masai are the direct descendants of those worn by a people with whom the ancient Egyptians were in contact during the Old Kingdom. At the end of his paper he says that we have now "proof positive that certain objects, and a very high degree of probability that certain customs, have survived in Africa without change these five thousand years".' We shall have occasion to refer to the conclusions here suggested later on.

Before passing on to the next line of illustration of this point, I might add that the third great period marked by the wide prevalence of a single script and a single language, the period of the Arab Empire, provided another opportunity for the transmission of many tales and legends whose origins demonstrably belong to the ancient East.

The second line of illustration may be taken from the field of religious art. Here again the material is abundant. Mr R. D. Barnett, writing in *Iraq*, ii. 2, Oct. 1935, on the 'Nimrud Ivories and the Art of the Ancient Phenicians', deals with a very common Oriental art motive, the cow and the calf type. Of this he says: 'The ancient Orientals dedicated to the statues of their god or kings, not to studies in genre, the labour of hewing massive blocks of stone. With the cow and calf type we can be quite certain of this divinity. A most interesting seal-impression, in which two priests worship the naked goddess holding her breasts, while above her head is the cow and calf, shows that in Mesopotamia from the time of Hammurabi this was a device of Ishtar. It is the form which Ishtar, Queen of Nineveh, assumed when she was said poetically to have suckled Ashurbanipal; note, too, that in her *akitu*-rituals a cow was milked. Parallel with this, the cow in Egypt as Hathor suckled the Pharaoh's son at Deir el-Bahri, Phœnicia probably being the intermediary for the transmission of the symbol, which was most popular; a cow with her calf formed the Egyptian hieroglyph meaning "to be joyful". The motive was imitated in Minoan art (though the animal there is a goat), *and in the subsequent Hellenic world found the widest acceptance*.' (Italics mine.)

[20]

Mr Barnett goes on to point out that Phœnician icono-graphic art also furnishes examples of illustrations of fables current in extended scenes, so that we have evidence for the transmission, not only of isolated art motives, but of the more complex and significant ritual and mythical scenes. One of the commonest forms of this type is the representation of a ritual combat, a type whose history we can trace from the earliest Sumerian seals to Greek vases of the sixth century B.C.

An interesting example of the transmission of early reli-gious art-forms, and of the problems created by changes in transmission, is the case of the *omphalos*, so frequently found represented in ritual and mythological scenes on Greek vases. Much ingenious learning has been directed to the explanation of the form and use of this object, and especially of the net-work with which it is often represented as covered. Anyone who is familiar with the representations on early Sumerian seals of the 'mountain' in which the dead god is imprisoned, and with the general convention in use throughout the ancient East, for the representation of any kind of mountainous country will at once recognize the origin both of the form of the *omphalos* and of the network which covers it, as it is repre-sented by the Greek artist. Furthermore, from the same source we have the explanation of the religious significance of the *omphalos*, and of the reason why it came to be regarded as the 'navel' of the world by the Greek mind. In actual practice the 'mountain' of the early seals was represented in the temple complex of the Mesopotamians by the *ziqqurat*, the great temple-tower, which was the scene of the central acts of the New Year ritual, including the dramatic representation of the death and resurrection of the god, and the sacred marriage. Father Burrows has shown that these buildings were known among the Babylonians as the *markasu*, the 'bond' between heaven and earth, and hence as occupying that place in their cosmogony which the Greeks attributed to the *omphalos*.[2]

The transmission of religious art-forms leads us naturally to the last of those elements in the culture of the ancient East

[2] See E. Burrows, 'Some Cosmological Patterns in Babylonian Religion', in *The Labyrinth*, pp. 47ff.

which we shall take as an illustration of the point under discussion.

Such elements as the ritual combat just mentioned are only organic parts of a general ritual pattern whose distribution throughout the ancient East is now beginning to be recognized outside the circle of purely Oriental scholarship. This ritual pattern with its associated myth rested upon and grew out of certain fundamental religious conceptions connected with the function of the king in the community. Its main features have been frequently discussed in recent publications, notable among which are those of a past president of this Society, Professor E. O. James. Hence we need only mention its chief features. They are dramatic representation of the death and resurrection of a god, a ritual combat with a dragon or other bestial form of adversary, a sacred marriage, and a ritual fixing of destinies. There were also, as I have attempted to show in the Schweich Lectures for last year, many ritual types of lesser importance which grew out of the central elements and were current throughout the ancient East. Many of the magical and mythical elements found in folklore can be traced back to this central source. Along the same channels by which scripts, languages, art-motives and material artefacts were carried beyond the boundaries of the inner circle, there were also transmitted in literary or oral form, by traders, soldiers, or settlers, the main elements of this ritual pattern.

The time is not far distant when it will be impossible to discuss the origin and significance of Greek ritual, or Celtic mythology, without reference to the great mass of fresh material from the Near East which recent archaeological research has placed at the disposal of the anthropologist and folklorist. This is the difficult and, in more senses than one, perilous task which the anthropologist who claims for his province 'the whole history of man' must be prepared to undertake.

The relation between the inner circle and the younger cultures comprised in the second circle is gradually becoming recognized, and only awaits a greater co-operation between anthropologists, archaeologists and historians, specialists in various departments of human studies, to produce a fruitful synthesis.

But the problems which arise when we come to examine the question of the relation of the primitive or savage cultures, of the outermost circle, to the older civilizations, of the two inner circles, are of a different character. In the first place these primitive peoples are, as Dr Marett has said, peoples who have no histories of their own in the documentary sense. Hence the perilous nature of the historical approach to anthropological studies here becomes most apparent, and it is not surprising that scientific workers in this field should, for the greater part, have confined themselves to the detailed study and description of the language, social structure, religion and material culture of these peoples. In this field the application of functional, psychological and sociological methods has yielded and continues to yield, year by year, most valuable results, and it is not surprising that anthropologists whose attention is primarily centred on this field should regard results of the historical approach to their material as uncertain, incapable of proof, and of no practical value.

Nevertheless, there is something to be said on the other side. History may be and occasionally has been a bad mistress but can be a good handmaid. Although the peoples of whom we are now speaking may have no documentary history, they have traditions which presuppose some kind of continuity with the past. It is impossible to eliminate the time aspect from human life anywhere. The passage already quoted from Mr Sayce's paper with its significant reference to the Masai armlets illustrates, by an established instance, the principle of continuity of culture. The work of Mr Hocart on *Kingship*, Dr Jeffrey's studies of kingship among the Ibo people, Mr Layard's illuminating examination of certain aspects of Malekulan culture, are examples chosen at random of the way in which historical method, rightly used, may supplement the results of the functional method in this field.

If once we accept the view of the general time and space relations of the different periods of human history and prehistory suggested in our metaphor of the three concentric circles, the essential importance of historical method in human studies follows as a necessary consequence.

Fourteen years ago a distinguished archaeologist could write: 'At present there is a real danger that the indiscriminate amassing of materials will by its sheer dead-weight retard the rate of progress.' The danger has not diminished in the meantime, and it is the particular task of historical method to discern the network of causal relation which gives meaning to the whole process, so infinite in its seeming complexity, of the growth and decay of civilizations. The magnitude of the task may well engender humility, but need not cause us to abandon it in despair.

There are certain definite things to be done, things which are within the compass of reasonable achievement. First there is the task, already hopefully begun, of establishing definite channels of communication between the various areas. Then there is the business of tracing the movement of various elements of culture along the various lines of communication. This has already made considerable progress in the field of material culture, as is shown by the many valuable maps which have appeared in recent years. But the application of the same method to the immaterial aspects of culture, owing to its greater difficulty, lags behind. I would venture to suggest that there is a profitable field of work here for collectors of folklore. A vast amount of material has been collected during the last half-century, and while it has been roughly classified according to countries, Scottish, Irish, Scandinavian, and so forth, very little is known about the distribution of particular folklore motives. The same holds good about local customs, an equally important part of folklore, since behind most folktales lies myth, and behind folk-custom lies some fragment of ancient ritual. Hence it would be of the greatest service to the studies in which this Society is interested if some enterprising student would embark upon the preparation of a series of maps indicating the distribution of particular folklore motives, and particular customs. A comparison between such maps and those already prepared for various artefacts would yield most valuable results.

These two lines of research lead up to the third and most difficult task of establishing a genetic relation between single culture elements, or between groups of culture elements, whose distribution in space and time has been determined. It is here, perhaps, that the application of historical method to the pattern of civilization has most proved to be a 'siege perilous'. We can see, as Sir Arthur Evans has said, that great symbol of divine kingship, the bull, journeying from Mesopotamia to Crete, perhaps by way of Egypt; thence we may trace him to Greece, and on to Spain, where he still holds ritual state; and so to the Brown Bull of Cooley in the magic fields of Eireann. But while the trail may be clear, it does not suffice to prove that the Brown Bull of Cooley is one end of a true cultural chain which ultimately leads us back to Sumer, or some other point in our inmost circle. The chief danger is of being satisfied with anything less than a completely rigorous proof of true descent. There is some cause for complaint that Clio has too many illegitimate children.

But that the task is difficult is a poor reason for abandoning it. It is rather a challenge to vindicate, in Dr Marett's brave words, the claim of anthropology, 'to be the whole science, in the sense of the whole history, of man'.

CHAPTER TWO

Time and Custom[1]

To the unceasing movement of Time Custom seems to present a certain rock-like permanence. Yet, as the hardest rocks are imperceptibly undermined and eaten away by the flow of rivers and the swing of tides, so Time, 'the hidden root of change', slowly transforms the contours of our customary life. Again, taking a metaphor from the etymology of the word, custom is like a garment, a costume, of whose ancient splendour Time makes a tarnished threadbare thing, consigned to the dust and darkness of the antiquarian's cupboard. In his epigrammatic way F. H. Bradley, in the course of his reflections on the nature of Time, remarks that 'we think forwards, one may say, on the same principle on which fish feed with their heads pointing up the stream'. While the strict accuracy of the simile might be challenged, since the poor fishes' tails would seem to be directed to the future, it might be taken without offence to the members of an ancient and honourable Society as symbolic of the attitude of the student of folklore who is ever on the watch to seize, devour and digest such fragments of ancient custom as the stream of Time may bring within his reach. The early makers of myths attributed to Time the unpleasant cannibal habit of devouring his own children. As the incidental embodiment of custom, a child of Time now about to be devoured, it may not be considered altogether inappropriate for a retiring president of this Society to offer some reflections on the relation between Time and Custom before vanishing into the limbo of forgotten vice-presidents.

Another philosopher, Professor Alexander, has characterized Time as the mind of space, a somewhat mystic utterance, which might be interpreted to mean that, as it is the function of mind to bring order into the chaos of experience, so Time

---

[1] Presidential Address to the Folk-Lore Society, 1937. First published in *Folk-Lore*.

imposes a pattern of order upon the otherwise meaningless succession of events. Mr Bradley charges science with such bad manners as to ignore the existence of Time: 'In establishing a law, itself without special relation to Time, science treats facts from various dates as all possessing the same value.' While such a charge is not without foundation, especially in the case of the physical sciences, yet on the whole those scholars who are at work in the field of the human sciences have not been unconscious of the significance of Time in their researches. Professor Gordon Childe's latest book, *Man Makes Himself*, is an illuminating example of the application of the concept of Time to the study of human behaviour. On the other hand it is impossible to consult some of the great collections of folklore material without feeling the need of discovering the 'hidden root of change' which causes the strange transformations through which customs pass in their age-long transmission.

The volume entitled *British Calendar Customs*, recently published by this Society, is a striking witness to the effect of Time on Custom. Here we may see Time both begetting his children and destroying them, and the material here collected by the labours of an eminent folklorist will serve as the text for this valedictory address.

Before we turn to the examination of some of the customs associated with the calendar of our own country, a few introductory remarks are necessary to explain the point of view and intention which will guide the course of our enquiry.

First of all we can hardly fail to observe that the movement of Time has a double aspect, reflected in the nature of its effect on Custom. Both of these aspects persist together in human consciousness, but in the earlier stages of the growth of civilization one aspect seems to be more strongly impressed upon man's ways of thinking and acting.

This aspect is what we may call the cyclic face of Time. It is the first, most obvious and most insistent way in which Time imposes its pattern upon human behaviour. It might be said to be the essential condition of a coherent existence. A state of existence in which recurrence was impossible, in which no event ever greeted man with a returning familiar face, would be a nightmare too appalling to contemplate. It would be as meaningless and fragmentary as the consciousness of a madman.

But it is this recurrent aspect of Time that has been the begetter of Custom, and by this element in man's experience he is linked with the instinctive patterns of behaviour in animals. A remarkable recent book by an eminent physiologist, Dr Lecomte de Noüy, entitled *Biological Time*, has demonstrated by a number of very interesting experiments that the organism has a Time of its own, a vital Time, very different from a Kantian category, far more than a convenient intellectual device, a yardstick of historical measurement. It is of the essence of the organism.

Hence the curiously tough and durable quality of the patterns which Time has imposed upon human behaviour.

From the beginnings of man's attempt to adapt himself to his environment, and to control it sufficiently to get a living out of it, he found that all the processes and events which were vital to him moved in cycles. Day and night, cold and heat, mating seasons, seasons of growth and flowering, seasons of decay and death, all moved round him in a cyclic dance, so that a cyclic pattern of behaviour was wrought into his blood. The strength of this pattern has always been most deeply felt by those who live in constant contact with the processes of Nature—the hunter, the agriculturist, the peasant. Professor Childe, in the book mentioned above, has described with vividness the consequences of the great urban revolution at the beginning of the second millennium B.C. One of those consequences, the one with which we are here more specially concerned, is a change in the feeling of Time. Instead of being felt and lived through as a cyclic and collective process, in which the sense of personal individuality is merged in a sense of oneness with all living and growing things in the ever-recurring cycle of death and rebirth, Time is felt as a stream, a succession of events, a string of dates, or, to the religious mind, the endless progress of the divine purpose towards some dimly envisaged ideal. To the priest Time brings round

the season for the payment of tithes; the king looks forward
to 'the time when kings go forth to war'; to the merchant
Time brings round the season propitious for prosperous trad-
ing voyages and the dates when bills mature. Collective consciousness grows weak and the importance of the individual
increases, and for religion the importance of the after-life of
the individual emerges.

But in addition to this double aspect of Time there is
another phenomenon which calls for remark and which is a
consequence of the overlapping of the cyclic and the historical
aspects of Time. This is the appearance of what we may call
Time-lag, which makes its presence felt both in the consciousness of the individual and in the life of the community. The
reason why people kiss under the mistletoe, throw salt over
their left shoulders, or refuse to accept the present of a knife
without ritual payment, is a Time-lag in the individual, unconscious, but none the less real. There is a submerged region
in the individual consciousness where the ancient patterns
survive, and the odds and ends of quaint irrational custom are
like the peaks of submerged continents appearing above the
sea. Further, as the urban and industrial way of life replaces
the agricultural, or at least relegates it to a secondary place
in the total social structure, the feeling of the cyclic pattern of
the seasons grows weak and its characteristic customs suffer a
sea-change. But here, too, the Time-lag operates; customs
belonging to the old pattern survive in the countryside after
they have disappeared from the city, and even in the new
forms which religious ritual assumes under the influence of
the changed feeling of Time, fragments of the ancient pattern
survive, often strangely incongruous with their new setting.

We shall now attempt to illustrate this thesis by an examination of some groups of customs selected from the volume
of *British Calendar Customs*, but before doing so we may close
this introductory section with a quotation from a Danish
scholar, S. A. Pallis, who has made an exhaustive study of the
ancient Babylonian New Year Festival, since his remarks are
peculiarly apt to the purpose of this address: 'But the scholar
knows quite well that though this division of the cultures into

strata (i.e. into agricultural and urban) is excellent for the purpose of obtaining a general view of the distinctive religious character of the various cultures, he very rarely, perhaps we may say never, meets with any of these cultures in the pure form. He must, therefore, take up for consideration the problem of how long the religious conceptions of one culture will survive in another culture. Or, to put it more concretely, how much is living substance, and how much is merely external form marked by tradition and sacerdotal interpretation when we meet with conceptions of the kind we call survivals in the urban culture?'[2]

In the volume of *British Calendar Customs* already referred to we find that the main part of the customs there collected are included in a section of cyclic Time whose pattern is imposed on it by the *hieros logos* of the most important events of the Christian Church. It is a section of time stretching from Shrovetide to Whitsuntide, a period of fourteen weeks. Its present appearance of unity is imparted to it by the thread of Gospel narrative which tells the story of the events which led up to the Crucifixion, followed by the Resurrection, the Ascension, and the coming of the Holy Spirit. But behind this unity there lies a far more ancient unity, an older *hieros logos*, telling of the death and descent into the underworld of the god, known by many names, who was the life of all young and growing things. It told also of the universal mourning for him, of the journey of his sister-consort into the lower world to seek him, and of his triumphant return.

The ancient significance of this section of Time is that it embraces the vital crisis, ever recurring, of the agricultural year. It contains the *hieros logos* of the corn, from the moment when the first green shoots appear above the brown earth, to be greeted with jubilation, through the anxious time of its growth and ripening, up to the triumphant moment when the last sheaf is cut and borne home with shouts of rejoicing.

There is something here older than history, something that cyclic Time has so deeply stamped into the racial consciousness of mankind that its pattern has survived through millen-

[2] S. A. Pallis, *The Babylonian Akito Festival*, p. 302.

niums of historical and religious change. We shall return later to the question of the change in Time-consciousness involved in this change from a pattern imposed by the cyclic drama of the seasons to that which has been imposed by the historical form of the Gospel narrative.

When we turn to the customs collected in the volume referred to above, we find many which have no recognizable link with anything in the Christian tradition which has given its unity to this section of the Christian year. Moreover, these customs fall into groups marked by common characteristics.

Such groups of customs are like islands appearing above the surface of the water. Apparently separated from one another, they are connected far below in the depths of the ocean, and if the sea should recede in some great tidal wave, it would reveal the islands as really the peaks of mountains in some great connecting pattern of land.

It would obviously be impossible to classify or discuss all the customs here collected, and a few groups, illustrating different but related elements of the cyclic Time-pattern, have been selected for discussion.

First there is a group of customs which we may call *heaving* customs; this brings together a number of customs which at first sight appear wholly dissimilar. Under this head we may group the various pancake customs still quite numerous, but once far more prevalent; in the same group we have the picturesque ritual chiefly practised on Easter Monday and Tuesday, of *lifting*, the men lifting the women on Monday, while the women return the compliment on the following day. Then there is the custom, connected with Whit Monday, of raising and lowering a tall pole, a custom which was carried on in Gloucestershire till shortly before the first World War, and may possibly still survive there.

In the pattern of Christian ritual the element of lifting or raising appears in the central moment of the great act of the Mass in the elevation of the Host, and also in the lifting up of the offertory by the priest before the altar. In Christian ritual the act of lifting has lost all significance save that of presenting or offering, but we find that in early Hebrew religion there was, at the beginning of harvest, a ritual elevation of a sheaf of the first corn, and later on, after an interval of seven weeks from the first act of lifting, that is, presumably, the period allowed for the ripening of the corn, two loaves of new meal were similarly elevated.

In the course of his discussion of this piece of ritual in his essay on 'Early Hebrew Festival Rituals', in *Myth and Ritual* (pp. 116-17), Dr Oesterley says: 'The waving of the sheaf, moving it towards the altar and back, no doubt symbolized the offering of a gift to Jahweh and receiving it back again, in recognition of the fact that he was the giver of the fruits of the earth. But it is possible that this rite had a history behind it. There is abundant evidence to show that among many peoples magical rites were performed in order to ensure abundant crops in the coming year; the waving of the sheaf may originally have been in an upward direction, in which case it was a magical rite to make the corn grow high.'

The existence of such rites has been abundantly illustrated from every part of the world in *The Golden Bough*, but it might be added with regard to the interpretation of the Hebrew usage and its original significance that Ex. 29.27, shows that the ritual acts of waving and lifting were so closely connected that they might almost be considered as one act, and further that the Hebrew word translated 'wave' has agricultural associations and is used to describe the motion of the sickle through the standing corn and also to describe the action of sifting corn. Hence there is a strong probability that the original intention of the ritual was mimetic and magical, just as hunting magic consisted in going through the actions of the chase.

Such an interpretation is supported by a scene in the early mythological and ritual texts from Ras Shamra in which the goddess Anat is represented as going through a series of acts which are evidently symbolic of the principal actions of the harvest—reaping, winnowing, grinding, and so forth.

Hence the pancake, tossed over the bar of Westminster School, takes us back to the cycle of customs connected with the vital interest of food and its growth, the Time-cycle from spring to harvest.

We shall not delay over the ritual of lifting referred to as connected with Whit Monday save to point out that it illustrates the way in which the symbols may change their form while their meaning remains the same. The lifting of the women by the men, and of the men by the women, has the same ancient significance as the tossing of the pancake. In the ancient cyclic pattern all fertility was felt to flow from the same source and to depend upon the performance of the same kind of mimetic ritual actions.

But the tossed pancake, the merry game in which lads and lasses lift each other, and the tall pole lowered to earth and raised again, take us back to a ritual which may well be even older than the beginnings of agriculture. Professor A. M. Blackman has pointed out that in the Egyptian spring festival of Osiris a central element of the ritual was the raising of the $\underline{Dd}$-column, a sacred pole, originally according to Andrae, a bundle of papyrus stems in flower bound together while still growing out of the ground. We have pictures of the ceremony of the lowering and raising of the sacred column being performed by the Pharaoh. Commenting on the ritual, Professor Blackman says: 'Surely all these performances reproduced in dramatic form the disappearance of vegetation, due to the inundation, and the renewal of growth following the subsidence of the waters. Osiris, dead vegetation, was buried and hidden out of sight, but not without expectation of renewal and regrowth. To ensure the fulfilment of this expectation was the object of the raising of the $\underline{Dd}$-column, the embodiment of Osiris.' (*Myth and Ritual*, p. 24).

In Egypt, evidently, the rite of lowering and raising the sacred pole was connected with agriculture, and part of the cyclic pattern which the rise and fall of the Nile flood with its life-giving consequences had impressed on the minds of the Egyptians. But in Sumer, in the ancient liturgies which bewailed the descent of Tammuz into the underworld, we find the fallen cedar-tree used as the symbol of the dead god, and when through the intervention of Ishtar he returns to life and light, she is said to have raised up her noble cedar-tree. That some such felling of a tree formed part of the early

Tammuz ritual is suggested by a scene represented on several pre-Sargonid seals, in which we see a sacred person or god in the act of cutting down a tree on a mountain within which a male and female divinity are engaged in some ritual act which might well represent the return of the dead god. Such a piece of symbolism could hardly have originated in Sumer, where the date-palm is the only tree of any size. Its home is in the high mountains, and it may have been part of some seasonal ritual of the mountain-dwellers before it found a place in the agricultural cycle of the river valleys.

Hence the apparently unrelated customs of tossing the pancake, of the lifting of men and women by each other, and of the raising of the tall pole, are survivals, like the island peaks of which we spoke, bearing witness to an ancient rhythm of actions so strongly impressed by Time upon human consciousness that they have survived the changes of more than six thousand years. Although they have no relation whatever to anything in the Christian tradition which, as we have seen, has given its own unity to this section of the course of Time, they have nevertheless retained their place here because this period of the year has stamped itself upon the consciousness of the race, and the ritual actions of which these customs are the vestiges are an essential part of that ancient cyclic pattern.

The next group to which we shall now direct our attention includes a number of very dissimilar customs. It brings together the various curious things done to cocks, such as cockkibbit, cock-throwing, cock-running, and cock-fighting, which are found from Shrovetide to Whitsuntide. Connected with these customs we shall consider the various games which make their appearance at this time of the year.

The link between the cock and Christian tradition is very slight. Like Judas, who also appears in some of the customs belonging to this season, the cock seems to owe his place here to his connexion in the Gospel narrative with the betrayal of Jesus. The unfortunate bird may possibly be one of the various forms in which the medieval anti-Jewish sentiment expressed itself. But the roots of the barbarous custom of throwing sticks at a tethered cock, and the related custom, somewhat less brutal, in which runners with their hands tied behind their backs gave chase to a cock whose wings had been cut, and endeavoured to secure it with their teeth, is far older than the coming of the Danes, with which local tradition connects it, or than the beginnings of Christianity. It has its place in a very early form of the cyclic Time-pattern of which we have spoken, and illustrates the emotional Time-lag characteristic of so many customs belonging to this period of the year.

A scene which frequently appears on early Babylonian seals represents a strange figure, half man, half bird, being brought in bound before the judgment-seat of a god. The ritual counter-part of this scene is found in one of the episodes of the Baby-lonian New Year Festival. Pallis's translation of the relevant lines of the text in which it occurs runs as follows: 'The foot-race taking place in the presence of Marduk and all the larger cities (*maḥazani*), that is when Assur sent out Ninurta to capture Zu . . . (Ninurta) said to Assur: Zu has been cap-tured. Assur (said) to (Ninurta): Go and tell (it) to all the gods. He told them and they rejoiced at it.'[3] Immediately after we hear of the priests beating Zu as part of the ritual.

Now it is well known that Zu was the storm-bird, one of the older gods, who was conquered by Ninurta, and Professor Langdon, commenting on the myth and its relation to the New Year festival, remarks: 'The myth of Ninurta and Zu is based upon the conflict between the spring sun and demons of the winter period of storms and darkness.'[4]

Hence the material suggests that one of the important epi-sodes of the festival consisted in a foot-race in which the priest pursued after a symbolic figure in a bird-mask, representing the storm-bird Zu, and that his capture and beating symbolize the victory of the gods of light and life and spring.

The mention of the foot-race leads us by a natural transition to the various games which, as we know without the help of calendar customs, suddenly appear at this season. The princi-pal games mentioned in *British Calendar Customs* as charac-teristic of the section of the year which we are considering

[3] Pallis, *op. cit.*, p. 232.   [4] S. Langdon, *The Epic of Creation*, p. 20.

are football, hurling, tug-of-war, marbles, whipping-tops, hoops, and tip-cat, together with many other special forms of sport which are rather customs than games. The mention of football is particularly interesting because, as we all know, the spring is not the time when organized football as an English game makes its appearance. The football which belongs to this season and which still persists in some parts of England is a ritual contest in which the whole male population of the town or village takes part. The ball is merely a symbol, and each side struggles to force it towards an appointed spot. At Derby the Shrove Tuesday football contest was between the two parishes of All Saints' and St Peter's. St Peter's sought to get the ball into the Derwent, while All Saints' strove to force it towards Gallow's Balk on the west of the town. The hurling matches had the same character. Marbles, whipping-tops, and tip-cat have the common feature of an object to be thrown at or struck, and the only reason why such games should begin at this season of the year rather than at any other is that they are all survivals of the same ancient cyclic pattern to which, as we have seen, the various lifting customs already mentioned go back.

One of the central features of the Egyptian Osirian festival was a ritual combat between the followers of Osiris and those of his enemy, Set. We have pictorial representations of the various symbolic ways in which this contest was carried out. We have wrestling, fencing or single-stick, boxing, tug-of-war, ball games of different kinds, and other sports. In early ritual texts we have the whipping of a figure representing Set. There are similar suggestions of games of a ritual and symbolic type carried on by priests and people at the Babylonian New Year Festival.

Hence, again we find that our British calendar customs contain elements which have no relation whatever to the Christian tradition, but which are survivals of a time when men did such things, not for amusement, but with the set purpose of influencing the powers of nature at the great crisis of the year, when death and life, light and darkness, were trembling in the balance.

Another group of customs of a somewhat different character is worthy of a brief notice. They are those usually designated as 'mothering' customs. The name is as old as the middle of the seventeenth century. The custom still survives in England, though it is gradually dying out, and takes the form of visits paid by children who have left home to their mother on Mid-Lent Sunday. They bring presents of various kinds, but especially cakes. The custom is connected with the special features of simnel-cakes, saffron, figs in some form, and frumenty. The mother is called the Queen of the Feast for the occasion.

Here we have to observe some strange transformations caused by Time. In the first place it seems certain that in medieval times the custom took the form of visits paid by parishioners to their cathedral or Mother Church, bringing offerings. But, going back further in time to the days of Jeremiah we find that the Jewish women in exile in Egypt declare their intention of continuing the custom which they had followed in Jerusalem, of making cakes for the Queen of Heaven, and of worshipping her with incense and drink-offerings. They also attribute the misfortunes which have befallen them to the fact that they have ceased to observe this custom (Jer. 44.17, 18). Thus behind the majestic medieval conception of Mother Church there lies the far older figure of Inanna, Ishtar, Persephone, Mother Goddess and Corn Mother, who, under the many names by which she is known, is inseparably bound up with some of the deepest emotions arising out of the collective activities belonging to this period. Saffron, as we know, is connected with the myth of Persephone, while the frumenty custom takes us back to the Corn Mother. It is also interesting to find that in one of the Babylonian ritual commentaries the central figure of the ritual enters the shrine holding in his hand a sweet fig which he shows to the god and the king. The precise significance of the act is not clear, but it probably has some connexion with fertility.

Time may be able to transform the Corn Mother into Mother Church, but the cakes, the saffron, the frumenty and the fig, cannot be so transformed, they remain, alien to their setting, a witness to the tough and enduring nature of the ancient cyclic pattern.

There is one more group of customs which finds a place in this period of the calendar, namely those customs connected with the temporary elevation to office of a king, as at Lostwithiel, in Cornwall, or of a mayor, as at Middleton and Randwick. This custom has been so abundantly illustrated by Frazer in *The Golden Bough* that it needs no discussion here, but it is worth while to quote Ebeling's interesting comment on the Babylonian ritual of the *šar-puḫi*, or substitute-king. His words are as follows: 'We know that among the Babylonians, as among many other peoples, the king was the embodiment of life. It was necessary that his life should not lose its strength, but that it should be renewed yearly. Originally the king must have been killed each year and his place taken by a new king and a fresh life. This custom probably prevailed in prehistoric times in Babylon, as is evident from the fact that when the king had gained sufficient power to avert his death at the end of the year, a substitute-king took the place of the real king and suffered death in his stead. That in the case of the death of the actual king during the festival the ritual was regarded as having been fulfilled and that the death of the substitute-king was no longer necessary is shown by the story of the king Ira-mitti, who died during the course of the New Year festival. As the result of his death it was no longer thought necessary to kill the substitute-king, Ellilbani, but the latter immediately assumed the crown.'[5]

But the purpose of referring to this central element of the ancient cyclic pattern is to point out that its traces are curiously faint at a period of the calendar year when we might have expected it to be specially prominent, since it is the period of the year when the death and resurrection of the god upon whom the new burgeoning of life depended was re-enacted in dramatic form as the central element in the New Year ritual.

In suggesting a reason for the almost entire absence of this feature from the calendar customs of the Easter season,

[5] E. Ebeling, *Tod und Leben usw.*, p. 62. Cf. *infra*, pp. 206f.

although it appears in many forms in other seasonal customs, we return to the questions raised in the introductory section of this address, and so to our conclusion, for 'Time is our tedious tale should here have ending'.

The Christian tradition, which, as we have said, has given its unity to this calendar period, has dealt with the cyclic pattern of Time in a curious way. In its origin Christianity was the result of a process which had already brought about a radical transformation of the old collective type of religion with its seasonal rituals. Through a series of events which cannot be described here the old nature religion of the Hebrews had been transformed into Apocalyptic, a form of religious emotion whose basis was historical in its Time-feeling, but which transcended Time in its forward vision. The individual consciousness, loosed from its collective participation in the ancient cyclic pattern of Time, looked forward to a consummation.

The form of the great Catholic tradition which emerged from the theological controversies and the political vicissitudes of the first five centuries of our era succeeded in combining the most important elements of the old cyclic pattern with the feeling of Time, not as a cycle but as an onward movement towards a 'far-off divine event'. The cyclic pattern of the ever-recurring death and resurrection of a fertility god was replaced by the drama of the death and resurrection of an historical figure, re-enacted yearly in the spring, and gathering up those emotions which had found their expression in the ancient seasonal rituals into a new collective form with a feeling of Time which was no longer cyclic but forward looking.

This is why the element previously referred to, namely that of the substitute-king, is almost wholly absent from this part of the calendar year, although it finds ample place in other seasons with their appropriate customs. The succession of nameless substitute-kings who 'died for their people' has been here replaced by the unchanging figure of a crucified and risen God.

Nevertheless, as we have seen, many elements of the

ancient pattern which could not be transformed have maintained their place in the season which belongs to them, and in spite of their incongruity, still form a part, although a slowly vanishing part, of collective activities at such times. The Time-lag, affecting even the central act of the Christian drama, is well illustrated by a story which Jane Harrison tells of her experience at an Easter Sunday celebration in Greece. She said to an old peasant woman whose joy at the celebration of the resurrection of Christ seemed particularly exuberant, 'You seem very happy'. 'Of course I am,' replied the old woman. 'If Christ were not risen we should have no harvest this year.'

The last stanza of Flecker's poem *The Bridge of Fire* may fitly serve as an *envoi* to this very inadequate valedictory address:

> *Between the pedestals of night and morning,*
> *Between red death and radiant desire,*
> *With not one sound of triumph or of warning*
> *Stands the great sentry on the Bridge of Fire.*
> *O transient soul, thy thought with dreams adorning,*
> *Cast down the laurel and unstring the lyre:*
> *The wheels of Time are turning, turning, turning,*
> *The slow stream channels deep and does not tire.*
> > *Gods on their Bridge above*
> > *Whispering lies and love*
> *Shall mock your passage down the sunless river*
> > *Which, rolling all it streams,*
> > *Shall take you, king of dreams,*
> *—Unthroned and unapproachable for ever—*
> > *To where the kings who dreamed of old*
> *Whiten in habitations monumental cold.*

CHAPTER THREE

Myth, Ritual and History[1]

THE culture area which is the source of the material dealt with in this paper is the ancient Near East, embracing Asia Minor, Mesopotamia, Palestine and Egypt in the third and second millenniums before Christ. In this area the invention of writing took place, and from it come the earliest written sources for the history of civilization. While much of this material, consisting of business documents, contracts, laws, and so forth, is of immense value for the reconstruction of the social organization of the period, our concern is with that part of the material which consists of documents arising out of the religious life of the time, such as myths, magical formulae, rituals and liturgies. In particular, there are a certain number of semi-mythical, semi-historical, texts which raise the question of the relation between ritual situations as embodied in the myths, and the beginnings of history.

The time at my disposal will not allow of more than a brief discussion of the three main points which form the subject of this paper.

First, an examination of the large number of myths contained in our texts leads to the conclusion that there are three types of myth, each representing a basic form which is to be found, with local modifications, throughout the culture area with which we are concerned. These three types, which I shall call *basic* myths, are as follows:

(*a*) The myth of Tammuz and Ishtar, embodied in the large number of Tammuz liturgies still surviving, and available for study in Witzel's great collection. This myth describes the death of the king-god at the hands of demonic adversaries, his imprisonment in the underworld, the lamentation of his sister-consort, Ishtar, her journey to the underworld to seek him and bring him back, and his triumphal

[1] Paper read before the British Association, 1938. First published in *Folk-Lore*.

return with its attendant processions and feasting. The basic nature of this myth is shown by its wide dispersion and long persistence throughout the ancient Near East. Tammuz 'yearly wounded', under the form of Adonis, was the object of cult and the theme of myth in Palestine, from Ras Shamra to Jerusalem, down to the end of the second century B.C. The myth and the ritual were taken over from the Sumerians by the Babylonians, and appear as constituent elements of numerous exorcism rituals as late as the Seleucid epoch.

(*b*) The Creation Myth, extant in our culture area in many forms, and most completely embodied in the so-called Babylonian Epic of Creation, of which Sumerian, Babylonian, Assyrian, and Hittite versions exist, bearing witness to its wide dispersion and long persistence. It has long been recognized that some form of the Babylonian version lies behind the two Hebrew accounts of Creation. Hence we may fairly claim this as a *basic* myth. The fact that the text was called an 'incantation' by the Babylonians is significant and will be referred to again later. The central features of the myth are the conquest of the powers of chaos and darkness, embodied in various dragon forms, by Marduk, the supreme god of Babylon, followed by the fixing in their stations of the heavenly bodies, and the creation of man out of clay and the blood of a slain god. This myth was recited during the great ritual of the New Year Festival in Babylon.

(*c*) The Deluge Myth. As its literature shows, no myth has a wider dispersion than the Deluge myth, being found in every part of the world, even in regions where no natural causes for a flood would appear to exist. This myth raises several interesting problems, being a kind of border-line territory, where historical, ritual, and aetiological elements seem to have some claim for consideration. The Mesopotamian form of the myth exists in Sumerian, Assyrian, Babylonian and Hittite versions. The Hebrew versions are clearly dependent upon the Babylonian form. The latter is known to us as the XIth tablet of the famous Epic of Gilgamesh, the semimythical king of Erech whose name occurs as the fifth king of the dynasty of Erech, which was, according to Sumerian tra-

dition, the second dynasty after the Deluge. The introduction
of the Deluge myth into the saga of a semi-divine hero raises
the question of whether a ritual element, unapparent at first
sight, may not lie behind the myth.

These three myths seem to stand out from the mass of
other myths with which our early sources have made us
acquainted, not only for their wide distribution, but for the
point which we shall now examine, namely, their character
as ritual myths. I have no intention of putting forward the
view that all myths are ritual in origin, and there can be no
doubt that many early myths from our culture area are aetiological myths. But such study as I have been able to make of
the myths of the earliest civilizations of which we have any
documentary evidence seems to suggest that the ritual myth
appeared earlier than the aetiological myth. It would be rash
to dogmatize on the point, but I cannot help feeling that the
ritual myth which is magical in character, and inseparable
from the ritual which is directed to certain fundamental needs
of an early society, whether pastoral, agricultural, or urban,
is older than the aetiological myth which has no magical
potency, and does not seem to satisfy any more fundamental
need than curiosity. From the point of view of a functional
anthropology the ritual myth would seem to be more important and likely to appear earlier than the aetiological
myth.

I am in entire agreement with Professor Rose when he
asks, in *Man* for November, 1937, that when a myth is
characterized as a ritual myth proof should be given, (*a*) 'that
it really is mythical and does not belong to *märchen* or saga,
(*b*) that a corresponding ritual, in a possible neighbourhood
to produce the myth in question, be shown reasonably likely
to have existed'. This is the second of the three main points
referred to at the beginning of this paper, and we shall now
go on to deal with it.

With regard to the first of the three myths which I proposed to call *basic*, namely the myth of Tammuz and Ishtar,
I think it will hardly be disputed that this is a genuine
myth. It is a story concerning the actions and sufferings of

gods, and shows none of the usual characteristics of folktale or saga.

The main outlines of the myth, in all its essential details, are embodied in a liturgy from the third dynasty of Ur, about the end of the third millennium B.C. It is clear, from the rubrics which occur at intervals throughout the text, that the liturgy was chanted by the priests at the annual Festival of Tammuz as the accompaniment of the various ritual acts in which the sacred drama of the death of Tammuz, the descent of Ishtar into the underworld, and the return of Tammuz in triumph, were enacted publicly. Hence the myth seems to satisfy Professor Rose's requirements and to present the undeniable characteristics of a ritual myth. It may be remarked that the frequent comparison of both Tammuz and Ishtar to a cedar, a tree which does not belong to the Mesopotamian plain, suggests that the Sumerians brought the ritual and its accompanying myth with them when they migrated from the highlands lying to the north-west of Mesopotamia.

Long after the Babylonian *akitu*-festival, with Marduk as its central figure, had taken the place of the ancient Tammuz festival as the principal event in the Babylonian religious year, the belief in the magic potency of the Tammuz ritual continued to find expression in various *puḥu* or substitution rituals intended to deliver a sick man from the power of evil spirits. In these rituals the sick man was identified with Tammuz by various ritual acts, so that by undergoing the ritual death and resurrection of Tammuz he might be freed from the evil spirit which had seized him.

In view of the wide distribution of the Tammuz-Ishtar myth, its late survival in magical ritual, and the extent to which it has entered into later mythology, folklore and literature, it seems to be useful, if somewhat obvious, to establish its character as a basic ritual myth, possibly the earliest example known to us.

There is one more point to mention before passing on to the second of our basic myths, a point which has a bearing on the subject of the third division of this paper. It is that embedded in the body of the Tammuz liturgy to which reference has been made, we find a list of deified kings of the third dynasty of Ur, who are represented in the liturgy as taking part in the procession which brings gifts to the returning god. These kings are attested from other sources and excavational evidence as historical figures, and the mention of their names in this connexion raises the question of the existence of a border-line region between ritual and history. We shall return to the point later.

Turning now to the second basic myth, the myth of Creation, we find the situation somewhat more complicated. Behind what one might call the canonical form of the Creation myth as contained in the Babylonian Epic of Creation, as it is commonly known, there are a number of early variants, most of which are concerned with a magic ritual by which the first man was created; some of these are also connected with a birth-ritual, and an accompanying myth. Time will not allow of a discussion of the variant forms of the myth, and we must confine our attention to the myth in the form in which it was used as an incantation in the New Year Festival at Babylon.

In outline the myth describes the conquest of the dragon Tiamat by the god Marduk, a conquest achieved mainly by magical means. Then follows the elevation of Marduk to the supreme place among the gods, and the subsequent activities of Marduk, including the ordering of the heavens and the heavenly bodies, and the creation of man for the service of the gods. The creation of man is a magical act depending on the ritual slaying of a god.

Although this myth, at least in the form in which we know it, has clearly undergone some transformation at the hands of the Babylonian priests in the interests of the cult of Marduk, yet there are two points to be noted which seem to bring the myth into the category of the ritual myth. First there is its use at the crucial point in the New Year ritual. When the god is lying dead in the mountain, the myth in the form which I have described is chanted by the priests in order to give life to the god, the chanting being accompanied by a sprinkling with holy water. Hence the myth has magical potency, it is life-giving. Secondly, the myth is an integral part of the more elaborate ritual of the New Year Festival, the whole of which consisted in the seasonal re-enactment of an original situation in which the present order of things, the whole cosmic order, and man himself, were brought into existence by magical means; and the purpose of the annual re-enactment was to keep the order of things going on by the use of the same magical ritual which had brought it into existence. Hence I think that the myth of Creation may rightly be claimed as a basic ritual myth, though I am perfectly ready to admit that in the course of time the Creation-myth tended to be separated from its ritual and to assume an aetiological character.

The third of the myths which I have selected for discussion, the Deluge myth, presents some difficult problems. In the first place, it might well seem to be a straightforward case of an aetiological myth intended to explain an unusual event on supernatural lines. But the matter is not so simple as it appears, and there are several points to be taken into account. First, excavational evidence from Ur, Kish and Erech has shown that these three cities, and especially Ur, suffered from a severe flood at a very early period of their history. In Sir Wallis Budge's description of the Babylonian story of the Deluge, an account which has been admirably revised by Mr Gadd, we are told that 'the Sumerians regarded the Deluge as an historic event, which they were practically able to date, for some of their records contain lists of kings who reigned before the Deluge, though it must be confessed that the lengths assigned to their reigns are incredible. After their rule it is expressly noted that the Flood occurred, and that, when it passed away, kingship came down again from on high.'

Secondly, it has to be noted that in the parallel Egyptian myth of the destruction of mankind there is no flood, but Hathor is the agent of the wrath of Re, and the destruction is connected with the senescence and rejuvenation of the god, while in the Babylonian story Ishtar, the Mesopotamian counterpart of Hathor, is the instigator of the destruction.

Thirdly, the Deluge myth is introduced into the Epic of

Gilgamesh as an espiode in that hero's search for immortality. The last three tablets of the Epic relate how Gilgamesh learning that his ancestor, Up-napishtim, the hero of the Deluge, was the only mortal who had been endowed with immortality, sets out to reach his ancestor in order to discover the secret of immortality for himself and his people. In the course of his quest Gilgamesh crosses the mountains of Mashu which no one but the Sun-god, Shamash, has ever crossed; then he is ferried across the waters of death by Ur-shanabi, the pilot of Ut-napishtim's vessel in the Deluge, and when he finally reaches his ancestor the latter tells him the story of the Deluge in answer to his request for the secret of immortality.

I have discussed elsewhere[2] the significance of the journey of Gilgamesh, and have suggested that there are grounds for believing that it represents a funerary ritual, a ritual journey of the dead such as Mr Layard has described in his study of the Malekulan Journey of the Dead, contributed to Professor Seligman's *Festschrift* volume.

Hence, while there is evidence for the occurrence of a severe flood, or possibly more than one flood, in the early history of Mesopotamia, and the presumption is justified that the various Sumerian forms of the Deluge story are examples of the aetiological myth, the other factors in the situation still remain to be accounted for. The myth of the destruction of mankind by Hathor is independent of a flood element, and is connected with a rejuvenation ritual. An *apsu*, or abyss of waters, in the form of a ritual laver or sea, such as was Solomon's laver, formed part of the equipment of a Babylonian temple. The expression is used of another of the ancestors of Gilgamesh, Meshkingasher, that 'he ascended the mountain and passed through the sea', by which is signified his death and deification. The motive of the story as it is found in the Epic of Gilgamesh is clearly that of a *rite de passage*, by which the ancestor of Gilgamesh passed through the waters of death and attained immortality. In a ritual text of the incantation type, published by Ebeling in his *Tod und*

[2] Chapter IV *infra*.

Leben, there is a reference to a journey in a ship undertaken by a dead man, under the guidance of the king of Dilmun, i.e. Ut-napishtim, to the place of the judgment of departed spirits. The passage is rather obscure, but the connexion of the journey of the soul across the waters with some kind of funerary ritual is clear (Ebeling, *op. cit.*, p. 14). There are several other texts, all belonging to the ritual class, from which it is clear that there was a well-established funerary ritual among the Assyrians and Babylonians, going back at least to the middle of the second millennium B.C., and that the ship, the pilot, the under-world river or sea, a judgment or fixing of destinies, and sometimes a conflict with demon adversaries, were elements of the funerary ritual. Hence, while we have not, so far, the complete text of a funerary ritual for Mesopotamia, as we have in the case of the New Year Festival and the associated Creation myth, yet there is clear evidence of the existence of such a ritual, and enough information about it to enable us to connect the myth of the crossing of the waters in a magic ship to obtain immortality, with such a ritual.

Thus it would seem that a conflation has taken place. The documentary evidence shows that, on the one hand, an aetiological myth explaining a great flood, or floods, in ancient Sumer, existed as early as 2000 B.C., independently of the ritual myth of the journey across the waters of death which is embodied in the Gilgamesh saga; the evidence shows, on the other hand, that the myth, or cycle of myths, relating to Gilgamesh, goes back much earlier. Hence the Gilgamesh story in its present form shows an original ritual myth, with which an aetiological myth has been incorporated at a very early date because it seemed to lend itself appropriately to the ritual intention of the earlier myth.

There is not time to discuss the wide distribution of the Deluge myth and the significance which it carries in the various regions where it is found, but I have a strong impression from an examination of its occurrences that in the great majority of cases, if not in all, the myth has the character of a ritual myth of the *rite de passage* type. Hence I think it may reasonably be classed as a basic ritual myth.

[48]

The third point of my paper can be dealt with briefly. The comparison of the material which Güterbock has collected in his most valuable monograph in *ZA* (' 38) on the historical tradition among the Babylonians and the Hittites, with other ritual material from various sources, shows a curious mingling of genuine historical material with mythical elements of a ritual character. Hence the suggestion arises whether one of the sources of written history may not be the sense of the magical importance of certain ritual situations in which the king is involved. Harper's collection of the Letters of the Assyrian Kings gives many illustrations of the close connexion of ritual with history, and one of Ebeling's ritual texts presents an interesting example of the way in which an historical event, the tragic death of Shamash-shum-ukin, the rebel king of Babylon, in 648 B.C., is used as a ritual occasion, the death of the king being treated as a substitution-ritual.

I do not wish to trespass on ground which belongs to Mrs Chadwick's paper, but only to point out that in the earliest examples of royal inscriptions and records from Mesopotamia it is the religious function or activities of the king which seem to be recorded, such as the dedication or restoration of temples, occasions for which we have the appropriate rituals preserved in Thureau-Dangin's *Rituels accadiens*. Moreover, in texts like *Sargon, King of Battle*, the *naru*-text of Naram-sin, the Hittite *zalpa*-text, and the much-discussed Anitta-text, we have a mixture of well-attested historical material and myths which generally seem to have a ritual intention. For instance, among Naram-sin's historical campaigns we have an account of a combat with a demonic adversary, Su-ila, which recalls the ritual myth of the sacred combat which belongs to the pattern of the New Year ritual. Again, in the Gurparanzahu myth from Boghazköi we have an account of a campaign against Akkad in the course of which a shooting-contest with bow and arrows takes place, Gurparanzahu being the victor over 60 kings and 70 heroes. His victory is followed by what appears to be the ritual of a sacred marriage. Forrer's comment is as follows: 'It relates how this king, in order that he may marry the princess Tatizuli, captures Akkad, the capital of the Babylonians, then, after the feast, a bow and arrow contest takes place, in which Gurparanzahu overcomes 60 kings and 600 heroes. The motive is identical with that of the bow and arrow contest between Odysseus and the suitors, where the prize is the hand of Penelope, as in this case it is the hand of the king's daughter, Tatizuli.'

CHAPTER FOUR

Some Parallels with the Gilgamesh Story[1]

I N his very interesting book, *Indo-European Folk-Lore and
Greek Legend*, Principal Halliday, discussing the problem
of the striking correspondences between many Greek and
Indian stories, says: 'The existence of correspondences of
this kind suggests that there must be some real connexion at
an early date between Eastern and Western stories, in fact
at a date earlier than any possibility of direct contact between
India and Greece.' He goes on to suggest that India and
Greece derived much of the common matter in these stories
from a common source in the Middle East. 'The Empire of
Darius unified the ancient civilizations of the Middle East
into a single entity with a common official language, Aramaic.
Its boundaries touched India on the one hand and Europe on
the other. That the ancient civilizations thus fused by the
Persian Empire possessed a story literature that is very old
we know, though unfortunately its content has been almost
entirely lost: we have a few folk-tales, romances and the
Admonitions of Ptah-hotep from ancient Egypt, the fragments
of the Gilgamesh Epic from Mesopotamia, and practically
nothing else of the secular literature except what has happened to be included in the Old Testament.'

Dr Halliday has indicated here a very fruitful field of research. Far more of the ancient story literature of the ancient
East has survived than is usually realized, and though its
amount may seem small in comparison with the wealth of
European folklore, yet every fragment yields some connexion
or parallel with later story forms. An interesting confirmation
of Dr Halliday's suggestion is to be found in the fact that the
early Babylonian myth of Adapa, which offers several striking
parallels with common folklore motives, was found on a tablet
among the Tell el-Amarna material. It had apparently been

[1] Paper read at a meeting of the Folk-Lore Society, 1934. First published in *Folk-Lore*.

used as a school exercise by Egyptian scribes in learning Akkadian, a language which was the speech of diplomatic and commercial intercourse in the Near East in the fourteenth century B.C., long before Aramaic had acquired the same status in the time of Darius.

One of the stories mentioned in the last quotation, the story of Gilgamesh, has survived from early Sumerian times in a sufficiently complete form to be used here as an illustration of the thesis suggested by Dr Halliday.

There are various elements in the story which offer parallels with Greek legend. It is possible that the legend of Medusa's head springs from the episode of the slaying of Humbaba, and that much of the material in the Hercules cycle has its source in the stories about Gilgamesh. A study of this ancient treasure of material embodied in the myths of Egypt and Babylon makes it very clear that many of the commonest and most important of the motives of folklore and fairy tale not only of Europe but throughout the world can be traced to this source.

But in this paper I have confined myself to one episode or group of episodes in the Gilgamesh Epic,[2] to which parallels appear in the Hebrew saga of Elijah, and in some extremely interesting material from Melanesia for which I am indebted to my friend Mr Layard.

As the story of Gilgamesh is not universally known, it may be permitted to give a brief account of it and of the significance of Gilgamesh in Babylonian saga. I say saga, rather than myth, because it seems possible that an historical person lies behind the mythical figure of the Epic. According to the old Sumerian king-lists, Gilgamesh was the fifth king of the 1st dynasty of Erech.[3] The first king of the 1st dynasty of Ur, Mesanipadda, was formerly regarded as a purely mythical figure. But his seal has been discovered, identifying him as an actual king. Hence it would be rash to deny the historicity of Gilgamesh.

[2] For an English translation see *The Epic of Gilgamesh*, by R. Campbell Thompson, to which reference may be made for the details given here; also an excellent translation in *ANET*, pp. 72-99.

[3] Meissner, *Babylonien und Assyrien*, vol. i, p. 441.

His position in the king-lists shows that he belongs to the border-line between pure myth and the beginnings of historical tradition, since after his time the fabulous length attributed to the reigns of the earlier kings gives place to rational numbers. In the epic his flesh is said to be the flesh of the gods, and he is described as being two-thirds god and one-third man. The whole story of Gilgamesh as given in the Epic is too long to be related here, but the situation which gives rise to the episodes with which we are here concerned must be briefly described.

In the course of the story Gilgamesh becomes closely associated with Enkidu, a strange figure who may represent in saga form the conquest of the early nomadic hunter and food-gatherer by the urban civilization of Sumer. Enkidu shares the adventures of Gilgamesh, and his untimely death fills Gilgamesh with fear of death and the desire for immortality. Impelled by this desire Gilgamesh declares his intention of going to find his ancestor Ut-napishtim, who, according to Babylonian tradition, had escaped the Flood by the favour of the gods and had been granted immortality, in order that he might learn from him the secret of immortality.

In the Sumerian version of the story of the Flood Ut-napishtim dwells on an island at the head of the Persian Gulf, a point of significance in connexion with our Melanesian material. But Gilgamesh is represented in the myth as journeying westward towards Mt. Mashu, where the sun was supposed to disappear at sunset. This apparent contradiction has probably a ritual origin. After various adventures Gilgamesh arrived at the mountain which was guarded by Scorpion-men,[4] whom it was death even to see. Gilgamesh falls prostrate with fear, but is recognized as being of divine origin, and is kindly received by the Scorpion-men. He is told that it is impossible for him to continue his journey, since none but the hero Shamash, the Sun-god, had succeeded in crossing the mountain, which required twelve double-hours to cross. Gilgamesh nevertheless persists, during the first twelve hours of the

[4] In *Bab. Bathra*, 74a, Mt. Sinai is encompassed by a scorpion.

journey the darkness increases, then it becomes lighter, until at the end of the 24 hours he reaches a region of bright daylight and arrives at the garden of the gods, where is the tree of the gods.

Here he is again dissuaded by Shamash, who tells him that his quest must be in vain, but Gilgamesh declares his intention of continuing. He then comes to the abode of the goddess Siduri by the sea. Dr Campbell Thompson's note on her name suggests a connexion with intoxicating drink, and a possible parallel with the sirens of the Ulysses saga. She is at first repelled by the appearance of Gilgamesh, but when he explains that he is in mourning for his friend and tells her the object of his quest she too tells him that his quest is vain, and advises him to enjoy life while he may since none can escape death. When he again declares his intention of proceeding, and asks for guidance, she tells him that no one but the hero Shamash has ever crossed the ocean, and that even if he succeeds in crossing the ocean he will still have to cross the waters of Death. As he still persists she tells him that Urshanabi, the pilot of his ancestor, Ut-napishtim, is available, and advises him if possible to cross with him. He finds Urshanabi, who tries to dissuade him, using the same formula as Siduri and Shamash. When he sees that he is determined to go on, he tells him to go into the forest and cut down 120 poles, each 60 cubits long. With these he punts the boat, letting each pole fall in turn, apparently to prevent his hands from touching the waters of death. The necessity for the poles seems to arise from the fact that Gilgamesh had destroyed some essential part of the boat, but the experts have not yet been able to explain the meaning of the term used to describe it. As they near the shore Ut-napishtim sees them coming and also notices that this unexplained part of the boat's equipment is missing. When they arrive Gilgamesh tells his ancestor who he is and why he has come. The reply of Ut-napishtim is discouraging. He tells Gilgamesh that Mammitum, the fixer of destinies, has settled the fate of every man with the Annunaki, and that there is no escape from death. Gilgamesh then asks him how he has himself escaped death. He proceeds to give Gilgamesh the account of the Flood and his escape, and the subsequent bestowal of immortality on him by the gods. The connexion of the Flood with the search for immortality is significant and will be discussed later.

Then Gilgamesh repeats his request and Ut-napishtim tells him that the first requirement is to abstain from sleep for six days and seven nights. Gilgamesh attempts to do this, but is overcome by weariness and falls asleep. While he is sleeping, the wife of Ut-napishtim bakes a loaf for him, and makes a mark on the wall for each day that he sleeps. On the seventh day, when the loaf is ready, Ut-napishtim awakens Gilgamesh and gives him directions about recrossing the sea. He also tells him that there is a magic plant which grows at the bottom of the sea which has the property of restoring youth. (*Shibu issahir amelu.*) Gilgamesh dives for it and is successful in bringing it up. He announces to Ur-shanabi his intention of taking it home to Erech in order that his people may enjoy the benefit of it. On the way back Gilgamesh stops at a pool to bathe. While he is doing so, a serpent discovers the plant by its smell and eats it; the result of this is that the serpent casts its skin and recovers its youth. But Gilgamesh sits down and laments the failure of his quest. He returns to Erech, and his further adventures, together with his attempts to call up the spirit of his friend, Enkidu, do not concern us here. It would appear, however, that he made further ritual experiments, as is shown by a new and interesting fragment of the myth discovered by Mr Gadd and recently published in the *Revue d'Assyriologie* (also included in the *ANET* translation).

We shall discuss the general significance of the story after we have examined the parallels from other sources, but the following points may be noted here:

1. The quest for immortality is essentially the search for the right ritual, the knowledge of what to do in order to secure a continued existence of the body after death.

2. This knowledge is possessed by the ancestors, and can only be obtained from them.

3. Two different ideas are confused in the myth:
   (*a*) The idea that the dwelling of the dead is in the west, the sun-set land, and that a mountain must be ascended or crossed in order to reach it.
   (*b*) The idea that the dwelling of the dead is on an island, and that the sea must be crossed to reach it.
4. The length and difficulty of the journey, the darkness that envelops it, and the attempts made to prevent its achievement.
5. Although the garden and the tree of the gods play no definite part in the story, they are mentioned and form part of the setting of the myth.
6. The need of a ferryman and a boat in order to cross to the land of the dead.
7. The vital importance of avoiding any contact with the water of death. In the Gilgamesh story this is secured by the device of the poles.
8. The significance of the seven days' sleep, the burden of mortality.
9. The supernatural food, the loaf prepared by Ut-napish-tim's wife to sustain Gilgamesh on the return journey.
10. The magic herb of immortality, growing at the bottom of the sea.
11. The theft of the herb by the serpent, and two very early mythical motives:
    (*a*) The idea that the serpent is the means of depriving man of immortality.
    (*b*) The idea that the serpent is connected with re-birth.
12. In general, the sense of frustration that pervades the Babylonian myth, and is found in other myths, such as the myth of Adapa and the myth of Etana. The secret of immortality has been lost.

We will turn now to the saga of Elijah. Jensen has observed the connexion of this story with the Gilgamesh Epic, but what is valuable in his study of the Epic has been so obscured by the vast amount of fantastic speculation which it contains that it has escaped general notice.

It is recognized by scholars that in the two books of Kings the sagas of the prophets constitute a distinct strand in the historical narrative. They are probably excerpts from an early *acta sanctorum*, a collection of stories about the prophets compiled in the various centres of 'schools' of the prophets which arose in and after the time of Samuel. While these stories contain undoubted historical material, they also contain a great deal of purely mythical matter whose form has been determined by existing story forms with which the Hebrews had become familiar in the course of their settlement in a country pervaded by the influence both of Egyptian and Babylonian culture.

The part of the Elijah saga which concerns our enquiry is found in I Kings 19, and II Kings 2. It begins by telling how, after Elijah's exploits in slaying the Tyrian priests of Baal, Jezebel threatened to kill him. In terror of his life he fled from the confines of Israel and came to Beersheba, in Judah. Here he left his servant and went on alone into the wilderness. After praying that he might die, he fell asleep under a juniper tree. An angel awoke him and said, 'Arise and eat. And he looked and behold there was a cake baken on the hot stones, and a cruse of water. And he did eat and drink and laid him down again. And the angel of the Lord came again a second time, and touched him and said, Arise and eat; because the journey is too great for thee. And he arose and did eat and drink and went in the strength of that meat forty days and forty nights unto Horeb, the mount of God.'[5] Here he lodges in a cave and experiences the effects of tempest, earthquake and fire, but, we are told, the Lord was not in any of these. Then there comes what our versions render as 'A still small voice'. The correct rendering is 'A thin whisper'. The word used here for 'whisper' occurs in a remarkable passage in Job 4.16. It is worth quoting for the light which it throws on our text.

Eliphaz is describing a nocturnal visitation which he had experienced: 'Then a spirit passed before my face; the hair of my flesh stood up. It stood still, but I could not discern the

[5] I Kings 19.5-8.

appearance thereof; a form was before mine eyes, and I heard a *whisper* and a voice.' Another instructive parallel occurs in Isa. 29.4: 'And thou shalt be brought down, and shalt speak out of the ground, and thy speech shall be low out of the dust; and thy voice shall be as one that hath a familiar spirit, out of the ground, and thy speech shall whisper out of the dust.' The last quoted passage curiously resembles the description at the end of the Gilgamesh Epic of the voice of Enkidu coming up out of a hole in the ground.

Hence it is an attractive suggestion that the sound which Elijah recognizes as supernatural is a spirit voice, the sound of the whistling voice of the dead. He receives the intimation that his own career is over, and that he is to anoint his successor. The saga continues in II Kings 2. Elijah takes his successor with him to the Jordan. He strikes the water with his folded mantle and the river divides so that they both pass over on dry ground. Then a chariot of fire and horses of fire appear and Elijah is taken up into heaven by a whirlwind. As he goes, his mantle falls from him and is assumed by his successor, Elisha.

The points which call for note in this story are:

1. The sleep which falls upon Elijah, so heavy that he needs to be aroused twice by the angel before he can continue his journey.
2. The supernatural food provided for him. He goes 'in the strength of this meat forty days and forty nights'.
3. The journey is no ordinary one. It is not 100 miles from Beersheba to Horeb. Hence the length of the journey is described in supernatural terms, forty days and forty nights is a period with special supernatural associations. Moses was forty days and forty nights with God on Horeb.
4. Horeb is definitely the abode of the God of the ancestors of the Hebrews. It was there that the ritual covenant between Jahveh and the Hebrew people was first established. In early Hebrew poetry Jahveh is represented as coming from Horeb to the help of his people.

5. Elijah takes up his dwelling in a cave. The connexion of the cave with the abode of the dead is obvious and will be referred to again when we come to our third section.

6. The real meaning of the voice which Elijah hears is particularly suggestive. It is the thin piping voice of the dead, as the other Hebrew parallels clearly show.

7. The next stage of the journey, the Jordan, has also ancestral associations.

8. The parting of the waters has a similar significance to the device by which Gilgamesh avoids touching the waters of death.

9. The mantle, like the staff, might serve as the double or representative of its owner. Parallels may be found in the use of the mantle of Assyrian kings as representing the actual presence of the king himself, and in the use of the staff of Elisha in the story of the Shunammite's son (II Kings 4.29).

10. The ascent into heaven, though it has no parallel in the story of Gilgamesh, has a striking correspondence in the myth of Etana's ascent to heaven on an eagle.

Fuller discussion of the implications of the various elements in this story will be resumed after we have described the Melanesian material.

This extremely interesting material, for which I am indebted to Mr Layard, was obtained by him from the inhabitants of the small islands off Malekula, named Vao, Atchin and Wala. It is concerned with the beliefs of the inhabitants of these islands regarding the journey of the dead to the place of departed spirits.

The material is very full and detailed, and I hope it will soon be published,[6] as it affords a striking illustration of the mechanism of culture spread within a small and controlled area. It will only be possible here to summarize the main features of the journey of the dead as they appear on each of the three islands, without discussing the changes in belief

[6] It will be published in the forthcoming volume of *Festschrift* for Professor Seligman.

and ritual which have taken place, and their causes, all of which are fully dealt with in the clearest possible way in Mr Layard's paper, from which I quote.

According to the belief current in these islands, the dead continue their existence on one of the volcanoes on Ambrim, a large island some 50 miles away, where they dance all night, and, according to the different accounts, either sleep or become disintegrated during the day. The accounts here summarized deal with their journey thither down the coast of Malekula, from a promontory on which they are invisibly ferried over to their future home.

After burial with due rites, the dead man first makes his way to the long black sand beach called Ghoramp, on the mainland between the islands of Atchin and Wala. Here he enters a cave called 'the Cave of the Dead'. As he goes in, his way is blocked by a Guardian Spirit called Le-hev-hev. It is not known whether this spirit is a man or a woman. After a conflict between Le-hev-hev and another spirit who takes the part of the dead man, he is allowed to enter the cave and join his friends.

He then proceeds on his journey down the coast until he arrives at sun-down at the promontory facing Ambrim. Here he makes a fire to attract the attention of the ghostly ferryman on Ambrim. The ferryman paddles over in his ghost's canoe, which consists simply of driftwood, and takes the newcomer back with him to Ambrim, where he joins in the nightly dance of the dead.

This is a brief summary of the Vao account which is supplemented by the fuller account from Atchin and Wala. According to these accounts, when the dead man sets out on his journey he first ascends a mountain on the mainland and climbs a tree and either eats of its fruit or gnaws its trunk. The name of the fruit of the tree is apparently the same as that of the S.W. Bay story of the 'forbidden fruit'. He then goes down to the shore and walks round a stone called 'the whistling stone', drawing in his breath with a whistling sound. He then walks through the cave of the dead and proceeds along the black sand beach until he comes to a river; he strikes its waters with a wand which had been buried with him, cut to the exact length of his height, and the waters divide to let him pass through, closing again after him. He continues southward until, at the end of the beach, he comes to a stone called 'Nose-devouring stone'. He presents the stone with the ghost of a fowl which he had carried with him, in order to avoid having his nose flattened. He then comes to the promontory and meets with a spirit represented by a stone associated with a shark and a bird and pentacles. This spirit must be propitiated with an offering, and corresponds to the Guardian Spirit of the cave in the Vao account.

Here the dead man lights a beacon with a brand stolen from a fire of living people. This attracts the attention of the ferryman on Ambrim, whose name is Shules, a name which, according to Mr Layard, is connected with the Atchin word used to designate the feast of communion with the dead. Shules comes over to see from what village the dead man hails, he then returns to Ambrim and tells the members of the dead man's village that one of their number is waiting on the other side. Then they all come over in their flotsam canoes, and take him back with them to the land of the dead.

On Ambrim the dead dance every night till the appearance of the Morning Star, when their heads fall off and their bones fall asunder till they join again the following evening. The newly arrived ghost joins in the dance, but his head does not fall off till the seventh night after his arrival, which is supposed to be the night when the body finally rots in the grave.

These are the main facts concerning the journey of the dead as it is believed to take place in these islands. It is clear that we have to do almost entirely with the performance of funerary ritual and its effect on the future life of the dead. In the Gilgamesh Epic and the story of Elijah, on the other hand, the ritual element is concealed behind a veil of myth and saga.

The points which offer parallels to the two previous stories are as follows:

1. There is a journey to the abode of the ancestors, marked by dangers and obstacles.

2. In all three accounts there is some confusion between the mountain and the cave as the abode of the dead.

3. There is water to be crossed. In the Hebrew and the Melanesian stories the water is divided by magical means, but in the Gilmagesh Epic contact is avoided by the device of the poles.

4. In the Gilgamesh Epic and the Melanesian traditions we have the presence of a ferryman and a boat. In both accounts the ferryman is connected with the ancestors. In the Melanesian account this is indicated by the meaning of the ferryman's name, and in the Babylonian story by the fact that the ferryman is the one who had piloted Ut-napishtim through the waters of the flood.

5. In the Melanesian account the magic tree and its fruit has a parallel in the garden and tree of the gods in the Gilgamesh Epic.

6. In all three stories there is a significant interval, Gilgamesh sleeps for seven days, Elijah sleeps for an unspecified period of time, while in the South Sea account an interval of seven days elapses before the dead man becomes fully united to his ancestors.

7. In the Elijah story we have the thin whisper, which I have suggested from other Hebrew parallels should be connected with the sound or voice of the dead. In the Melanesian account we have the whistling intake of breath, the sound which the dead man makes as he walks round the 'whistling stone'. There is a parallel in the Gilgamesh Epic in the description of the sound like the wind which the spirit of Enkidu makes as it comes up through the hole in the ground.

8. There is the magic food, prepared by supernatural means in both the Semitic stories.

9. Lastly, there is the point already noted, that both in the Gilgamesh story and in the Melanesian account the abode of the ancestors is on an island only to be reached by a voyage.

I think it is clear from the above account that these three stories exhibit a sufficiently large number of striking parallels to make the theory of independent origin a difficult one. In his masterly analysis of the various traditions from the three islands concerned Mr Layard has shown that the correspondences and differences between the three accounts arise from culture spread connected with a change from an older dolmen and contracted burial culture to a later monolith and extended burial culture. He has also shown important connexions with the development of Egyptian funerary ritual.

In the parallels described here we have to do with a possible spread of culture extending over a far wider range both in time and space, and involving a far more complicated problem of transmission. In Egypt, where funerary ritual was most fully developed and where we have the amplest evidence, the problem of securing immortality by ritual means may be said to have been solved. The early coronation ritual of which the Ramesseum papyrus gives us evidence, and what we know of the Sed Festival, show that the ritual by which the king was installed as the centre of the life and well-being of the community, and that by which his vigour was prolonged and renewed, were patterned on the funerary ritual by which he was united after death to the Sun-god, his divine ancestor, and took his place in the realm of the blessed dead.

In Mesopotamia, on the other hand, the situation is different. As has been already suggested, throughout the remains of Babylonian myth there seems to run an undertone of frustration. There is a quest for immortality which is continually defeated by the craft or malevolence of jealous gods. But there are also traces that what has been lost was once known and enjoyed. The first king of the first dynasty of Erech, the predecessor of Gilgamesh, Meshkingasher, is called the son of the Sun-god, has the divine determinative prefixed to his name, and is said to have ascended the mountain and passed through the sea. It has been suggested, with some probability, that Meshkingasher is to be identified with Utnapishtim, the only ancestor of Gilgamesh who had attained immortality. In connexion with the material we have been

discussing the mention of the mountain and the sea is significant. Gilgamesh, in the course of his journey in search of
immortality, both ascends the mountain where the sun sets,
and crosses the sea. In the general pattern of Babylonian
religious ceremonial, the *ziqqurat*, or great temple tower held
a central place. It was the 'mountain' where the dead god was
shut up, from which he emerged risen and triumphant, and
the place where the sacred marriage was consummated. But,
in the main, Babylonian ritual, as far as the great seasonal
festivals were concerned, seems to have been directed to
securing the continued potency of the king as the divine
centre of the well-being of the community.

There is little trace of funerary ritual, but it is possible that
behind the myth of Gilgamesh there lie the outlines of such a
ritual; it is also possible that the Flood-myth so closely bound
up with the Gilgamesh story, has its origin in the same ritual
motive, a suggestion which lies beyond the scope of this
paper to discuss.

The influence of Babylonian culture on the religion and
civilization of the Hebrews has long been recognized in details, but that the general pattern of early Hebrew religious
ceremony, through the mediating influence of Canaanite culture, was largely determined by Mesopotamia, is only recently
beginning to be admitted. The later trend of Hebrew religion
under the direction of the prophetic movement was towards
the complete obliteration of this early pattern. Hence the
Elijah saga is particularly interesting, as showing that it is
not only in the early myths of Genesis that clear traces of this
older pattern are to be found. In its present form many of its
elements have been rationalized, and of course there can be
no doubt that Elijah was an historical figure who played an
important part in the struggle against the introduction of the
Tyrian Baal cult in the reign of Ahab. But, as other historical
examples show, an historical figure may become the nucleus
of a legend, and the form assumed by the legend betrays the
influence of an older culture pattern which had once been
dominant in the region where the legend or saga takes its rise.

In this case, it seems indubitable that the form taken by the story of the closing acts of Elijah's life is due to the influence of the Gilgamesh story, and that originally this section of the Elijah story was a description of what might be called a Hebrew journey of the dead, with its corresponding funerary implications.

Archaeological evidence shows that an early dolmen culture existed in Canaan, and that, at a later date, there was a wide-spread monolith culture which was prevalent there at the time of Hebrew settlement in Canaan. All the evidence of excavation also goes to prove that there was a well-established funerary ritual, as shown by the universal presence of funerary furniture and offerings in tombs and burial places. There are also traces in Hebrew legislation of an earlier funerary ritual, seen in the prohibition of ancient mourning customs, ritual disfigurements and taboos. Hence, it is possible that the remarkable correspondences between the Elijah story and the Melanesian journey of the dead, point to the transmission on a larger scale, of such a ritual pattern as Mr Layard has shown in process of transmission and transformation on a smaller scale in the limited area of the small islands of Malekula. His evidence suggests the transmission of Egyptian elements to that area, a possibility which Professor Elliot Smith's demonstration of the identity of the mummification practised in certain of the South Sea islands with the practice of the twenty-second dynasty confirms.

The present evidence suggests that such spread was not limited to Egyptian elements but that elements from the Mesopotamian area may also have travelled along the same route. In Mr Layard's words: 'There is evidence from a wider field to show that successive elements of belief, not necessarily originating in a common centre have spread in a series of waves over a large portion of the globe, and such local amalgamations, each laying varying stress on the individual component elements is precisely what we should expect, and what, in fact, is occurring under our very eyes to-day.'

CHAPTER FIVE

Cain and Abel[1]

THE ancient biblical story of what is commonly regarded as the first fratricide has been the subject of innumerable monographs and endless learned discussions. The only reason for attempting a fresh study of the material is, first, that it seems possible in the light of recent researches into the nature of the religious pattern of the early civilizations of Mesopotamia and the regions under its cultural influence to place the story in a fresh setting, and, secondly, the new texts from Ras Shamra seem to offer new light on the subject.

In his *Folklore in the Old Testament*, at the end of his chapter on 'The Mark of Cain', Sir James Frazer, after suggesting that the deity may have decorated Cain with red, black, or white paint, or perhaps with a tasteful combination of these colours, after the manner of various savage peoples, concludes his study with the following extremely humorous remarks: 'Thus adorned, the first Mr Smith—for Cain means Smith—may have paraded the waste places of the earth without the least fear of being recognized and molested by his victim's ghost.

'This explanation of the mark of Cain has the advantage of relieving the Biblical narrative from a manifest absurdity. For on the usual interpretation God affixed the mark to Cain in order to save him from human assailants, apparently forgetting that there was nobody to assail him, since the earth was as yet inhabited only by the murderer and his parents. Hence by assuming that the foe of whom the first murderer went in fear was a ghost instead of a living man, we avoid the irreverence of imputing to the deity a grave lapse of memory little in keeping with the divine omniscience. Here again, therefore, the comparative method approves itself a powerful *advocatus Dei*.'

[1] Paper read before the British Association, 1937. First published in *Folk-Lore*.

Far be it from me to speak against my father Parmenides, and it is hardly necessary to say that in Sir James Frazer's hands the comparative method has abundantly justified itself, but this particular case is an example of the vital importance of combining the comparative method with the historical and genetic method. In other words, the saga of Cain and Abel can only be understood in the light of a knowledge of the religious and social conditions of the time and of the region from which it sprang.

In its present setting the saga of Cain and Abel forms a part of a series of ancient myths, grouped together by the latest editors of the Pentateuch, and representing the earliest traditions of the Hebrews about the origin of their race. It requires a very slight examination of the stories to show that in their original form they were independent of one another and owe their present connexion to the hand of the editors who gave the book its present form. It is at once clear that the story under discussion was originally quite unconnected with the Paradise stories since it reflects the existence of two types of primitive social organization, pastoral and agricultural, and Cain's words 'every one that findeth me shall slay me' imply, not the fear of a ghost, but the existence of other hostile members of the human species.

Hence it is necessary to study the story in isolation from its present artificial connexion with the Paradise stories and with the genealogies which follow it. Thus regarded it presents the picture of a pastoral and an agricultural community, each performing its own characteristic rituals, presumably at the same time of year. The ritual of the pastoral group is successful, while that of the agriculturist is not.

Now we know that the Hebrews begin to make their appearance upon the stage of history about the middle of the second millennium B.C., and their own traditions take back their origins to the district about Harran, in the N.W. of Mesopotamia, and the Aramaean region lying to the N.E. of Palestine. Hence their traditions will reflect the general social and religious pattern characteristic of the ancient Near East about the beginning of the second millennium B.C., or slightly earlier.

From the sources at our disposal we know that by this time the change which Professor Childe has called the urban revolution had taken place and that in Mesopotamia and Canaan city-states prevailed, surrounded by dependent agricultural areas, with a fringe of semi-nomadic pastoral population. The general ritual pattern of the period was one of seasonal fertility rituals. One of the earliest Hebrew seasonal rituals, the Passover, presents the form of a mixed pastoral and agricultural character, with the slaying of a lamb or kid together with the ritual eating of unleavened cakes.

Hence we may legitimately assume that the purpose of the ritual in the original form of the Cain and Abel story was fertility, and that the probable time of such a ritual was the spring, when the main seasonal fertility rituals took place.

The next point which arises is that Jahveh is said to have accepted the pastoral offering and to have rejected the agricultural offering, involving the question of how the distinction was indicated. At the time when such rituals were practised only one criterion of success or failure was recognized, namely the pragmatic test of increased fertility or the opposite. The shepherd's flocks increased and multiplied while the unfortunate tiller of the soil saw his crops wither as the heat of the year increased in strength towards the summer.

Then comes the so-called fratricide, but there are some details in the story which call for discussion. We have first a communication from Jahveh to Cain which is very obscure and corrupt and has evidently suffered in the course of transmission. Its form seems to suggest an oracular reply, and it is possible that the original form of the story recorded that the unfortunate agriculturist consulted the oracle to learn what he should do under the circumstances. The answer seems to suggest that the enquirer knows what the proper ritual is, and that there is a *robeṣ*, a hostile demonic power waiting to be propitiated. The word translated 'lieth' or 'croucheth' is the same as the Akkadian *'rabiṣu'*, 'the evil croucher', who lies in wait for his offering, and is frequently mentioned in Babylonian magical texts. We shall return to the connexion with Mesopotamian ritual later.

The next step is introduced by a significant phrase which is omitted in the Hebrew text but is supplied by the LXX, 'And Cain said unto Abel his brother, Let us go into the field'. It is in the *field*, the tilled soil whose infertility has brought about the situation, that the slaying of the shepherd takes place, and the suggestion here made is that the slaying was a ritual one, not an impulsive murder instigated by jealousy, but a ceremonial killing intended to fertilize the soil by drenching it with the blood of the victim, in the words of the Hebrew text, 'the earth has opened her mouth to receive thy brother's blood'.

Then follows the curse of Cain, his flight from the scene of the slaying, and the protective mark which he receives from Jahveh. The incompatible elements in the present form of the story have long been a cause of trouble to commentators; Jahveh curses the killer and at the same time places him under his protection. Also the problem of the nature of the mark has given rise to much speculation, as illustrated by the extract from Sir James Frazer quoted above.

These difficulties tend to disappear if we relate the rest of the story to the interpretation suggested above. But there is one apparent difficulty which may be dealt with first. We have suggested that the object of the ritual slaying was the fertilization of the soil, whereas the terms of the curse suggest that as the result of Cain's nefarious deed the earth will henceforth refuse to yield her strength to her defiler. The answer to this difficulty is that the story has been edited from the religious standpoint of a much later time and that we have a double element to deal with. We have to disentangle the original intention of the story from the later colouring which it has received from the hands of an editor to whom the ritual of human sacrifice had become abhorrent. Later Hebrew writers, forgetting or ignoring the fact that their ancestors had once participated in such rituals, came to regard the whole ritual pattern with all its implications as purely Canaanite, and spoke of the land as rejecting its former inhabitants on account of such practices, while they attributed its infertility to the same cause. The story of Abraham and Isaac similarly illustrates the point of view of a later time which had revolted against the barbarity of human sacrifice. But a well-known passage dating from the time of Hezekiah (Micah 6.7) shows that as late as the end of the eighth century B.C. the average Hebrew believed that such sacrifices were acceptable to Jahveh.

Hence we may regard this element in the story of Cain and Abel as due to the hand of the later editor of the saga. But the flight and the mark raise important points of contact with the general ritual pattern which we are considering. In the ritual of the Babylonian New Year Festival, whose main features are extremely ancient, a sacrificing priest and an exorcist purify the shrine of Nabu with the carcase of a slain sheep, smearing the walls of the shrine with the blood of the sheep, after which they were obliged to flee into the ṣeru, the desert, until the Festival was over, because they are defiled by their ritual act. In the Hebrew ritual of the Day of Atonement, originally part of the New Year ritual, we have a similar combination in the ritual of a slaying and a flight, but here the original human participants in the ritual are replaced by animal victims, the two goats, one of which is slain, while the other is driven out into the desert. In the ancient Athenian ritual of the Bouphonia an ox was slaughtered by two men who were then obliged to flee.

These parallels seem to suggest that the flight of Cain represents the motive of the ritual flight. The sacrificer is defiled by his act and is driven out by the community until he is purified, his guilt is a communal not an individual guilt. It is this which explains why the slayer enjoys ritual protection. He is no common murderer but a priest or sacred person who has performed an act for the benefit of the community, an act which involves ceremonial defilement and the consequent temporary banishment of the slayer, but his person is sacrosanct. This, moreover, suggests that the most likely explanation of the mark is that it represents a tattoo mark or other indication that the fugitive belonged to a sacred class. We have evidence from Hebrew sources that the prophets bore such marks, and the existence of such marks to distinguish the members of temple staffs as the property of the god is abundantly attested in ancient literature.

There are two further points to be discussed. First, in view of the region and the period to which these traditions belong, it is difficult to avoid the conclusion that the ritual slaying of a shepherd which we find in the Hebrew story has connexions with the Tammuz ritual and its associated myth, belonging to early Mesopotamian religion, and characteristic of Canaanite cults down to a comparatively late date.

From the Tammuz liturgies, now available for study in Witzel's fine collection, we find that the god Tammuz, who bears the title of 'the shepherd', dies, or is ritually slain, during the period of summer drought. The time of mourning for him while he is in the underworld is terminated by fertility ceremonies which finally result in his resurrection and return to the earth at the time of the spring revival of vegetation.

Moreover, we find from the Tammuz liturgies and from many later Babylonian magical texts that one of the commonest symbols of Tammuz was the kid or lamb, and that in various apotropaic rituals where a demon is to be exorcised or propitiated, the sick man is identified with Tammuz by means of the animal victim; he undergoes a ritual death by the slaying of the victim, and is thus freed from the power of the demon.

Hence the wide-spread existence in this area of this type of ritual from a very early date supports the suggestion that in the saga of Cain and Abel we have the survival in Hebrew literature of the tradition, worked over by a later hand in the interests of an entirely different religious point of view, of a fertility ritual of the Tammuz type, where a shepherd was ritually slain at the time of the summer drought, and his official slayer was obliged to flee in order to remove the ceremonial guilt of the slaying from the community.

The other point is that this suggestion receives further support from the new material from Ras Shamra. These very interesting texts recently discovered at a site in the north of

Syria date from about the middle of the second millennium B.C. and are contemporary with the period of Hebrew settlement in Canaan. They give us a very full and detailed picture of early Canaanite myth and ritual.

Various types of fertility rituals occur, especially the ceremony of pouring a libation into the earth. Professor Schaeffer says, 'We must consider the possibility of the relation at Minet-el-Beida between the cult of the dead and fertility. A great number of the deposits discovered, especially those with stone or pottery conduits leading to a well or pit, in which vases were often intentionally buried, correspond exactly to the ritual for making plants grow, which has been found on one of the Ras Shamra tablets.' M. Virolleaud translates it as follows: 'Place the pots in the ground. Pour into the heart of the ground the *slm* (Hebrew *shelem*). Pour into the heart of the fields the *arbdd*. If you do this, your tree will be with me (i.e. will be fertile).'

But more important from our point of view is the representation in the myth of Aleyan-Baal and Mot, of a conflict between these two lesser gods who correspond respectively to the principles of fertility and drought. Aleyan is slain by Mot, and goes into the underworld. During his absence there is no rain and all living things wither. Just as Tammuz is brought back by his sister-consort Ishtar, so Aleyan is sought for and brought back by his sister Anat, to the accompaniment of various fertility ceremonies.

In the recently published Ras Shamra text, entitled *La Légende de Danel*, there is a further important parallel to the element of ritual murder in the story of Cain and Abel. In this text we have the account of what has every appearance of being a ritual murder, with the subsequent flight of the slayer to a sanctuary designated for him. The point has been discussed in a paper by Mr T. H. Gaster, contributed to the *Studie Materiali di Storia delle Religioni*, 1936.

It does not seem that the fratricide motive is original to the story, but comes in as the result of the artificial connexion between the Cain and Abel story and the Paradise myth which makes Cain and Abel the children of the first human pair.

Hence when we take the Hebrew story, the Ras Shamra ritual myth of Aleyan and Mot, the ritual slaying of Aqhat, and the Tammuz myth and ritual so early prevalent in Mesopotamia and Canaan, together, the fundamental connexion between them seems to be inevitable.

CHAPTER SIX

The Way of the Initiate[1]

IN the preceding essays of this volume the attention of the reader has been directed mainly to those characteristics of the Age of Transition belonging to the Jewish communities scattered throughout the Roman Empire. But we turn now to an important element in the religious and social life of the Empire which takes us outside the comparatively narrow limits of the Jewish communities. As we shall see, its roots are far older than Judaism, older even than the beginnings of that prophetic movement out of which the Hebrew religion, the parent of Judaism, sprang. This element is that vivid and many-coloured manifestation of religious needs and emotions comprised under the general name of the Mystery Religions.

The subject is a vast one, and it is impossible to do more, in the brief compass of an essay, than indicate the chief features of those strange and alluring cults which, while differing in many ways, all exhibit a similarity of aim and pattern pointing to their common origin in the religious life of the ancient East.

Recent studies in this field have made it clear that in the beginning of the second millennium B.C. the kingdoms of the ancient Near East were dominated by a common religious outlook. A study of the myth and ritual complex of this region, comprising Egypt, Crete, Babylonia and Canaan, shows that under the bewildering variety of their pantheon lie certain common fundamental concepts which express themselves in a ritual pattern whose main features show a remarkable resemblance to one another.

These central concepts are, first, the place of the king in the community. We find that he is the pivot round which the life of the community revolves. Upon his physical vigour and the continuance of his life depend the various aspects of the

---

[1] First published in *Judaism and Christianity*, vol. I, 1937.

well-being of the community, and this feeling finds expression in ritual acts of which the king is the object and centre. The close association of the king with the god in these rituals, and the many ways in which the king is identified with the god, suggest the possibility that originally the king and the god were one.

Next, we find that the ritual life of these early communities is determined by the course of the seasons. In the Tammuz ritual, possibly the earliest organized Mesopotamian ritual, now made available for study in P. Witzel's great collection of Tammuz Liturgies, we find that the ritual re-enacts the death of the god, the desolation of the land and the withering of the crops, the mourning of the goddess, his consort, her descent into the underworld to seek him, his resurrection and return, and the celebration of his victory. In Babylonian ritual texts from the Seleucid period we find that out of the earlier and simpler Tammuz ritual there has developed an elaborate New Year Festival, celebrated in the spring month of Nisan. The main outline of this festival was the same, and consisted of the dramatic representation of the death, resurrection and triumph of Marduk, followed by a sacred marriage and a ceremony known as the fixing of destinies, intended to ensure a happy and prosperous New Year for the community.

Similarly, in Egypt, from the Old Kingdom period down to the decay of Egyptian civilization, the ritual surrounding the myth of Osiris, his death and resurrection, was the central feature of Egyptian religion, and is abundantly illustrated on Egyptian monuments and in Egyptian ritual texts.

The recently discovered Ras Shamra texts show that the same general ritual pattern existed in such an important centre of Canaanite civilization as excavation shows the ancient city of Ugarit to have been. Nor are traces of the same pattern wanting in early Hebrew literature. There is not space in such an essay as this for detailed illustration of this position, but those who may be interested in a fuller exposition of the subject may be referred to the recent volume of essays entitled *Myth and Ritual*, published by the Oxford Press.

While the complex of ritual practices comprised under the

description given above was closely bound up with the political structure of ancient society during the second millennium B.C., it constituted the atmosphere, so to speak, of the religious life of the community, and penetrated deeply into the religious consciousness of the individual, so much so that it was able to survive the decay of the political framework of the ancient empires which took place towards the end of the first millennium B.C.

But in order to estimate the significance of this survival, it is necessary to touch briefly on two important lines of religious development which are characteristic of this Age of Transition.

In the first place, as the result of the prophetic movement which began in the eighth century, together with the subsequent political extinction of Israel, a religion and a people came into being, namely, Judaism and the Jews, completely emancipated from the atmosphere and influence of the ancient ritual pattern. The lofty conception of the Holy One of Israel, the Eternal God who fainteth not, neither is weary, the Maker and Sustainer of all things, who had chosen Israel from the womb to be his servant, was utterly incompatible with the conception of a dying and rising god. Fragments of the ancient pattern might survive in Hebrew poetry, bearing witness to a time when Hebrew religion shared the same general characteristics as did the religion of their neighbours, but the picture of the Jew which we gather from the records of the Age of Transition is of one who is at once at home and a stranger in every city and country of his wide dispersion. Carrying with him his own atmosphere and his own spiritual heritage, bearing the yoke of the Kingdom of Heaven in prosperity and adversity, he is almost completely immune from the influences of the flood of Oriental Mystery-cults which overflowed the Roman Empire during the period with which we are concerned. It is only in the various forms of the Apocalyptic movement in Jewish thought that we can trace the late survival and the transformation of the elements of the old ritual pattern,[2] but this movement left no abiding stamp on later

[2] See Chapter IX, p. 140f.

Judaism. As we shall see later, this fact is of great importance in estimating the influence of the Mystery Religions upon early Christianity.

Secondly, the effect of what we may call the Greek Enlightenment had been to make the fundamental ideas of the ritual pattern, with its sacramental and magical attitude to life, intellectually impossible. We see this reflected in Paul's polemic against Greek rationalism. To the Greek a crucified and risen God was foolishness.

Hence a large section of the more educated and intelligent laity of this period would, like the Jew, but for a different reason, be immune from the emotional influences of the Mysteries.

But these two classes constituted a comparatively small minority of the population of the Roman Empire. For the vast majority other factors were at work which favoured the eager acceptance of the various Oriental cults which, even before the beginning of the Empire, had started to work like leaven in the West. There is not space here to describe these factors in detail, but in brief they are as follows.

First, the destruction of older forms of national government and the obliteration of political boundaries resulting from the conquests of Alexander, a process still further developed by the expansion of the Roman Empire, led to the loss of political consciousness and of that sense of solidarity which the individual derives from his membership of a state or nation. Citizenship in the Roman Empire, in spite of its privileges, could not replace this loss, and for innumerable individuals the close ties and intimate fellowship which membership of one or other of the new religious communities afforded them served to supply this sense of solidarity.

Further, the same process of destruction of ancient states and political units involved the discrediting of the gods with whom the fortunes of these states were bound up. Greek philosophical scepticism tended in the same direction, and although the statues of the Olympians might occupy their ancient places in the temples, their worship had become little more than a respectable convention, and they themselves, as

Jane Harrison has said, were little more than *objets d'art*, decorative but devoid of religious significance.

Lastly, the destruction of ancient political and religious beliefs and hopes lay at the root of that failure of nerve already mentioned. While the belief in the vast potency of evil spirits and the sense of their ubiquity, surviving from the older religions, had lost none of its hold upon the common mind, the old safeguards and protective rituals had lost their power with the decay of the older gods. Hence men felt themselves naked and helpless amid hostile spiritual forces. Even in Paul's letters we can feel the ever-present menace of this lowering cloud of evil in the universe. A famous passage from Harnack's *Mission and Expansion of Christianity* may be recalled in this connexion: 'The whole world and the circumambient atmosphere were filled with devils; not merely idolatry, but every phase and form of life was ruled by them. They sat on thrones, they hovered around cradles. The earth was literally a hell, though it was and continued to be a creation of God.' (I.131).

While these factors, together with the growth of Greek as an international language throughout the Mediterranean area, were specially favourable to the spread of Christianity throughout the Empire, they also provided a congenial soil for the growth of the many forms of Oriental religion which had already begun to invade the Empire before the rise of Christianity.

We turn now to a brief survey of the main types of Oriental Mystery-cults which gained a footing in the Roman Empire during this period of transition.

There were, no doubt, many obscure local cults of which no record has remained, but even such would be embraced under the four main types of which we have evidence from contemporary sources. These are as follows:

(*a*) *Phrygian.*—This wild and remote region of Asia Minor was not only the home of a very early form of the cult of the Mother-goddess, but was also a channel from the earliest times by which various influences from Mesopotamia were transmitted to the West. It is possible that the Cretan form of the cult of the Mother-goddess, which is abundantly

illustrated on early Cretan seals and in cult-objects, was derived from Phrygia. But the three best known forms of
Mystery-cult of Phrygian origin which had a wide vogue in
our period were the cult of Ma-Cybele, the Dionysiac mysteries, and the cult of Sabazius. A valuable study of the last-
named cult and its history by Professor W. O. E. Oesterley is
to be found in the volume of essays entitled *The Labyrinth*[3]
(S.P.C.K., 1935). For fuller details of the other two the
reader may be referred to Professor Cumont's book *Oriental
Religions in Roman Paganism.*

(*b*) *Syrian.*—From Syria, which was closely linked with
the West during our period, there spread into the Empire the
cult of Attis, a form of the far more ancient cult of Tammuz,
and the cult of the Syrian Goddess, mainly known to us from
Lucian's treatise *De Dea Syria.* The latter was derived from
the Mesopotamian cult of Ishtar, the origin of the many
forms of Astarte worship prevalent in Canaan in earlier times.

(*c*) *Egyptian.*—From Egypt came two of the most popular
forms of Mystery-cult prevalent in the early period of the
Empire, the cults of Isis and of the Lord Serapis, which were
closely intertwined with one another. We have a full contemporary account of the mysteries of Isis in the amusing
treatise, or romance, known to English readers under the
title of *The Golden Ass* of Apuleius, a convenient edition of
which exists in the Loeb Classical Library. The name Serapis
has been derived, with some doubt, from the names Osiris
and Apis, but the rites of Serapis were based upon the very
ancient Egyptian myth and ritual of Osiris, one of the central
elements of Egyptian religion. From the well-known treatise
of Plutarch, *Concerning Isis and Osiris,* we can gather something of the nature of the influence which these cults exercised
upon the religious life of the Empire.

(*d*) *Persian.*—The main contribution of Persia to the
movement with which we are concerned was the widespread
cult of Mithra. This was the latest of the four forms here
described to make its influence felt in the Empire. As is well
known, it was carried to the farthest western bounds of the

[3] *Op. cit.,* pp. 115 ff.

Empire by the legions, and its monuments and sanctuaries are known to us from the magnificent work of Cumont. It is, moreover, the only one of the Mystery-cults of which a liturgy has survived. This has been published by Dietrich under the title of *Eine Mithras Liturgie* (1910). In the third century A.D. Mithraism was the most serious rival to Christianity in the Empire, and for this reason its main features will be dealt with more fully later on in this essay, since space will not allow of a detailed account of each of the various forms of Mystery-cult enumerated above.

Such a detailed description is the less necessary for our purpose in that all the various forms of Mystery-cult possessed certain characteristics in common, and we shall now go on to describe those central elements in these cults which constituted the main reason for their success, that which they offered to men and women who had found the more orthodox forms of established religion incapable of giving them what they sought.

In the first place, as their name indicates, all these cults were Mysteries. In order to enjoy the benefits which they offered it was necessary to be initiated, to undergo certain secret rites. These rites all possessed the common character of being *rites de passage*, to use a convenient French anthropological term, by means of them the participant passed from one condition to another. From the dangers and darkness and ignorance of a world which lay under the domination of hostile spiritual powers he passed into a region of enlightenment, privilege and hope.

Secondly, the central feature of these initiatory rites consisted of a symbolic identification of the initiate with the god or goddess whose myth gave its distinctive character to the cult in question. There were two main types of Mystery, differentiated by the nature of their central rite. This consisted either of the symbolic representation of the death and resurrection of the god, or the symbolic enactment of a sacred marriage. As we have already seen, both these rites were essential features of the ancient ritual pattern.

In the rites of Dionysus, Attis, Serapis, and above all in

the Mithraic ritual, the death and resurrection of the god were the central feature of the myth, and by some ritual act the initiate was identified with the god in his death and resurrection. On the other hand, in those rites in which a goddess was the central figure, such as those of the Syrian Goddess, or of Isis, other forms of initiation were practised: for instance, the sacrifice of virility, or the ritual of sacred prostitution.

Thirdly, in nearly all these cults attainment was progressive. A common symbol of the Mysteries was the ladder, representing the successive stages of enlightenment through which the initiate passed in his upward journey. It is interesting to observe that the ladder enters into the very ancient Egyptian coronation ritual preserved in the Ramesseum Papyrus. There it is the magical means by which the dead king attains his deification.

This leads us to the last point, namely, that the goal of the Mysteries in general was deification, the attainment of the age-long desire of man to become as God. The words of an early Father, although intended to apply to Christianity, are borrowed from the language of the Mysteries, and illustrate well the feeling which drew men to them: 'Thou shalt avoid hell when thou hast gained the knowledge of the true God. Thou shalt have an immortal and incorruptible body as well as a soul, and shalt obtain the kingdom of heaven. Thou who hast lived on earth and known the heavenly King, shalt be a friend of God and a joint-heir with Christ, no longer held by lusts, or sufferings, or sicknesses. For thou hast become divine, and all that pertains to the God-life hath God promised to bestow on thee, seeing that thou, now become immortal, art deified' (Hippolytus, *Philosophumena*, x. 34).

While many of the Mystery-cults undoubtedly provided opportunities for the indulgence of the lower elements in man's nature, the more reputable Mysteries demanded of their devotees a long course of training, strict asceticism, and patient endurance of many severe tests, before the higher stages of initiation were reached. Even Christianity never completely divested itself of a certain magical element attach-

F   [81]

ing to its rites, especially to baptism, and the pagan Mysteries to a great extent depended on the general belief of the uneducated in the magical potency of the secret rites, the spells and mysterious *abracadabra* with which they were surrounded. Nevertheless, there is evidence that the initiate did at times experience that sense of enlightenment and enlargement, of union with a vaster richer life, which is characteristic of the mystic experience, whether Christian or pagan.

But the main objects which the initiate believed himself to have attained through deification were the deliverance from the power of the demons and evil forces which threatened him with disease and misfortune in this present life, deliverance from the sense of guilt, the feeling that he might have broken some unknown taboo, or unwittingly offended some vengeful deity; he also believed that through union with Mithra or the Lord Serapis he was assured of a happy immortality after death. In addition to these inestimable gains he enjoyed the warmth and enrichment derived from fellowship in a community whose sacramental meals and common rites sustained him in the trials of his daily calling. It is not surprising that the Mysteries which offered such privileges to their devotees attracted vast numbers of adherents in every corner of the Empire.

We have already referred to the comparative immunity of the Jew from the influence of the Mystery-cults. There were exceptions, as Professor Oesterley has shown in his essay on the Cult of Sabazius mentioned above (p. 79), but the exceptions may well be considered to prove the rule, since a Jew could not become an initiate of any of the Mystery-cults without losing his Jewish privileges. The reasons for this immunity have been touched on above. The more difficult question of the extent to which Christianity was influenced by the Mysteries is dealt with in a short essay later on in this volume. The rest of this essay will be devoted to a description of the characteristic features of Mithraism, since it is the cult concerning which we have most evidence, and, as we have already pointed out, it was the most serious rival to Christianity for the conquest of the Empire.

Like the religions of the ancient East whence it sprang, the cult of Mithra not only possessed an elaborate ritual, but also an imposing myth explanatory of the various stages of the ritual. In addition to these elements there was a body of esoteric teaching of which the priests were the depositaries, and which they communicated to the initiates.

The cult of Mithra goes back to the earliest period of Persian history, possibly to the time when the ancestors of the Hindu peoples had not yet separated from their Iranian kinsmen. But the Mithraism of the period with which we are concerned had undergone many changes and borrowed from many sources. Its doctrine contained elements of Oriental theosophy and Greek philosophy, its myth had borrowed largely from Babylonian myths, and its ritual was compounded of early Magian rites, fragments of Babylonian ritual and elements assimilated from other contemporary Mystery-cults, especially that of Attis which had close connexions with Mithraism in our period.

The theology of Mithraism is too complicated to describe in detail, but its principal features as set forth by Cumont in his *Mystères de Mithra* (1913) may here be briefly summarized. First we find that the characteristic dualism of Persian religion underlies the Mithraic system. The universe is the scene of the age-long struggle between Good and Evil, personified in the figures of Ahuramazda and Ahriman. In Persian apocalyptic the ultimate triumph of Light and Goodness over Darkness and Evil is envisaged, but in the meantime men are exposed to the attacks and constant malevolence of hostile demonic powers, although, on the other hand, they can, by suitable rites and prayers, obtain the help of good spirits, and in this long conflict Mithra, the god of light, is the Mediator, the most powerful aid whom suffering men can invoke.

Secondly, Mithraism had borrowed elements from Babylonian astrology, which played an important part both in the theology and in the ritual. The seven planets and the twelve signs of the Zodiac, taken up into the Mithraic system, together with the conception of Zervan, or Endless Time, were regarded as divine beings, exercising potent influences for good or evil upon human destiny. Of the planets Cumont says: 'Each of the planetary bodies presided over a day of the week, to each some one metal was consecrated, each was associated with some one degree in the initiation, and their number has caused a special religious potency to be attributed to the number seven. In descending from the empyrean to the earth, the souls, it was thought, successively received from them their passions and qualities.'

Thirdly, the apocalyptic element in Mithraism, like that in early Christianity, exercised a very powerful influence upon the minds of its devotees. Cumont's vivid description of it is worth quoting: 'The struggle between the principles of good and evil is not destined to continue into all eternity. When the age assigned for its duration shall have rolled away, the scourges sent by Ahriman will compass the destruction of the world. A marvellous bull, analogous to the primitive bull, will then again appear on earth, and Mithra will redescend and reawaken men to life. All will sally forth from the tombs, will assume their former appearance, and recognize one another. Humanity entire will unite in one grand assembly, and the god of truth will separate the good from the bad. Then in a supreme sacrifice he will immolate the divine bull; will mingle its fat with the consecrated wine, and will offer to the just this miraculous beverage which will endow them all with immortality. Then Jupiter-Ormazd, yielding to the prayers of the beatified ones, will cause to fall from heaven a devouring fire which will annihilate all the wicked. The defeat of the Spirit of Darkness will be achieved, and in the general conflagration Ahriman and his impure demons will perish, and the rejuvenated universe enjoy unto all eternity happiness without end.'

Those who are familiar with Jewish Apocalyptic of this period will recognize the resemblance between its general outline and the picture here set forth, a resemblance which is due, in part, to the influence of Persian religion upon Jewish thought after the Exile.

The last point to be noticed in this summary of Mithraic

theology is its high ethical standard. This was probably an inheritance from Zoroastrianism. The metaphysical dualism of Good and Evil provided a natural basis for an ethic of action. The initiate was from the first imbued with the idea that he was being enrolled in a holy war against every form of evil. That sense of the inherent evil of the flesh, which pervaded all the various forms of Gnosticism, was strongly present in Mithraism, and strict asceticism was the rule for all who sought the privileges of initiation. In this respect Mithraism stood out in sharp contrast with many of the contemporary Mystery-cults.

We turn now to a brief description of the central myth of Mithraism, which underlay the ritual, and which is represented in the rich variety of symbolism depicted in the many monuments of the cult. Like the theology and the ritual, the myth is of a syncretistic character, containing elements borrowed from Babylonian sources intermingled with the original Iranian legend.

According to the myth, the god was born from a rock by the side of a river, under the shade of a sacred tree. His birth was witnessed by shepherds who saw him emerge from the rock, wearing a Phrygian cap, and bearing a knife and a torch. The shepherds made offerings to the new-born god from their flocks and their crops. He then concealed himself in a fig-tree, whose fruit provided him with food and its leaves with clothing. The first of his exploits was a combat with the Sun, with whom, after he had vanquished him, he made an alliance, and whose help he sought in his subsequent adventures. These, which are depicted upon the various Mithraic bas-reliefs, show the influence of the myths of Gilgamesh and of Heracles. The next exploit was the conquest of the primeval bull, the first creature created by Ahuramazda. Mithra caught the bull, subdued it, and brought it to his cave. The central event of the myth is the favourite theme of the Mithraic monuments, and is familiar to us from the great bas-relief of Heddernheim and similar monuments. Here we see Mithra, by divine command, slaying the bull, whose dying body becomes the source of life for mankind. The evil emissaries of

Ahriman, symbolized by the scorpion, the ant, and the serpent, vainly endeavour to poison the life at its source. In the words of Cumont, 'The seed of the bull, gathered and purified by the Moon, produced the different species of useful animals, and its soul, under the protection of the dog, the faithful companion of Mithra, ascended into the celestial spheres above.'

Then came the creation of the first human couple, the attempts of Ahriman to destroy them, and the frustration of his designs by the intervention of Mithra. In this part of the myth we have the representation of a universal deluge and the deliverance of mankind by an ark. The myth closes with the celebration of a Last Supper by Mithra with the Sun and other companions of his labours, and the departure of the god, in the chariot of the Sun, to the celestial abodes.

Such, in brief outline, was the story which formed the ideas and inspired the actions of the soldier of Mithra, playing the same part in his experience as the Gospel records played in the life and thought of the early Christian, who in like manner was imbued from his baptism with the conception of an unceasing warfare to be waged against the powers of darkness. For the Mithraic initiate, his god, immortal and victorious, was his leader in the stern fight, his defender from the demonic powers by whom he was surrounded, his mediator, the source of his life here and hereafter, and in the ritual he became identified with his god, in symbolic actions he passed along the road by which his forerunner had gone towards the apotheosis which was his goal.

The close resemblance between many of the principal ideas and practices of Mithraism and those of the Christian mysteries was the cause of much bitter recrimination on the part of the early Christian writers, who accused the guardians of the Mithraic rites of shameless plagiarism. But while Mithraism was undoubtedly influenced by certain Christian ideas and practices, nevertheless, the main stock of Mithraic myth and ritual is derived from elements which are far older than Christianity. The questions raised by such similarities will be dealt with in the next essay.

There is one point of connexion between the myth and the ritual which calls for comment here. It has already been remarked that the central element in all the various Mystery-cults is some form of *rite de passage* by which the initiate passes from a state of darkness and sin to light and freedom. In many of the cults this element is a symbolic identification of the devotee with the death and resurrection of the god, whose passion and triumph is related in the myth. In her valuable book *From Ritual to Romance* Miss Weston has remarked on the apparent contrast between the two closely connected cults of Attis and Mithra as follows: 'There is thus a marked difference between the two initiations; the Attis initiate dies, is possibly buried, and revives with his god; the Mithra initiate rises direct to the celestial sphere, where he is met and welcomed by his god. There is here no evidence of the death and resurrection of the deity' (*op. cit.*, 157-8).

Now although this statement is justified by the superficial aspect of the myth and ritual of Mithra, yet a closer examination points to the presence of this element of identification with the death and resurrection of the god in the Mithraic mysteries. In the first place, it is generally recognized that the very ancient rite of the Taurobolium was practised in the cults of both Attis and Mithra. In this rite the initiate was placed in a pit with a grating over it; the sacred bull was then slain on the grating and the initiate was drenched with the blood of the slain bull.

From the knowledge which we now possess concerning the early stages of Mesopotamian religion, we know that the bull was a substitute for the king-god in the ancient ritual of the killing of the king. Hence, it can hardly be doubted that the true significance of the Taurobolium in the mysteries of Attis and of Mithra was the identification of the initiate with the death of the god. It was also a λουτρὸν παλιγγενεσίας, 'a washing of regeneration', if we may use the phrase employed by the author of the Epistle to Titus (Tit. 3.5), a phrase which is no doubt borrowed from the language of the Mysteries. Hence the initiate of Mithra, like the initiate of Attis, undergoes a symbolic death before he ascends the ladder which leads to the celestial spheres and ultimate deification.

Most of our knowledge of the ritual of the Mithraic mysteries is derived from references in the writings of the early Christian Fathers, although, since the appearance of Cumont's account in his *Mystères de Mithra*, much light has been thrown on the liturgical formulæ of the rites by Dietrich's publication of the text of a Mithraic liturgy under the title of *Eine Mithras Liturgie*. From this we learn that the general pattern of the rite consists of a series of magical formulæ by means of which the initiate is successively conducted by the priest, or mystagogue, through the seven stages of initiation until he is finally brought by Mithra himself into the presence of the supreme god. It is clear that each stage of the initiation was accompanied by symbolic acts.

The seven stages of initiation, not necessarily taken by all initiates, were denoted by symbolic names derived from elements in the myth. These stages were: the Raven, the Occult, the Soldier, the Lion, the Persian, the Sun-runner, and the Father. The first three ranks were known as the Servants, and were of a lower degree of importance than the last four ranks which bore the title of Participants, since only the members of these ranks were entitled to partake of the full privileges of the mysteries, and probably only these were allowed to participate in the sacramental meal which was the central act in the Mithraic mysteries, being the re-enactment of the Last Supper in the myth, partaken of by the god with his companions before his return to the celestial regions.

Each of the various stages of initiation had its own ritual. Cumont tells us that 'conformably to the ancient Iranian rites, repeated ablutions were prescribed to neophytes as a kind of baptism designed to wash away their guilty stains. As with a certain class of Gnostics, this lustration doubtless had different effects at each stage of initiation, and it might consist, according to circumstances, either in a simple sprinkling of holy water, or in an actual immersion as in the cult of Isis.'

Apparently, initiates were signed or 'sealed' on their foreheads, probably with a red-hot iron, a custom which Paul may have had in mind when he says 'I bear in my body the *stigmata* of the Lord Jesus' (Gal. 6.17). The custom was an exceedingly ancient one in Oriental religion. When the stage of the Lions was reached, we find new methods of purification used. Honey, much in evidence in the Hermetic rites, was poured on the hands and placed on the tongue of the initiate to preserve him from sin. The preservative properties of honey were known to the ancients, and we may recall that the earliest means of deification was the magic ritual of mummification in ancient Egypt.

A further element in the initiatory rites which accompanied each stage of the neophyte's progress was the element of trial. From what we know through the allusions of early Christian writers, the initiate might be said to have died many times, and, as we have already seen, continuous and prolonged asceticism and other austerities marked the whole period of initiation.

Finally, it is clear that the Mithraic sacramental meal was derived from the earlier Mazdean Haoma ritual, which is intimately connected with the kindred Soma ritual preserved in the Vedic literature. Haoma and Soma were both herbs possessing intoxicating properties, and were regarded as a means of partaking of the life of the gods, that is, of deification. In the Mithraic sacramental meal wine took the place of the Haoma. One of the bas-reliefs published by Cumont in his *Mystères de Mithra* is a representation of a sacramental meal. He describes it as follows: 'Before two persons stretched upon a couch covered with pillows is placed a tripod bearing four tiny loaves of bread, each marked with a cross. Around them are grouped the initiates of the different orders, and one of them, the Persian, presents to the two a drinking-horn; whilst a second vessel is held in the hands of one of the Participants. These love-feasts are evidently the commemoration of the banquet which Mithra celebrated with the Sun before his ascension. From this mystical banquet, and especially from the imbibing of the sacred wine, supernatural effects were expected. The intoxicating liquor gave not only vigour of body and material prosperity, but wisdom of mind; it communicated to the neophyte the power to combat the malignant spirits, and what is more, conferred upon him, as upon his god, a glorious immortality' (*op. cit.*, p. 160, English trs. 1903).

Resemblances with the Christian Eucharist are obvious, and were the subject of much controversy in the early Church, but need not be discussed here, as they are dealt with in the next essay.

Enough has been said to show the general character of the Mystery-cults and the place they occupied in the strange melting-pot of races and religions which was the Roman Empire in the Age of Transition.

CHAPTER SEVEN

Christianity and the Mystery Religions[1]

T HE problem of the extent to which early Christianity was influenced by the ideas and practices of the many forms of Mystery-cult in the Roman Empire is one which has been abundantly discussed in recent years, and the purpose of this essay is not to re-argue the question, but to state one aspect of the problem which was ignored by Harnack, and has not received much attention in recent discussions.

In his *Paul and his Interpreters*, Albert Schweitzer was the first, so far as I am aware, to point out the immunity of the Jew to the influences of the Mystery-cults, and it is the significance of this fact, to which attention has already been drawn in the previous essay, that we shall now go on to consider.

In the vivid description of the religious condition of the Gentile given in Eph. 2.12, the writer is consciously contrasting the spiritual wealth of the Jew with the destitution of the Gentile. The Jew had a Messiah, for the Jewish Christian one already revealed, a polity, a covenant rich with promises, a hope, and above all, a God whose achievements and moral character stood out in strong contrast with the objects of Gentile worship. In the Torah, which had become the centre of the Jew's devotion, the moral character of that God was revealed, and in it the application of the will of God to the minutest circumstances of daily life was to be discovered by patient study. The pursuit of righteousness, which Paul designates as the object of Israel's passionate search, was, in reality, the pursuit of the attainment of likeness, moral likeness, to God. The hope of the righteous lay in a blessed and sinless immortality after death in the presence of God, although, for many Jews, this hope included also a transformation of terrestrial conditions, the manifestation of the life of

[1] First published in *Judaism and Christianity*, vol. I, 1937.

'the age to come' on earth through the agency of the Messiah, by whom the purposes of God were to be fulfilled.

Between the eternal, immortal, invisible, and only wise God, and the dying and rising gods of the Mystery-cults, there was a great gulf fixed. There is a striking utterance of one of the later prophets, Habakkuk, which bears witness to the existence, centuries before our period, of the sense of this contrast. In Hab. 1.12, following the older MSS. tradition embodied in the reading of the R.V. margin, we read, 'Art not thou from everlasting, O Lord my God, mine Holy One, *thou diest not*'.

Hence, while it was easy enough for a Gentile to be a member of one of the many Mystery-cults and at the same time remain attached to one of the orthodox forms of religion, and there is also evidence to show that in the second century the line between Christianity and the Mystery-cults was somewhat blurred, a Jew could only enjoy the benefits of the Mystery-cults at the cost of the surrender of his Jewish status and privileges.

Moreover, as I have endeavoured to show in my Essay on 'The Myth and Ritual Pattern in Jewish and Christian Apocalyptic' (Chapter Nine), the same ancient ritual pattern which was the source of the most important elements in the Mystery-cults had already given to Jewish Apocalyptic many of the same elements in another form. The place of baptism as an initiatory rite preparatory to the coming age of the Messiah, the Messianic banquet, the preliminary tribulations (the πειρασμός), the triumph over hostile forces, and, above all, the figure of the Apocalyptic Messiah as Hero-God and *Heilbringer*, these are all elements having their source in the ancient ritual pattern, and taking the place in Jewish Apocalyptic hope of the parallel features in the Mystery-cults which ministered to the needs of those described in the passage quoted from the Epistle to the Ephesians as spiritually destitute.

But the point of our insistence on this immunity of the Jew to the influences of the Mysteries lies in the fact that the first Christian community was wholly Jewish, and that the first great original Christian thinker was a Jew. The language which Paul uses concerning the Christian sacraments is the inevitable starting-point for any discussion of the presence of elements derived from the Mystery-cults in early Christianity, and it is from Paul's teaching that our enquiry must begin.

But there is one important point to be examined before we proceed to deal with Paul's doctrine of the Christian sacraments and certain related conceptions.

We have seen the cleavage which the prophetic movement had effected between the conception of dying and rising gods, current in the ancient world, and the prophetic conception of God as a purely moral and spiritual being; but in the armour of immunity which protected the Jew from the influences of the Mystery-cults there existed a vulnerable point. This point was the nature and function of the Messiah.

For our purpose it is immaterial whether we place the date of those great poetic passages known as the Servant-Songs in the sixth century B.C. or in the fourth. In any case they bear witness to the rise of a new moral conception in Jewish religious thought, that of vicarious suffering. Few scholars would now maintain that to the author of these poems the Servant was a Messianic figure, but by the time that the tradition of the Aramaic paraphrases of the Hebrew scriptures known as the Targums had established itself it is clear that the Servant of Jahveh had come to be identified with the Messiah. But in the Targum of Jonathan on Isaiah 53, the passage in which the Servant is unequivocally depicted as a suffering, dying, and triumphant figure, we find a curious phenomenon. Throughout that passage all references to the sufferings of the Servant are skilfully transferred to sinful Israel or to her persecutors, while those parts which refer to the glory and triumph of the Servant are referred to the Messiah.

The date of the fixing of the Targum tradition is too early to allow of an explanation of this phenomenon as the result of Christian influence, that is, as an attempt to refute the early Christian use of the passage as a prophecy of the death and resurrection of the Messiah. It is rather to be explained as part of that general tendency to react against everything that might suggest the possibility of suffering or death in anything related to the divine or possessing the divine nature, and in the later Jewish conception the Messiah might at least be said to be regarded as a semi-divine person. This is borne out by the fact that in the Synoptic Gospels the confession of Jesus that he was the Messiah, whether we accept it as authentic or not, was immediately received by the Sanhedrin as blasphemy.

Here, then, we have the point of divergence between the earliest Christian community and their fellow-Jews. While both were Jews in every essential respect, observing the Mosaic law, strict in attendance at the Temple, and awaiting the consolation of Israel, the sect of the Nazarenes believed that, in the person of Jesus of Nazareth, the Messiah appointed by God for Israel had appeared, suffered for the sins of his people, died, and risen again, and was about to return in order to inaugurate the 'age to come' foretold by the prophets. The main body of Judaism remained steadfast in their rejection of the conception of a suffering Messiah.

Thus the breach was made in the Jewish defences, but it fell to one who could describe himself as 'a Hebrew of the Hebrews', a scholar of the Rabbinical schools, to develop the consequences of the acceptance of a suffering and risen Messiah.

Before we turn to the examination of Paul's sacramental teaching, it may be well to touch briefly on the four main elements which determined the course of his religious experience. In the first place, by the circumstances of his birth and upbringing Paul belonged to the liberal Hellenistic side of Judaism. He was familiar with the thoughts and feelings of the Greek world which formed his immediate environment. The terminology and practices of the Mystery-cults were not strange to him. Secondly, his youth was spent in the discipline of the Rabbinical schools which left their ineffaceable mark upon him. He never ceased to feel and reason as a Rabbi. Thirdly, his outlook was profoundly Apocalyptic. Any account of Paul's teaching which fails to take this fact into consideration is bound to misinterpret his meaning. All his great concepts, justification, the life in Christ, the doctrine of the Spirit, the Church, are coloured and determined by his Apocalyptic convictions. Lastly, he was a mystic, and the significance of the fact that Judaism had a place for the mystical experience is not always realized. While the possibility of the *unio mystica* was not for all, it was, nevertheless, an object of earnest desire, and is recorded to have been attained by a few Rabbis. Paul's account of his experience in II Cor. 12, where he speaks of himself as having been caught up into the third heaven, shows that he was one of those who had attained. This last point is of importance in connexion with our subject because it offers another reason for the immunity of the Jew to the influences of the Mystery-cults. That experience of deification which the initiate sought by way of the Mysteries could be attained by the Jew in a more direct and more spiritual way.

The first impression that arises from an examination of Paul's language concerning the two principal sacraments of the early Christian community, baptism and the Lord's Supper, is of a strong similarity between his description of the working of these sacraments and the terminology of the Mysteries. For Paul baptism is essentially a rite of identification of the participant with the death and resurrection of the Messiah. In Romans 6.3-5, the key-passage for his view of the significance of baptism, he says, 'Are ye ignorant that all we who have been baptized unto Christ Jesus have been baptized unto his death? We have been buried with him through baptism unto death, that as Christ was raised from the dead by the glory of the Father, so we should walk in newness of life.' Again, in Col. 2.12, he says, 'buried with him in baptism, by which also you have been raised by faith in the activity of God who raised him from the dead'.

It is clear that for Paul baptism is a *rite de passage* by which the believer, through a symbolic identification with the death of Christ, dies to all the implications of his old life, and enters upon a new life with Christ. The special significance of this for him, as a Jew, was that he had passed from under the power of the law, whose claims had been vicariously satisfied by the death of Christ. Death has no more dominion, either over the risen Christ, or over the believer. For the Gentile the same rite implies a passage from 'darkness to light, from the power of Satan to God', and participation in a life for which the old distinctions between Jew and Gentile have become meaningless.

The two classical passages in which Paul deals with the other great Christian sacrament of the Eucharist are I Cor. 10.14-22, and 11.23-34. In the first of these passages he draws a contrast between 'the table of the Lord' and 'the table of demons', showing that he regarded participation in the communal meals of the Mystery-cults as of real significance. The partaker was thereby identified with the life of the hostile spiritual powers to whom these rites belonged. For Paul it was impossible to partake at the same time of the life of the risen Lord, and of another alien life, since the cup and the bread were the *koinōnia*, the common participation in the blood and body of the Lord. In the second passage he implies that participation in the elements of the Eucharist is not only a symbolic but a real participation, bearing consequences of life or death according to the worthiness or unworthiness of the participant. It is also important to observe that the operation of the sacrament has in view the ultimate event which is the goal of the whole divine process, the *parousia* of the Lord, 'until he come'. We shall return to the question of this Apocalyptic element in Paul's doctrine of the sacraments later on.

There are other points of resemblance with the language of the Mysteries in Paul's treatment. In writing to the Corinthians he makes use of the conception of complete initiation, perfection, and draws a distinction between the 'babes' and the 'perfect'. 'We speak wisdom among the perfect', the τέλειοι, he says, and in this connexion uses the word 'mystery' (I Cor. 2.1 and 7). Those who have reached the stage of full initiation are the illuminated, those who are able to understand the hidden wisdom, the inner meaning of the mystery of God. In this connexion we also find in Paul the beginning of the conception of the three grades of attainment which we meet with later in Clement of Alexandria and Origen, the choïc, or earthly, the psychic, and the pneumatic or spiritual. According to Origen, those who have attained the last grade of enlightenment are those who have transcended both the literal and the symbolic meaning of the scriptures, and apprehend their full spiritual significance.

Hence, the external resemblance between Paul's presentation of Christianity and the advantages which the Mystery-cults offered to their adherents is sufficiently striking, and it is not surprising that many scholars have argued for the dependence of Paul's sacramental teaching upon the Mystery religions. But there are two strong grounds for rejecting this view.

First, if the argument for the relation between the ancient ritual pattern and both Jewish Apocalyptic and the Mystery-cults be accepted, it follows that the resemblance just referred to need not prove the dependence of early Christianity upon the practices of the Mystery-cults, but is due rather to the fact that they both spring from a common source. But the second and most convincing ground for rejecting the theory of dependence lies in the nature of what we may call Paul's Apocalyptic mysticism.

A fundamental element in Paul's thought was the conception, derived from his Jewish theology, of the 'life of the age to come'. For him the Apocalyptic idea of the age to come, present in the teaching of Jesus, was the central object of the purpose of God, and, like Jesus, he believed that it was very near at hand. Indeed, the horizon of his Epistles does not go beyond the generation then living. 'We which are alive and remain unto the *parousia* of the Lord', is his point of view.

But the new and distinctive element in his presentation of the Apocalyptic expectation of the age to come is based upon his intensely realistic interpretation of the consequences of the death and resurrection of the Lord, the Messiah, Jesus of Nazareth. This also explains the little interest which the earthly life of Jesus held for him. He had arrived at the belief that by his death and resurrection the Messiah, having died

G

to the life of 'the present age', with all its evil, had entered upon a new life, the life of the Spirit, the life of the age to come. By the power of the Spirit, raised and glorified, he had become the 'firstfruits of them that slept', the pattern already of what those who shared in this new life would become.

This brings us to the next point in Paul's sacramental teaching. Those who believed in the 'good news' of the Messiah, both Jews and Gentiles, and underwent the initiatory rite of baptism, received the gift of the Spirit, the life of the risen Lord. Hence, while in appearance they still belonged to the present age, in mystical reality they already possessed the life of the age to come after the pattern of their Lord. This life was actually in operation in those who had received it, transforming them into the likeness of the risen Christ, and its full results would be manifest at the *parousia* of the Lord, when their mortal bodies would be changed into the likeness of the 'glorious body' of him whose death and resurrection had made this consummation possible. Meanwhile, during the short interval before the consummation of the process, the life thus imparted when the seal of faith through baptism was received, was fortified and sustained by the communion of the body and blood of the Lord in the second of the two great sacraments, the Lord's Supper or Eucharist.

The shortness of the interval is repeatedly emphasized in Paul's letters, and the relative insignificance of mundane affairs in the light of the near approach of the *parousia*.

Two more points remain to be touched on before we sum up the bearing of Paul's teaching on the problem with which we are occupied in this essay. First, the possession of this 'new' life not only united the recipient to the risen Lord, but all who partook of the life were equally united to one another by the same mystic, yet real, bond. Hence, all believers, living or dead, constituted one living body, animated by the life of the Spirit, suffering together in the trials of the present age, and destined to be glorified together at the revelation of the Messiah.

Secondly, this realistic conception of the nature of the new life entered also into Paul's characteristic conception of 'righteousness'. For Paul righteousness involved much more than 'forensic' justification from guilt, important as this was. It was also a δικαίωσις ζωῆς, 'a justifying of life' (Rom. 5.18). The believer was not only cleared from past guilt and freed from the claims of the law; he further received a new kind of life, belonging to a new sphere of existence, in Paul's language 'a new creation'; he was 'in Christ', living a life governed by a new law, the 'law of the spirit of the life in Christ Jesus'. He was already living in this world the life of the age to come. This aspect of Paul's doctrine of righteousness passed almost entirely unnoticed in the Reformation theologians' formulation of the Pauline doctrine of justification.

While these ideas have their origin in Jewish conceptions of the law, the Messiah and the age to come, Paul, working from his own religious experience, developed them in an entirely new way, and created a world of ideas far removed from Jewish modes of thought, possibly only fully understood by the author of the Fourth Gospel.

Hence it follows that the resemblance between Paul's language, in his description of the Christian sacraments of baptism and the eucharist, and the technical terms of the Mystery-cults is merely superficial. We have already seen that Paul would have been familiar with the language and practices of the Mysteries in his early environment, and would have been in constant touch with them in the course of his missionary labours. He has told us that he sought to become 'all things to all men', and it has often been suggested, with good reason, that he adapted his language to the needs of a world which was seeking for spiritual satisfaction in the forms of the Mystery-cults. It is also clear that to the average citizen of the Roman Empire the preaching of a dying and rising Lord, with the offer of deliverance from sin and the powers of the hostile demonic world by which he was surrounded, and the prospect of a blessed immortality, accompanied further by an initiatory rite of baptism and a communal sacred meal, would seem extraordinarily like the appeal of the various Mystery religions with which he was familiar. Nor would it be surprising if such a person should think that when he received Christian baptism he was being initiated into a new and better Mystery-cult.

But it is equally clear that Paul's fundamental ideas are far removed from those of the current Mystery religions, and are drawn from an entirely different source. Hence, so far as Pauline Christianity is concerned, and it seems permissible to assume that the Christianity of the Hellenistic and Gentile churches founded by Paul and his fellow-workers may be so described, we are justified in claiming that it owes nothing to the Mystery-cults of the period save a superficial resemblance in terminology.

We do not know enough about the extent to which the sacramental teaching of the Fourth Gospel was understood by the churches of Asia in the beginning of the second century A.D. to be able to make any positive assertions about it. Two points, however, may be suggested.

First, the author of the Fourth Gospel has developed the Pauline doctrine of the *parousia* in a remarkable way. Although it may seem a paradox, Paul's doctrine of the life of the risen Lord contained implicit in itself the destruction of the Jewish antinomy between the present age and the age to come. The author of the Fourth Gospel perceived the implication. The presence of the life of the divine Word in the believer was the true *parousia* or presence of the Lord, and there was no need to wait for a single divine event. Resurrection, judgment and *parousia* were all eternally present. Hence the elaborate framework of Paul's Apocalyptic fell away, with its interim state, its transformation of the mortal body, and all the curious metaphysics of I Cor. 15.

The other point is that the author of the Fourth Gospel has similarly divested Paul's sacramental teaching of its Apocalyptic colouring. It is significant that he does not record the institution of the Last Supper, to which Paul attaches so much importance. We have, instead, the discourse in the sixth chapter of the Gospel in which is developed the sacramental conception of eating the flesh of the Son of Man and drinking his blood as the means of receiving and sustaining the true life. Like Paul, the author thinks of a real participation in the life of the Spirit. But whereas the former connects the life with the state of the risen Messiah, and regards it as the means by which the believer will ultimately attain the same glorified state, the latter conceives of it as the life of the eternal and incarnate Word imparted to dying man, or rather to those who are already dead, that they may here and now live the life, not of the age to come, but of eternity, the timeless life.

But since the author of the Fourth Gospel develops Paul's ideas to their full consequences, ideas whose sources we have already seen, the argument which holds good of Pauline Christianity is, *a fortiori*, valid for the Christianity represented by the author of the Fourth Gospel. He must be held to share in that same Jewish immunity to the influences of the Mystery cults which we have argued for the earliest Christian communities in Palestine, and for Paul.

The teaching of the Didache is too obviously of the early Jewish Christian type to reflect the influence of the Mysteries. Beyond this point we need not carry the argument, since we are concerned only with the period of transition, with the beginnings of the Christian movement, and for this period it seems safe to say, whatever may have been the results of the contact of the Church later on with the Græco-Roman world, that the Jewish origin of the movement rendered it immune at the outset to the influences of the Mystery-cults.

CHAPTER EIGHT

The Emergence of Christianity from Judaism[1]

W E have been reminded more than once of late of the saying of one who was a great Christian and a sound historian that whatever is good history is also good religion. History is concerned, not with eternity, but with time. By its nature it does not view things *sub specie æternitatis*. Hence the truth of history is never the whole truth, and this essay, especially in that part which deals with the earthly life of Jesus of Nazareth, makes no attempt to do more than set forth the historical aspect of the relation between that life and the religious developments which preceded it and followed it.

On the *façade* of the cathedral at Strasbourg there is a well-known piece of sculpture representing symbolically, by two female figures, Christianity and Judaism, the New and the Old dispensations. Judaism is represented as discrowned, mourning, with bandaged eyes, as Paul saw her—'but unto this day, whenever Moses is read, a veil lieth upon their heart' (II Cor. 3.15). Paul, dazzled by the glory of his experience on the Damascus road, henceforth saw all things in that light, in whose shadow lay his Jewish past. But it would be truer to say that the Jew was dazzled by his vision of the glory of the one Eternal God, and could not see the glory of the Son of Man. It would also be true, in the light of history, to say that the blindness has not been all on the side of the Jew. In the sinister shadow of the Cross the Church has forgotten, not only the words, 'Father, forgive them, for they know not what they do', but the vast extent of her indebtedness to the Jew. It is necessary to remember that the Church emerged from the womb of Judaism, and that the metaphor has the profound truth in it that the

[1] First published in *Judaism and Christianity*, vol. I, 1937.

bones of the Christian Church were shaped in that womb.

It is this aspect of the Age of Transition that is all too briefly dealt with in the present essay.

Although the statement may lie open to the charge of over-simplification, it may serve as a convenient summary or graph of a vast curve of religious history to say that in passing from the eighth century prophets of Israel to Paul, we pass from man to God, and back again to man in Christ.

We have already alluded, in the previous essays, to the general character of the pre-prophetic religion of Israel. In order to make clear the meaning of the prophetic protest, it may be as well to give a brief description of the salient features of the religious background of the pre-monarchic and early monarchic period of Hebrew history. We know very little of the type of religion which the ancestors of the Hebrew people brought with them when they first came into Canaan. But recent research has made it clear that the earlier theories of the predominantly Bedouin origin of Hebrew religion and social organization need some correction. Hebrew tradition assigns the origin of the first movement of Hebrew settlement to Ur, a city whose ancient and highly developed civilization has been made familiar to us by Sir Leonard Woolley's excavations. It is an attractive suggestion that the motive which impelled the leader of this first wave of Hebrew settlement in Canaan to leave his home in Mesopotamia was a religious one, a protest against Babylonian polytheism, but for this there is no definite proof.

The general result of recent excavations in Palestine and Syria has been to show that there is no sharp line of demarcation between Canaanite and Hebrew culture in the second millennium B.C., and from the early historical records of the Hebrews we get a picture of a religion which must have been hard to distinguish from that of the neighbouring peoples. A quotation from Professor S. A. Cook's valuable book, *The Old Testament* (S.P.C.K., 1936), illustrates this point: 'Indeed, the points of contact between Old Testament religion and the neighbouring religions are such that the earliest Jahvism of the Israelites—the nature of which is keenly discussed—and the native religion of the land must have deeply influenced each other. Both the native Canaanites and the immigrant Israelites would practise the same agricultural rites at the old-time sacred places, for all newcomers must learn "the manner of the god of the land" (II Kings 17.11, 26 ff).'

Hence it seems to follow from the evidence now at our disposal that the early Hebrew settlers brought with them a knowledge of the religion and culture of their Mesopotamian home; that the religion of Canaan, which had already long been subject to Mesopotamian influence, partook of the general character of the anthropocentric nature-religions of the ancient East at that time; and that the religious practices and beliefs of the Hebrews during the early period of settlement closely resembled those of their Canaanite neighbours.

The first point to be emphasized is the agricultural, and hence the seasonal, nature of early Hebrew religion. The central object of such a type of religion is the control, by magical rites, of the forces underlying the fertility of crops and cattle. The most striking symbols of such a religion may seem to us now, as they seemed to the prophets, crude and repellent, but they represent the way in which men felt and thought about the powers of nature. The common occurrence of the bull as the symbol of the god, not excluding Jahveh; amulets representing the male and female organs of fertility; the rite of the sacred marriage, and its derived institution of sacred prostitution; these are elements found in both Canaanite and Hebrew religious practices, for which we have evidence from excavation and from literary allusion, attesting the fertility character of the religion.

Secondly, what we have referred to as the anthropocentric character of this early religion is shown by the central place of the king in the seasonal ritual. In the various seasonal rites which are intended to represent the waxing and waning of the vegetation, the king represents the dying and rising god. The nature of these rites is best seen in the New Year Festival of Babylon, a full description of which is given in Mr C. J. Gadd's admirable essay on 'Babylonian Myth and Ritual' in

Myth and Ritual (Oxford Press, 1932). The place of the king in Hebrew religion is obscure for two reasons. First, the Hebrews seem to have been later than most of their neighbours in adopting the institution of the kingship, and secondly, the whole history of the monarchy from its earliest beginnings has been drastically edited by the prophetic historians in a hostile sense. Yet this hostility itself has evidential value, since it suggests that the prophets found in the conception of the king and his religious functions something fundamentally opposed to their conception of Jahveh. For a valuable study of the place of the king in the early religion of Israel the reader may be referred to Dr Aubrey Johnson's essay in *The Labyrinth* on 'The Place of the King in the Jerusalem Cultus'.[2]

The third characteristic of the early religion is that the religious significance of the individual is limited to his status as a member of the group. His relation to the god is collective, and early conceptions of guilt and punishment are mainly concerned with the breach of taboos which affect the community's well-being.

It is also important to note that even the class of religious persons designated as prophets, from whom the protest whose nature we are now to consider took its rise, was originally a part of the same religious pattern. In the Babylonian religious economy the *ašipu*-priest, or exorcist, and the *barû*-priest, or seer, who interpreted dreams and omens, were attached to the temples and belonged to the general order of priests. As the early source of the story of the choice of Saul to be king, in I Sam. 9.10 shows, the seer was attached to the local sanctuary and performed the functions of sacrificer as well as those of a *barû*. From the ninth century and onwards we find a class of prophets attached to the court, in both the Northern and the Southern kingdoms, with whom the representatives of the class usually regarded as the genuine prophets of Jahveh were in continual conflict. Indeed, the bitterness of the conflict was possibly not merely due to different conceptions of Jahveh, but to the fact that the court prophets exercised

[2] See also Professor A. R. Johnson's *Sacral Kingship in Ancient Israel* (University of Wales Press, 1955).

functions in connexion with the old seasonal ritual order, and that the attitude of the new prophets towards the whole business of ritual threatened their existence as a class.

These considerations bring us naturally to the point where we may begin our discussion of the prophetic protest and its significance for the subsequent development of Hebrew religion. Although there is much in the codes, both in the Book of the Covenant and in the Deuteronomic Code, relevant to our enquiry, since the prohibitions contained in those codes are evidence for the existence of the practices which are there condemned, we shall nevertheless confine our attention to the evidence of the historical books and the writings of the prophets themselves. Neither is there space in this essay to discuss the problems concerning the origin of this particular class of prophets, and concerning their psychological characteristics. For these points readers must be referred to the abundant literature on this aspect of the subject.

The first considerable protest recorded is the patriotic movement associated with the names of Elijah and Elisha. Here we find no protest against the worship of Jahveh under the form of a bull-image, nor against any of the ritual practices. The object is to free Israel from the presence of a foreign Baal, probably Hadad, and to assert the principle that Jahveh will not share his land or his people with any rival god. The story of Naboth seems to indicate that the prophet regarded Jahveh as the guardian of social justice. The story of Micaiah, the son of Imlah, and the 400 court prophets has the further implications for this period that the court prophets were regarded as prophets of Jahveh, that a southern king, Jehoshaphat, was not satisfied with their pretensions, and that in Micaiah rather than in Elijah or Elisha we find the beginning of that divergence between the official prophets and the true messenger of Jahveh which becomes more clearly marked as we pass on to the so-called 'writing prophets'.

With the writing prophets, Amos and Hosea, we get the beginnings of the long-continued protest against the whole ritual order as incompatible with the conception of Jahveh which these prophets and their successors set forth with ever-increasing clearness. We also find that these prophets reject the imputation of any association with the class of official prophets. There is a striking episode described in I Kings 22 which throws light on the functions of the official prophets and on the beginnings of the divergence between these prophets and what we may call the 'new' prophecy.

Ahab and his ally, Jehoshaphat, the king of Judah, are contemplating an attack on the Syrians at Ramoth-Gilead. In accordance with the universal custom of those days Ahab, before embarking on the enterprise, consults the omens through his court prophets. Behind the account as we have it there lies the picture of a ritual. The leader of the court prophets puts on what was probably a bull-mask or *protomé*, and goes through the dramatic or mimetic actions of goring a fallen enemy, a symbolic scene which is often found pictorially represented on both Egyptian and Babylonian monuments and seals, where the bull is the symbol of the victorious king-god. The rest of the prophets accompany the dramatic action with a refrain announcing the victory of the king and the success of the undertaking. The whole action has magical significance. It is not merely a prediction of victory but a ritual intended to procure victory. Micaiah is then introduced with the suggestion that Ahab is aware that he represents another type of prophetic activity hostile to the king and his official prophets with their ritual. When he is consulted by the king, Micaiah replies with an ironical echo of the encouraging refrain of the court prophets. Ahab perceives the ironical intention of the prophet's reply and adjures him to speak the truth in the name of Jahveh. Micaiah's reply is interesting for three things. First he delivers his message in the form of a vision, introducing it with the words so characteristic of the 'new' prophecy, 'I saw'. Like Amos, Isaiah and Ezekiel, he has a vision of Jahveh in his exaltation. Secondly, in contrast to the official prophets whose business is to speak comfortable words (cf. Jer. 23.17), Micaiah utters words of doom, words echoed and re-echoed by his successors until the final destruction of the old order in 586 at the fall of Jerusalem. Lastly, we find the first suggestion of the lying spirit, the falsehood with which the 'new' prophets charged the whole official order of prophets against whom they are henceforth arrayed in the long conflict that marks the prophetic protest.

In considering the nature of this protest as we find it expressed in the utterances, actions and writings of the canonical prophets, from Amos to Malachi, it is necessary to remember that it is directed, not against details of the ritual, such as sacrifice or specific cult objects, but against the whole ritual order with the idea of the divine which it embodied. It is not possible here to discuss in detail the contributions of the different prophets to this movement, and we must confine ourselves to a brief consideration of the main characteristics which mark the divergence between the old and the new order of prophetic activity.

The first and focal point of divergence is to be found in a new idea of God, certainly arising from a religious experience, which, if not new, broke into Hebrew life with all the force of newness. The many names of the Canaanite or Babylonian pantheon represent, not distinct personalities, but the manifold embodiment of the desires and fears of the various social groups, and while a god, such as Shamash, might be regarded as the guardian of truth and social justice, there is no evidence that any one of these gods was conceived of as an ethical personality, still less any suggestion that the ethical character of the god is the basis and source of both individual and social morality. But with Amos begins the explicit announcement that the God of the prophet's experience is a distinct personality whose activity in the universe is neither arbitrary nor controlled by the potency of ritual, but is the expression of moral judgments based on a moral character. The second point, which is directly connected with the first, is the discovery of the possibility of a relation of a personal nature between Jahveh, the God of the Hebrews, and his people, both as a community and as individuals. This relation did not depend on offerings or any other ritual actions, but only on a sincere desire to know and to do the will of a God who had a moral character to be known, and who desired to be known.

Such a conception cut at the root of the whole pattern of the ancient religious life. It was impossible that a God who could be described in the magnificent words of Amos as 'he that formeth the mountains and createth the wind (or spirit), and declareth unto man what is his thought, that maketh the morning darkness, and treadeth upon the high places of the earth; the Lord, the God of hosts is his name', should be conceived of as a dying and rising god, as a god who could be compelled by incantations, or persuaded by offerings, to do what men desired, as a god who could be incarnate in a king of flesh and blood, or represented by a bull-image.

Hence, in the conception of God set forth in the utterances of the shepherd-prophet, amplified and elaborated by his successors, there is implicit the gradual rejection of every element of ritual until the climax of the process in Jeremiah's rejection of the holy city itself, with temple, ark, sacrifices, seasonal festivals, leaving nothing but a relation based on the will of God written on the heart. It is only fitting that the author of the Epistle to the Hebrews should take the great passage in Jer. 31.31-34, where the New Covenant is laid down, as the charter of the new order which we call Christianity.

But this process involved death as well as rebirth, pain and disillusionment, and a long agony of change, which took centuries to accomplish, and which may be said to be still incomplete.

The first thing to be observed in this process of change is the gradual transformation of the central elements in the ancient religious pattern. The most fundamental idea, that of the dying and rising god, was, as we have seen, so completely incompatible with the prophetic conception of Jahveh, that it could not, at least in the early stages of the prophetic movement, be transformed or spiritualized. It disappears, leaving only such traces as the denunciations of the kingship which we find in Hosea, or the passionate assertion in Habakkuk 1.12 that Jahveh cannot die.[3] It is, however, possible that the conception of the nation as passing through a symbolic death and resurrection (cf. Ezek. 37 *et al.*), and the picture of the

[3] Reading with Tiq. Soph. לֹא תָמוּת, '*Thou* diest not'.

sufferings and death of the Servant of Jahveh in Isa. 53, are derived from deep-rooted feeling of the religious value of this element in the ancient pattern. We shall return to this point later on.

Further, the conception of a monarchical order of society and of a divine king was too strongly entrenched to be discarded. Mowinckel in his *Psalmen Studien* has shown that there are good grounds for believing that in the early period of the Hebrew monarchy the central element of the annual New Year Festival was the ritual enthronement of Jahveh as King, and while the prophets might condemn the cultus they laid increasing emphasis on the eternal Kingship of Jahveh, independent of any connexion with ritual or local habitation. On the other hand, we find that the figure of the King as the focus of the well-being of the community returns in a new form in the Apocalyptic Messiah (see Chapter IX, p. 129).

Similarly, another closely connected element of the ancient religious pattern, the sacred marriage, is spiritualized by the prophets under the symbol of a marriage relation between Jahveh and Israel (cf. Hos. 2.2 ff; Jer. 2.2, 3.1; Isa. 50.1), and, like the conception of the Messiah, survives in an Apocalyptic form, especially in early Christian Apocalyptic (cf. Rev. 19.7, etc.).

It would be possible to go through all the principal elements of the early religion against which the prophetic protest was directed, and to show that they were not eliminated, but transformed and spiritualized, retaining much of their value as the vehicles for the expression of religious emotion.

But it would be a mistake to suppose that the process which we have been describing followed a steady and triumphant course, producing a complete change in the religious ideas and practices of the people and their leaders. On the contrary, the deeper and more revolutionary aspects of the prophetic protest were probably confined to a very limited circle, and it is only when we come to the circumstances which led to the emergence of what afterwards came to be called the Christian movement from its Jewish environment, that we discover the persistence of these deeper elements in the prophetic protest.

Hence we must now turn our attention to a brief survey of the various streams of religious tendency which appear during the course of what is called the post-exilic period of Jewish history.

In the first place, the catastrophe of the destruction of the monarchy and the fall of Jerusalem did not avail to destroy the traditional association of Israel's God with a definite locality and a definite ritual order. While we may find, perhaps late in the Persian period, such a rejection of the localization of Jahveh's dwelling in a particular spot as is expressed in the words of the author of Isa. 66.1, later quoted in Stephen's speech, 'Thus saith the Lord, The heaven is my throne, and the earth is my footstool: what manner of house will ye build unto me? and what place shall be my rest?' We also find another post-exilic writer saying, 'Even them will I bring to my holy mountain, and make them joyful in my house of prayer; their burnt-offerings and their sacrifices shall be accepted upon my altar, for mine house shall be called a house of prayer for all peoples' (Isa. 56.7).

Hence it is not surprising that the efforts, sometimes rather half-hearted, of the returned exiles were directed to the restoration of the Temple and its services. From the time of the rebuilding of the Temple under the stimulus of the messages of Haggai and Zechariah, up to the final destruction of the Temple by the Romans in A.D. 70, the whole ritual order of sacrifice, priesthood, and seasonal festivals was the obvious external focus of Jewish life, although purified from most of those elements against which the prophetic protest had been directed.

But other significant tendencies were at work. That section of the Jewish people whose history is reflected in the later canonical literature, namely the returned exiles, constituted but a small part of the nation. The larger portion remained dispersed in settlements from one end of the ancient world to the other. Deprived, partly by their own choice, and partly by force of circumstances, of the opportunity of observing the ancestral religious rites of the Temple worship, they developed the institution of the Synagogue. For the presence of Jahveh, enthroned on the mercy-seat in the Holy of Holies, they had the *Torah* in its sacred ark. The men of the Great Synagogue, with Ezra as a second Moses, began the process of what we may call the deification of the *Torah*. A class arose, destined ultimately to replace the priesthood, of professional students of the Law, the written expression of the will of Jahveh. The attempt to apply the provisions of a body of law intended to regulate the lives of an agricultural people in Canaan in, let us say, the ninth century B.C., to the conditions of life in the Græco-Roman world, led to the creation of a unique literature embodied for us to-day in the Talmud.

Hence, in both of these tendencies we may see a reluctance to accept the implications of the prophetic protest. For Jeremiah's rejection of the Temple, ark, and sacrifices, we have the restoration of all these things after the Exile, and for his vision of the Tables of the Law replaced by the inward knowledge of Jahveh, we have a passionate worship of the letter of the written law, a devotion to the will of Jahveh thus revealed which was capable of producing the highest type of piety, as in the moving and heroic figure of Rabbi 'Aqiba, but was also capable of yielding the Dead Sea fruit of formalism and hypocrisy so bitterly denounced by Jesus.

The tendency which produced the institution of the Synagogue and the Scribes, and indirectly the Pharisees, has been the main factor in determining the subsequent history of Judaism. But other important tendencies call for notice.

Earlier studies of Jewish Apocalyptic, such as those of Volz and Gressmann, have suggested that the main elements in the pattern of that Apocalyptic are to be found in early Oriental mythology and cosmogonies. More recent study along these lines has tended rather to suggest that those elements belong to a well-established ritual pattern which dominated the ancient East about the beginning of the second millennium B.C., a pattern to which we have shown that early Hebrew religion to some extent, at least, conformed. While eschatological conceptions of varying definiteness are characteristic of all early religions, Hebrew Apocalyptic developed along special lines. Its imagery and central ideas are largely drawn from the ancient myth and ritual pattern, but its impulse came from the new conception of Jahveh and his relation to the nation and to the individual worked out by the writing prophets. Hebrew and Jewish Apocalyptic was in fact a theodicy. The failure of the hopes of Israel's greatness and prosperity, based on the belief that Israel was the special object of the purposes of an omnipotent God, instead of destroying that faith led, in at least certain sections of the community, to the projection of those hopes into the future. The adulatory expressions characteristic of the *Hofstil*, grandiose descriptions of Israel's king as 'higher than the kings of the earth', and of the bounds of his kingdom as extending 'from the river to the ends of the earth', are transferred with heightened emphasis to the ideal future, and centred in the figure of a Messianic king who is to be the agent of the execution of the divine purpose of glory for Israel. There is no need here to elaborate the details of the Apocalyptic vision of the future, as it may be found in its varying forms in the Jewish and Christian Apocalyptic literature of our period. The main point to observe is that the Apocalyptic impulse is an offshoot of the prophetic protest, over-emphasizing and distorting certain of its features, and that it was an important stream of tendency, strongly influencing the minds of certain sections of the community during the Age of Transition. We have already seen its effect on the mind of Paul, and, although the point is still a matter of dispute, there are strong grounds for believing that in a special form it profoundly influenced the mind of Jesus.

In the main, the Apocalyptic vision was nationalistic, and only occasionally do we find gleams of an ideal order of society in which distinctions of nationality will disappear. Before we touch on that aspect of the prophetic protest which gave expression to such an ideal, there are one or two other streams of tendency to be referred to.

That intense spirit of nationalism which, as we have seen, characterized the earliest stage of the prophetic protest under Elijah and Elisha, gathered fresh intensity from the Maccabæan successes, and about the time of Christ found its expression in the fanatical patriotism of that body of sectaries known as the Zealots, described in the writings of Josephus. These patriots believed in the Apocalyptic vision of Israel's future, but also believed that it was their duty to assist God, so to speak, to make the Apocalyptic vision a reality by political activity.

Two more streams of tendency make their appearance in this period, both of which may owe their rise to the influence of Greek thought. Neither of them exercised a deep and lasting influence on the development of later Judaism, though one of them has left its traces in the canonical literature of the Old Testament. The one referred to is that represented in the books of *Job* and *Ecclesiastes*. Like the Apocalyptic literature, it may be regarded as an escape from the religious problem bequeathed by the prophetic protest. But while the Apocalyptists found escape by the projection of the hopes which had failed into the future, such writers as the authors of *Job* and *Ecclesiastes* found escape, if such it may be called, in scepticism. They abandon the moral problem as insoluble. The author of *Job*, in a loftier vein, takes refuge in the inscrutability and apparently arbitrary nature of the divine activity. The author of *Ecclesiastes* falls back upon what we can only describe as a despairing Hedonism. Nothing could be farther removed from the ardent impulses of faith and hope which characterize the early Christian movement.

The other movement takes its rise in the liberal atmosphere of Hellenistic Judaism, and finds its expression in the writings of Philo of Alexandria, and, to a lesser degree, in certain of the extra-canonical books, such as *Ecclesiasticus*. In its allegorizing methods, and in its use of the conception of the divine Logos, it has left some traces in late Jewish and early Christian literature; but the blend of Hebrew monotheism, Jewish Wisdom, and Stoic philosophy was a somewhat tenuous and artificial product, and can hardly claim to have been one of the fundamental tendencies of the Age of Transition.

Before we come to the actual historical moment of the emergence from its Jewish *matrix* of the movement afterwards known as Christianity, we must turn back for a brief glance at that aspect of the prophetic protest which was the most important factor in determining the direction of the early Christian movement.

We have already seen that Jeremiah, in the shadow of the final destruction of the Hebrew monarchy, had risen to a conception of God and his relation to his people which was independent of any external ritual forms. But even Jeremiah had not abandoned the vision of a restored Israel enjoying the divine favour in their own land, under the rule of a Davidic king, that is, if we accept such passages as Jer. 23.5 and 30.9 as from the pen of Jeremiah.

But in the series of poems by an unknown author, commonly referred to as the Servant Songs, and contained among the oracles in Chapters 40-55 of the book of Isaiah, we find the implications of Jeremiah's teaching developed to their limit. The author of the oracles composing the book of Second Isaiah believes that the time has come for Jahveh to favour Zion. He looks forward confidently to the restoration of Israel to her own land, and to the rebuilding of Zion. He is dazzled by the vision of the future glory of his people. He sees nations and kings bowing down before Israel and taking part in her restoration.

But the author of the Servant Songs[4] reads the future far otherwise. He goes beyond Jeremiah in his rejection of the ancient order, and is prepared to abandon the idea of the restoration of the national independence of Israel. For him the dispersion is not a temporary state of chastisement and purging, but an essential element in the purpose of Jahveh for Israel. The key-note of the second Song in Isa. 49.1-6 is the contrast between the past history of the people, with all its vanity and disappointment, and the new conception of a future in which Israel's destiny is seen to lie, not in a restored national greatness in their own land, but in carrying, by the very fact of their dispersion, the precious knowledge of Jahveh to the ends of the earth.

With such an interpretation of the past history of Israel in

---

[4] I no longer regard the Servant passages as by a different author from that of the rest of Deutero-Isaiah.

his mind, it was natural that the author of the Servant Songs should have arrived at a new view of the sufferings of the Israel of his vision. For him these sufferings were no longer to be regarded as the chastisement of national apostasy. 'She hath received of the Lord double for all her sins' could not have been said by the author of these poems. For him the sufferings were vicarious; the words 'he was wounded for our transgressions, he was bruised for our iniquities', represent this prophet's attitude towards the meaning of such suffering as he describes in 50.6 and 52.13-53.1-9.

For our present purpose it does not matter whether we regard the Servant as an individual or as a community. Any individual or any group entertaining such a view of the history and destiny of Israel as these poems represent would be bound to come into the sharpest conflict with any purely nationalist view of the future of the nation. The persecution to which Jeremiah was exposed on account of his attitude towards the political situation of Judah in his day may serve to illustrate and explain the sufferings described in the Servant Songs.

The book of Jonah is evidence that the point of view of the Servant Songs was not without influence on the thought and literature of later Judaism, but it was not the prevailing influence. There are traces of it in the more liberal Rabbinical circles, but we can regard such an influence only as an underground stream, so to speak, which reappears at the beginning of the Christian movement.

We may turn now to the situation of the Jewish people at that point in their history in which the events took place which led to the emergence of the new movement.

Outside Palestine there existed a large and relatively prosperous body of Jews, the Jews of the Dispersion, scattered throughout the Roman Empire in all its important cities, as the records of Paul's journeys testify. Philo's statement that the Jews resident in Egypt in his day amounted to a million is the chief basis for the estimate that the total number of Jews in the Empire was about four to four and a half million, or about seven per cent of the total population of the Empire.

In these scattered communities the Synagogue became the centre of religious life, and, moreover, a centre which attracted large numbers of Gentiles. Until the fall of Jerusalem in A.D. 70 the Temple still remained the place where Jahveh dwelt, and where alone the great seasonal festivals could be celebrated with the full ritual prescribed by the *Torah*. Hence, so long as the city stood, it continued to be the centre of Jewish pilgrimage, and at the times of the festivals its walls were full of pilgrims from every part of the Empire.

But, as Harnack points out, the Jew 'was unable in a foreign country to fulfil, or at least to fulfil satisfactorily, many other precepts of the Law. For generations there had been a gradual neutralizing of the sacrificial system proceeding apace within the inner life of Judaism—even among the Pharisees; and this coincided with an historical situation which obliged by far the greater number of the adherents of the religion to live among conditions which had made them strangers for a long period to the sacrificial system. In this way they were also rendered accessible on every side of their spiritual nature to foreign cults and philosophies, and thus there originated Persian and Græco-Jewish religious alloys, several of whose phenomena threatened even the monotheistic belief.'[5]

A further quotation from Harnack will serve to illustrate the relation between this historical situation and the point which here concerns us, the emergence of Christianity from Judaism: 'To the Jewish mission which preceded it, the Christian mission was indebted, in the first place, for a field tilled all over the Empire; in the second place, for religious communities already formed everywhere in the towns; thirdly, for what Axenfeld calls "the help of materials" furnished by the preliminary knowledge of the Old Testament, in addition to catechetical and liturgical materials which could be employed without much alteration; fourthly, for the habit of regular worship and a control of private life; fifthly, for an impressive apologetic on behalf of monotheism, historical teleology, and ethics; and finally, for the feeling that self-diffusion was a duty. The amount is so large, that one might

[5] *Mission and Expansion of Christianity* (E.T.), vol. I, pp. 10-11.

venture to claim the Christian mission as a continuation of the Jewish propaganda.'[6]

But in Palestine itself this tendency, which might be said to represent the development in a modified form of the outlook of the Servant Songs, was being countered by the growth of a sharply nationalistic and exclusive point of view. The controversy between the liberal school of Hillel and the exclusive school of Shammai ended shortly before the destruction of Jerusalem in a victory for the latter. Among the famous eighteen rules of Shammai were the prohibition against learning Greek, and against the acceptance of presents from pagans for the Temple. Intercourse with Gentiles was strictly limited and gradually began to cease. This opened the way for the Judaism of the Mishnah and the Talmud.

The influence of the various forms of Apocalyptic expectation tended in the same direction, since Apocalyptic, in general, looked, not for the conversion, but for the destruction, of Israel's Gentile foes.

The actual germinating point of the new movement is to be found in the small circle attracted by the preaching of the prophetic figure described in the Gospel narrative as John the Baptist. The account of the man and his message there given makes it clear that it was an Apocalyptic expectation of the near approach of the kingdom of God and of the coming of the Messiah which he presented to his hearers.

According to the Synoptic narratives, Jesus of Nazareth was attracted to John's movement and attached himself to it, accepting baptism from John. The same source relates that at the time of this occurrence Jesus had a spiritual experience of a similar type to those of the prophets, an experience which is generally, and probably rightly, interpreted to mean that Jesus felt that he was divinely marked out to be the means of bringing in the Kingdom, that is, that he was in some way the predestined Messiah. The fact of the Messianic consciousness of Jesus can only be eradicated from the Gospel narratives at the cost of the almost complete destruction of their historical credibility. On the other hand, it is not necessary to assume

[6] Harnack, *op. cit.*, vol. I, p. 15.

either that Jesus' conception of his Messianic destiny under-went no development, or that it conformed exactly to any of the accepted types of Messianic expectation current in his time.

It is not possible here to discuss the details of the Gospel narratives, still less what we may call the supra-historical implications of the life and death of Jesus of Nazareth. But we are concerned with the historical conditions of the emergence of Christianity from Judaism, and however much Paul and his successors may have concentrated their attention on the heavenly Christ of spiritual experience at the expense of the historical Jesus, we must come back to the fact that the move-ment received its initial impulse from the events of the life of Jesus. In some way he constitutes the link between the pro-cess which we have been tracing out and the subsequent de-velopments. Hence we are bound to attempt to discover the attitude of Jesus towards the various streams of religious tendency which we have described as existing in his time, and to make a brief estimate of the direction which he gave to the movement which sprang into existence as the consequence of his impact upon the history of his people.

In the first place, three of the tendencies already mentioned may be dismissed as having no place in his consciousness. There is no trace in his recorded utterances of the spirit re-flected in later sceptical Wisdom literature, nor of the philo-sophical speculations of Philo. His attitude towards the Zealot movement and its methods was one of definite rejec-tion of any kind of political activity. Recent studies of the parables of Jesus, such as those by Professor Oesterley and Professor Dodd, have shown that the Rabbinical use of the parable as a vehicle of teaching had some influence upon the form of his teaching, but, unlike Paul, who remained a Rabbi to the end in his modes of reasoning and his use of the Scrip-tures, Jesus was far removed from the Rabbinical teachers of his time in his attitude towards the Law and what he called 'the traditions of the elders'.

But on the positive side there are three fundamental ele-ments to be noted in the attitude of Jesus towards the religious history of his people. In the first place, he is the direct descendant of the great prophets in his experience of the relation between God and the individual. That experience is direct, intense, and unmediated, and assumes, in visual and auditory experiences, the character of the experiences of the great prophets. He is in the same descent in his attitude towards the religious organization in the forms which it had assumed in his day, and towards the conception of the will of God, as contained in a body of precepts. With him we are back in the atmosphere of Amos, Hosea, and Jeremiah, 'mercy and not sacrifice' is his word.

But in this first element there is newness, or rather, the development of an earlier element to the point where it appears as something new. His experience of the relation between God and the individual as a relation between father and child already existed in germ, and is to be found in the best Rabbinical experience, but in his experience it is carried to a degree of intimacy and intensity which makes it a new thing, providing the basis for subsequent theological speculations which lie beyond our purview.

Secondly, the Apocalyptic element is of great importance in the outlook of Jesus. His conception of God's action on the course of history is, like that of all the prophets, an Apocalyptic one. The kingdom comes with power, it ends the present age and ushers in the age to come, the *'olâm habba*, the age of the Messiah. It is not a remote, far-off divine event, but 'nigh, at the doors'.

But it is in connexion with the problem of the nature and functions of the Messiah that the third of the fundamental elements with which we are dealing comes up for discussion. It is here that we find that element in the thought of Jesus which presents the widest divergence from the general conception of the Messiah current in his time, and indeed from the whole Jewish outlook. Here lies the direction which led away ultimately from Judaism and was to make of the Christian movement what Paul so aptly called 'a new creation'.

First, it may be said that in this respect there seems to be a development in the thought of Jesus. During the early period of his activity, immediately after the imprisonment of John the Baptist, Jesus seems to have thought that the mission of the Twelve would be directly followed by an act of divine intervention and his own public manifestation as Messiah. This is the atmosphere of Matthew 10 and 11, where we find a description of Jesus' emotions and utterances which can hardly be the reflection of a later period of Christian thought.

The non-realization of this early expectation brought about a vital change in Jesus' conception of the nature of the Messiah's function and of the basis of the divine intervention for which he looked. Here, to put it briefly, Jesus brought together two elements which had not previously been associated in Jewish Messianic ideas. The Gospel narratives bear witness that the Servant Songs had early been connected with the life and character of Jesus, and the narrative of the Last Supper further suggests that this connexion had its source in Jesus' own use of passages from the Servant Songs in relation to himself.

The Targum of Jonathan is evidence for the fact that the Servant of Jahveh in the Servant Songs was equated with the Messiah in the late Jewish period. But the well-known paraphrase which the Targum gives of the fifty-third chapter of Isaiah is also the strongest possible evidence that the Jews refused to admit any idea of a suffering and dying Messiah.[7]

It would appear that Jesus had come to the conviction that John was the Elijah, whose return, as the forerunner of the Messiah, was an element in the popular Apocalyptic belief of the time. Hence, the death of the forerunner, together with the influence of the Servant-passages upon the mind of Jesus, had brought him to regard his suffering and death as necessary for the inauguration of the Kingdom; the Messiah must go the way of the forerunner, and his death would have the vicarious value which the author of the Servant Songs assigned to the sufferings and death of the Servant of Jahveh.

Hence we may see in Jesus' acceptance of death as essential to the function of the Messiah, even if he was not conscious of

[7] This statement should be limited to the Tannaaitic period. Cf. Klausner, *The Messianic Idea in Israel* (Macmillan, 1955), pp. 405f.

all its implications, the crowning point of the process which we have been following. In a symbolic sense it has been a long process of dying. Beginning with rejection of the ancient ritual pattern by Amos and Hosea, we find the surrender of one element after another that had seemed essential to the existence of the national religion. Jeremiah goes very far, abandoning Temple, Ark, the holy city, and even the tables of the Law, the external symbols of that knowledge of Jahveh's will which was Israel's unique possession. The author of the Servant Songs goes further and accepts the symbolic death of the nation, the surrender of the cherished hopes of the restoration of the ancient glories of Zion, taking the dispersion as the indication of the missionary destiny appointed by Jahveh for his people, a destiny for which the whole previous history had only been a preparation. Now, in accepting the death of the Messiah as part of the purpose of God, Jesus surrenders the last thing that the national hopes could cling to.

Moreover, he does not surrender it in theory, he undergoes it. Believing himself to be the Messiah he nevertheless accepts death as the portion of the Messiah, leaving the issue of his choice to God whose will he believed himself to be thus fulfilling.

It remained for those who came after him to work out the consequences of his act. From the outset the first group of disciples found themselves separated from their countrymen by their acceptance of a suffering and dying Messiah. Good Jews though they were and desired to remain, they found themselves reluctantly being forced farther and farther away from Jewish ground by the internal logic of the Cross. Some were unable to go all the way, and the community which Paul found living as a respected sect of Jews at Jerusalem under the guidance of James, the Lord's brother, represents the last vestige of the early movement which clung to the old position and perished with the fall of the holy city.

It was Paul's destiny, by birth a liberal Hellenistic Jew, by training a Rabbi, than whom no Jew was ever prouder of his national heritage, to work out the consequences of the death of Jesus of Nazareth. His life-work was to lay the foundations for a spiritual city, a community where distinctions of race and nationality had ceased to exist. For him the Death of Christ had severed all the old links with the past. The Law had no further dominion over one who had died with Christ. Sin reigned no longer, and death itself was slain when Christ died. Even Jesus himself, the focal point of the whole process, is replaced in Paul's new creation by the heavenly Christ—'Though we have known Christ after the flesh, yet henceforth know we him no more.'

Only one thing remained to Paul of his old ways of thought: his Apocalyptic expectation. The heavenly Christ becomes the centre of his hope, and apparently he died in the belief that the Lord Jesus would shortly return to set up the Kingdom of God on earth. But, in a sense, we may say that Apocalyptic never dies, it is essentially bound up with the nature of history and of man from which the element of the incalculable and the catastrophic can never be eliminated.

With Paul the emergence of Christianity from Judaism, although it has never been completed in actuality, became a fact of history.

One more remark may be made in closing. Looking back at the process in the long perspective of history, we can see that with the emergence of Christianity from Judaism the wheel had come full circle. The old conception of the dying and rising god which was such a vital element in the ancient ritual pattern as the centre of collective emotion and desire, destroyed by the protest of the Hebrew prophets in the interests of the new idea of God as an ethical personality, eternal, immortal, invisible, returns in a new form. God becomes man again, suffers and dies, lives again, victorious over the enemy in a sacred combat which has been lifted to the spiritual plane.

CHAPTER NINE

The Myth and Ritual Pattern in Jewish and Christian Apocalyptic[1]

THE literature commonly known as Apocalyptic came into existence as the expression of an outlook on history and of a state of mind peculiar to late Judaism and early Christianity. The beginnings of Apocalyptic appear even before the downfall of the Hebrew monarchy, and its influence has continued down to the present time, but most of the literature so designated came into existence during the period extending from about 200 B.C. to A.D. 100.

It is hardly necessary to give a detailed account of the nature and contents of the apocalyptic books, since much has been written about them in recent years and their general character is well known. Hence this Essay will be confined to three main points. First, the relation between the attitude implied by the existence of those religious beliefs and practices which can be described as the myth and ritual pattern, and the general outlook of the apocalyptic literature. Second, a discussion of the characteristic symbolism of this literature and its relation to the ritual forms and symbols which appear in the ritual pattern of the ancient East. Lastly, it will be suggested that the general plan to which the apocalyptic visions conform is based on the early myth and ritual pattern referred to, and is evidence for its persistence long after the social structure and outlook of the early civilizations which had given birth to it had decayed and passed away.

1. The picture which emerges from a study of the great seasonal rituals of the ancient East and their associated myths is that of a community seeking to bring under control by

[1] First published in *The Labyrinth*, 1935.

means of an organized system of ritual actions the order of nature upon the functioning of which its well-being depends. It is also clear that behind the later stage of that civilization with its sharp differentiation of gods from men, its hierarchy of divinities and its ordered cult of prayer, praise and sacrifice, there lies an older stage, dimmer but still distinct, when the focus of the attempt to secure the well-being of the community was a single individual possessing qualities of strength or knowledge, or both, which indicated him as the centre of the ritual life of the community. He was both king and god, the term god implying nothing more at that stage than the king in his ritual aspect with all the magical potencies which he embodied.

It is this relation between the king and the community which constitutes the first main characteristic of the outlook of the early state of society where the myth and ritual pattern prevailed. The hopes and desires of the community were centred in the king. Behind the long list of titles, purely conventional in later times, there lies this original reality, the dependence of the people upon the king.

Thus we find that 'individual kings boast with magnificent assumption that "their rule is beneficial to the bodies of men as the plant of life", or courtiers, with exaggerated loyalty, declare that "he causes them to live by putting the plant of life into their nostrils"; seal cylinders frequently depict a scene in which the enthroned god presents to his worshipper a vase containing the water of life and the plant of life, but such exaggerated forms of speech and symbolic representations were only the natural expression of the desire for health and well-being.'[2]

The same conception is also attested in the valuable body of material collected by Mrs Douglas E. van Buren in her book *The Flowing Vase and the God with Streams*, where the life-giving potency of the king-god is represented on many seals by streams of water issuing from his body or from a vase which he is holding.

A more detailed illustration of this central point of view

[2] Meissner, *Babylonien und Assyrien*, vol. II, pp. 123 f (1924).

will be found when we come to discuss the symbols connected with the pattern and its main elements in the next two sections of this Essay.

The second general characteristic of this early outlook has been admirably illustrated by Father Eric Burrows in *The Labyrinth*, and need only be briefly indicated here as one of the features which reappear in the apocalyptic literature. It is the tendency, appearing extremely early, to regard the pattern of the ritual order on earth as being reproduced in the heavenly world.

The third general characteristic to which attention must be called is the ancient attitude to the progress of time. This attitude is closely connected both with the fact that the ritual order of religious life in the ancient world was mainly determined by the seasons, and also with the second feature mentioned above, the relation between the earthly and the heavenly order. Both the seasonal aspect of life to those who depended for their well-being upon the orderly procession of the seasons and their fruits, and the cyclic character of the movements of the heavenly bodies, inevitably tended to produce a view of Time as a vast circle in which the pattern of the individual life and of the course of history was a recurring cyclic process.

Such a conception of time and the emotional experience connected with it are in strong contrast to the modern experience of time, based largely on the concept of evolutionary process, and tending to express itself in the spatial metaphor of a line infinitely produced, without definite beginning and with no conceivable end.[3]

These three general characteristics may suffice to provide a picture of the *Weltanschauung*, the orientation of the ancient world where the ritual pattern of which we have spoken prevailed, determining its emotions and actions.

Turning now to the period of history which gave birth to the apocalyptic literature, we find that, roughly speaking, two millenniums have elapsed. From the ritual which describes the deification of King Lipit-ishtar, dated by Zimmern at

[3] Cf. J. E. Harrison, *Themis*, p. 273 (1912).

about 2270 B.C.,[4] to the beginning of the Seleucid era when Jewish apocalyptic was beginning to flower, the course of time had seen the dispersion and disintegration of the ritual pattern together with the decay of the civilizations in which it had flourished.

During that period the Hebrew people had passed from their early stage as a group of invading clans in process of settling in a country already long under the domination of the culture and ritual of Egypt and Babylon, to the attainment of an independent political existence and a national consciousness.

Dr Aubrey Johnson has shown, in *The Labyrinth*, that to an extent perhaps hitherto unsuspected the urban religion of the Hebrews shared in the ritual pattern dominant in the ancient East, and was characterized by a cultus in which the king had a central place and still retained much of the ancient divinity attaching to the person of a king.[5]

This independent political existence, early weakened by the schism between the North and the South, lasted barely 500 years. During the next 500 years, up to the fall of Jerusalem in A.D.70, save for a transient gleam during the Maccabean period, the political history of the Jews is a story of futility and frustration. During the last 200 years of the independent national existence of Israel, a religious movement unparalleled in the ancient world had succeeded in destroying the characteristic features of the ancient ritual pattern, or at least in eradicating them from the religion represented in the history and laws of the Hebrew people as we have them from the hands of those responsible for this movement.[6] The separation between God and man had been made absolute; the idea of God had been completely spiritualized, and the relation between God and man presented

---

[4] H. Zimmern, *Berichte der Kgl. Sächsischen Gesells. der Wiss.*, 68, 1, 1 ff. For the nature of this text cf. G. R. Driver, *The Babylonian Laws* (O.U.P. 1952), vol. I, pp. 15-17.

[5] But cf. now A. R. Johnson, *Sacral Kingship in Ancient Israel* (University of Wales Press, 1955).

[6] Cf. W. C. Graham, 'Isaiah's Part in the Syro-Epraimitic Crisis', *A.J.S.L.*, vol. L, 1934, p. 213.

as purely ethical and spiritual, unmediated by priesthood and ritual. This at least represents the peak of the movement as it culminated in the work of Jeremiah and the author of Second Isaiah.

In the ancient East the conception was familiar that a country or a city was under the special care of its own gods, whose glory or humiliation was reflected in the varying fortunes of their people. But this conception had passed through a strange history in Israel. As their estimate of the power and moral character of their God developed, so the idea that Israel was his peculiar people grew until it resulted in a world view which made their God the omnipotent ruler of the universe, the one real God, and his people, Israel, the centre of world history. The contrast between their actual political condition and status, and the vast and grandiose aspirations based on these beliefs constituted the central religious problem of Israel from the first attempts at solution in Isaiah's time up to the period of the apocalyptic solution with which we are dealing in this Essay.

For the only explanation of the rise of this literature, as distinct from its characteristic form, lies in the fact that it was an attempt, the attempt of a hope creating 'from its own wreck the thing it contemplates', to vindicate the claim of Israel to be the centre of world-history, and therefore the central object of the purpose of God.

It should also be added here, since we are dealing with Christian as well as Jewish Apocalyptic, that the early Christian movement, which was wholly Jewish in origin, not only inherited the Old Testament as its sacred book, but was itself the offspring of a Jewish apocalyptic movement, and that the causes which operated to produce the apocalyptic literature in late Judaism operated still more effectually to produce an even more brilliant burst of apocalyptic writing in the early Christian community. There is really no breach of continuity between Jewish and Christian Apocalyptic, but certain special circumstances brought about an increased emphasis upon particular elements in the pattern, as we shall see when we come to discuss the symbolism and the details of the pattern.

Before we go on to the task of pointing out the presence in apocalyptic literature of the three characteristics of the ancient ritual pattern and its outlook which we have already indicated, there is one point to be observed which serves as a link, a vital link, between these two periods so widely separated in time.

It is this, that in spite of the profound changes which the prophetic movement had effected in Hebrew religion, one element had remained practically unchanged, namely, the belief that it was possible to alter the course of nature, to direct it and control it to human ends. The whole system of ancient ritual embodied in the king had this as its purpose. With the separation of God from man the functions and potencies of the ritual were transferred to the god, and ritual became a means of influencing the actions of the gods. In the case of the God of Israel the influence of ritual diminished and disappeared from the religion of the prophets, but the conception persisted of a power that controlled the order of nature at its own will, that is, in the last resort, arbitrarily, even though the controlling will might be conceived of as a righteous will.[7]

Hence, in their 'last giddy hour of dread endurance', the Jewish people, or at least that circle which produced the apocalyptic literature, clung to this very ancient conception of the possibility of a catastrophic interference with the order of the world.

When we come, then, to examine this literature we find first of all that, with one or two unimportant exceptions, the Messianic element is central. The frustrated aspirations of an oppressed and persecuted people project into an imaginary future the figure of a king, a *heil-bringer*, a half-divine, half-human figure, upon whom the realization of their hopes depends, who is the incarnation of their most passionate desires.

The central element of the ancient ritual pattern, the king-god, banished from the effective religion of the people by the prophetic purge, returns again in the guise of the Messiah of apocalyptic expectation. The point is too evident to need labouring.

[7] Cf. Isa. 44.24; 45.7 *et al.*

Coming to the second main characteristic, that the earthly cosmic order has its counterpart in the heavenly, we find in the apocalyptic books a sudden and striking resurgence of this preoccupation with what is happening in heaven. Most of the pseudonymous authors of the various apocalyptic books are caught up into heaven, or have visions in which they see the heavenly order and the revelation of the ideal future of their desires. While the tradition that the pattern of the tabernacle was given to Moses in the Holy Mount, and that of the temple to David by divine revelation (Exod. 25.40; I Chron. 28.12, 19) does not belong to the apocalyptic literature, its presence in the Priestly redaction is a sign of the reviving belief in this correspondence between the earthly and the heavenly patterns. It may also be regarded as evidence for the survival of the ancient belief that the temple was the bond between heaven and earth.

But the most striking illustration of the presence of this element in apocalyptic literature is found in the Christian Apocalypse. In Rev. 11.19, and 15.5, the seer, who has been caught up into heaven, sees the temple of God together with the ark of the covenant which it contains. Other cult objects belonging to the temple are also seen in heaven, such as the seven golden candlesticks (1.12), the great sea or laver (4.6), the altar of incense (8.3), etc.

Examples might easily be multiplied, but one more interesting parallel may be quoted. In the Jewish apocalypse of Daniel the author sees a 'Watcher' coming down from heaven (cf. I En. 12.2-3; 20.1), and we also find the conception that the various territorial divisions of the world in the apocalyptist's time were represented in heaven by angels who, in their relations to one another, reflected the relations, friendly or hostile, that existed between the nations whom they represented (Dan. 4.13, 23; 10.13, 20.21. For Christian apocalyptic cf. Rev. 1.20). This conception corresponds to the early belief in Babylonia that the terrestrial divisions of the time were represented in heaven by special stars.[7] Also we learn from Diodorus, whose information was, doubtless,

---

[7] Meissner, *op. cit.*, pp. 409-10.

derived from Berossus, that the planets, not being fixed, but having definite orbits, were regarded as interpreting to men the purposes of the gods, and were called 'Interpreters' or 'Watchers'.[8] It is also interesting to note that the fixed stars were called 'sheep', and the planets 'goats', a distinction which is probably the source of the apocalyptic division between the sheep and the goats in the great assize scene in Matt. 25.31-33.

We turn now to the third main characteristic, the cyclic conception of time. We have already pointed out that the great rituals of the ancient world were seasonal, and based upon a cyclic experience of life. In the Hebrew expression *tequphath hashshanah* (Exod. 34.22), 'the circuit of the year', we have a reminder of the way in which the yearly festivals with their regular round re-enacted with magical potency the secular changes of nature, death, re-birth and consummation. The early development among the Babylonians of the study and the movements of the heavenly bodies strengthened the tendency derived from observation of the revolution of the year, and led to the belief in a close relation between celestial cycles and terrestrial affairs. It also led to the conception of vaster cycles than the first simple cycles of the sun and moon. Each of the three great Babylonian gods, Anu, Enlil and Ea, had his own 'way', or territory in the heavens, with special control over the heavenly bodies which each 'way' contained. Finally, the discovery of the precession of the equinoxes led to the conception of the great cycle of world history of 28,000 years.

Already in the earlier prophetic period, when apocalyptic ideas were beginning to make their appearance, we find traces of this cyclic conception of history. For example, in Isa. 11.15-16 there appears the prophecy that the miracles of the parting of the Red Sea and the Jordan will be repeated 'in that day', a characteristic apocalyptic phrase. In Isa. 41.18 and 43.19-20 it is suggested that miraculous inci-

---

[8] In the Babylonian Epic of Creation, Marduk appoints *Watchers* over Tiamat. See S. Langdon, *The Babylonian Epic of Creation* (1923), p. 147.

dents of the wilderness wanderings will be repeated when the exiles cross the desert on their homeward journey from Babylon. Such passages illustrate the frequently occurring conception that the early stages of Israel's history will be re-enacted when Jahveh 'turns the fortunes' of his people.

But in the apocalyptic books themselves we find abundant evidence of the dream of one great final revolution of the wheel of the divine purpose, setting all things right, in the New Testament writer's phrase, the *apokatastasis*, the restitution of all things. Here the preoccupation with time in its apsect of recurrence finds expression in calculations of mystic periods, days, weeks, half-weeks, weeks of years and an appearance of strange minuteness and accuracy. Thus the author of Daniel has a mystic period of seventy weeks, counting from the rebuilding of Jerusalem. The last week of this period is the critical point when the coming of the Messiah, the final tribulation of Israel, and the great consummation will take place (Dan. 9.24-7). In Dan. 12.11-12 we have a similar calculation in days reckoned from the profanation of the temple by Antiochus Epiphanes and the seer is told: 'Blessed is he that waiteth and cometh to the thousand three hundred and five and thirty days.'

Similar calculations occur in I En. 9.1-3 and Rev. 11.2-3. In Jubilees 1.29 we hear of the great cycle from creation to creation, and in 23.27 a return to the old length of life before the Flood is announced. The significant expression 'the consummation of the ages' occurs in the Testament of Benjamin 2.3 and elsewhere. Here, again, evidence might be multiplied, but the above quotations will suffice to establish the point.

Hence, we find that there is abundant proof of the presence in Jewish and Christian Apocalyptic, not merely incidental but predominant, of the three main characteristics of the ancient pattern, the central importance of the king-god, the conception of the correspondence between the earthly and the heavenly order, and of the cyclic conception of time.

2. The second section of our enquiry deals with the characteristic symbolism of apocalyptic literature, and we shall

attempt to show that the most important elements in this symbolism have their origin in certain fundamental elements in the myth and ritual pattern of the ancient East.

It has been long recognized that most of the luxuriant growth of symbolism in the apocalyptic writers has a mythological origin. Our purpose is rather to prove that the most striking of these symbols play an essential part in ancient myth and ritual and help to impart the same peculiar shape and colour to the drama of the last things. The field of this symbolism is very large, and owing to the fact that in the late period with which we are dealing many symbols had become detached from their original setting and had acquired an independent life and meaning, it is often difficult to determine the origin of a particular symbol. This will be noticed in Professor W. O. E. Oesterley's contribution to *The Labyrinth*, where a number of symbols derived from various sources have gathered round the figure of Sabazios. Hence our discussion in this section of the Essay will be confined mainly to the most important group of animal symbols, although a few other significant symbols will also be discussed.

Space will not allow of a detailed enumeration and description of the sources from which we receive our information concerning the form and functions of the various types of animal symbols found in early Babylonian myth and ritual. It must suffice to say that these sources consist of the early king-lists, the religious texts such as the Creation Epic and the Epic of Gilgamesh, the various collections of magical texts, of which almost the only available example in English is Dr Campbell Thompson's *Devils and Evil Spirits of Babylonia*, and the very difficult class of texts containing commentaries on the rituals for the use of the priests. For the pictorial representations needed to supplement the descriptions contained in the texts mentioned above we have to depend mainly on the seals with some help from the *kudurru* or boundary stones.

The position here adopted, that these animal symbols are immediately connected with ancient ritual, is confirmed by the evidence contained in Dr H. Frankfort's valuable paper

'Gods and Myths on Sargonid Seals', in Vol. I, Pt. I of *Iraq*. In this paper Dr Frankfort shows that the seal-groups discussed, containing examples of all the most important animal symbols dealt with here, focus round 'the greatest religious annual event in the Babylon of later times which is known to us through the texts: the New Year Festival'.

While there are many animal forms which come into some kind of relation with early myth and ritual, some of which belong to no recognizable species, but are what the Germans call *mischgestalt*, there are three main classes which occur more frequently than the rest, and which concern the purpose of this Essay more directly.

These are:

(i) The various dragon and serpent forms so often seen on seals and described in the Epic of Creation and elsewhere. There are various examples of such forms combined with the human form. The scorpion-man mentioned in the Epic of Gilgamesh and often represented on the *kudurru*, may be included in this group.

(ii) The different types of bird-forms and their numerous combinations, the most familiar examples of which are the man-bird, often identified with Zu, frequently found on seals, and the vulture or eagle-headed human figures, so often seen engaged in some ritual action connected with a sacred tree.

(iii) The important group containing bull, lion and goat or capridæ forms. These, again, are often found in mixed forms. The bull-man is a common and widely distributed form, also the *lamassu*, or winged bull, and the winged lion or sphinx.

Our next task is to examine the chief functions which these animal forms appear to possess in relation to the ritual and its explanatory myth. We find, first of all, that in one of the central elements of ancient myth and its dramatic representation in the great rituals, the sacred combat, the antagonist of the hero of the combat is most frequently represented by a dragon or serpent form of some kind, although in some of the older forms of the myth a bird form occupies this place, the Zu-bird. In one of the seals from Tell Asmar published by

The Dragon-Beast of Marduk
(Gressmann, *T.u.B.* CXLIX. 371)

Dr Frankfort (*op. cit.* above) there is a representation of a seven-headed dragon or Hydra being slain by two gods. There is also a well-known representation of what is believed to be the fight between Marduk and Tiamat, where Tiamat is shown as

The Defeat of Tiamat
(Gressmann, *T.u.B.* CLI, 374a)

[135]

a dragon of serpent form in flight before the god. Representations of the bird-man, conquered and captive, being brought before the god for judgment, are also common on early

Judgment of the Bird-Man
(Meissner, *B.u.A.* II, Abb. 30)

Akkadian seals. The scorpion-man in an attitude of combat is often figured on the *kudurru*.

The second point that emerges from an examination of the pictorial evidence is that animal forms, or mixed animal and human forms, are found in what may be described as ritual positions, performing some ritual function in relation to a god or goddess, king, or sacred tree. It may be assumed with some certainty that in the performance of the rituals these parts were taken by masked priests.

Thirdly, we find that on many of the early Akkadian seals some kind of contest is represented between a human figure with divine insignia and a bull, a lion, or some mixed form. Fuller discussion of this material and its significance has been given elsewhere by the writer,[9] but the main inference to be drawn from it for our present purpose is that these forms represent the divine king in one aspect of his functions, namely, as the dying king, an element in the pattern not to

[9] *Congrès International des Sciences Anthropologiques et Ethnologiques, Londres,* 1934. *Compte-rendu,* p. 302.

be confused with the similar place of the dragon on the seals.

Space will not allow of a further discussion of the animal symbolism in the early myth and ritual. But one or two other interesting symbols also call for notice. We have already seen that the sacred tree enters frequently into the pictorial representations of the ritual. The conception of the plant of life, or herb of life, some plant with magical potency, is also a frequent element in the myths (cf. also p. 125, above). As we have suggested, the interchange between the god, the king and the sacred tree seems to point to the fact that the tree, which it may not be misleading to call the tree of life, is a symbol of the life-giving functions of the king.

Another important element which must be noticed is the 'tablets of destiny'. This symbol occurs frequently in the religious texts, and the action of the myth often turns upon the possession of these tablets. They appear to represent the secret, magical knowledge upon which the power of the god, or king, depended, and their possession is a symbol of divinity and supreme power. They give the power to fix the destinies, a ceremony which constituted a very important element in the New Year ritual at Babylon. Thus we find, to take only one example, that the possession of these tablets is one of the consequences of Marduk's victory over Tiamat.

One more curious element of animal symbolism which appears in both Jewish and Christian Apocalyptic may be mentioned. It affords an interesting illustration of the way in which a symbol may be detached from its original context and acquire an entirely fresh significance. This is the symbol of the eyes which are found in the wheels of Ezekiel's vision and again in the four living creatures of the Apocalypse. In representations of the Minotaur on early Greek vases we find the figure of the monster as a man wearing a bull's protome and a bull's skin covered with eyes. In Egypt we have the ubiquitous Eye of Horus, which plays a central part in the Osiris myth and its associated rituals. It is a most potent symbol of the sun's vivifying and fertilizing power, and we do not need to be reminded that this power was incarnate in the king-god. By a natural extension of its significance it has become in the apocalyptic literature a symbol of divine omni-presence and omnipotence (cf. Ezek. 1.18; Zech. 3.9, 4.10; Rev. 4.6).

We must now turn to the apocalyptic literature for parallels to the symbols enumerated above. It has already been pointed out by Professor T. H. Robinson in his Essay on Hebrew myths in *Myth and Ritual* that the myth of the combat be-tween Jahveh and the Dragon has been preserved in several passages of the Old Testament.[10] One of the most striking of these passages, Isa. 27.1, projects the myth into the future and represents Jahveh as the conqueror of the Dragon 'in that day'. But in the Jewish apocalyptic literature the serpent-dragon form does not play a very prominent part in the visions. In the Zadokite fragment, 9.19-20, the kings of the Gentiles are seen under the symbol of dragons; in the Psalms of Solomon 9.29, Pompey is represented as a dragon, possibly under the influence of the passage in Jer. 51.34, where Nebuchadrezzar is symbolized by a dragon; but the clearest reference is in the Testament of Asher 7.3, where the Messiah slays the dragon in the waters (cf. Ps. 74.13). The principal form which the serpent-dragon of the ancient pattern has taken in Jewish apocalyptic is the monster Leviathan whose flesh is destined for the Messianic banquet (IV Ezra 6.52).

But it is in the Christian Apocalypse that the Dragon appears in the clear outlines of the ancient myth as the anta-gonist of the Messiah and his saints. With the dragon, who is identified with Satan in the Apocalypse, there is associated a beast with seven heads (cf. p. 135, above) and ten horns, who is overcome by the Lamb in the last fight.

Bird forms do not play a prominent part in the apocalyptic literature. The one exception is the great Eagle vision in IV Ezra 11, where the eagle is clearly the Roman Empire, and is destroyed by the Messiah. Scorpion forms occur in Rev. 9.10.

The bull appears in I Enoch 85-86 *al.* In 91.37 the Messiah is represented as a white bull. But, although the bull is a frequent symbol for the might of Jahveh in the Old Testa-

[10] *Myth and Ritual*, ed. S. H. Hooke (1932), pp. 175 ff.

ment, it is not much used in apocalyptic literature outside the Book of Enoch. The same holds good of the lion. In IV Ezra 11.37 the Messiah is seen as a lion who destroys the eagle, and in Rev. 5.5 the Messiah, the triumphant Lamb, is called the Lion of the tribe of Judah. But it is impossible to go through the apocalyptic literature without becoming convinced that the abundant animal symbolism found there implies the resurgence of those ancient forms which embodied so much of the emotion attaching to the early ritual pattern.

Two other types of symbol mentioned above still call for notice. The tree of life is found in an important vision in I Enoch 24-25. There it is seen growing on the mystic mountains. It may not be touched until the great judgment, when its fruits will be given to the righteous, endowing them with long life on earth. The corresponding vision in Christian Apocalyptic is in the well-known passage in Rev. 22.1-2, where the tree of life grows in the holy city in the midst of the paradise of God.

Lastly, the tablets of destiny, which play such an important part in the ancient ritual pattern, appear in a very interesting way in both Jewish and Christian apocalyptic literature. In I Enoch 81.1-3; 103.2, the seer is allowed to see the 'heavenly tablets', containing the future destiny of mankind. But the most striking parallel occurs in Rev. 5.1-8, where the seer beholds in the right hand of him who sits upon the throne a seven-sealed scroll which none can open or read. The Lamb appears and by virtue of his triumph takes the book as the symbol of his victory. The parallel with the assumption by Marduk of the tablets of destiny as the result of his victory over the dragon, Tiamat, is too obvious to need elaboration.

It may be added that the symbol of the Lamb, so central in Revelation, has one parallel in Jewish apocalyptic, in the Testament of Joseph, where the Messiah is seen in the guise of a lamb triumphant over his enemies, but this is very probably due to Christian influence.

We might easily spend more time in the discussion of the symbols with which this type of literature abounds, but enough has been said to suggest that the source of the most characteristic elements in apocalyptic symbolism lies in the ancient myths and rituals of Egypt and Babylonia. It is so easy, however, for symbols to become detached from their original context and to acquire a separate life of their own, that the mere proof of a connexion between individual symbols and the source of which we have spoken is not sufficient. Hence the main burden of the proof of our thesis falls upon the third part of this Essay, namely, the relation between the ritual pattern of the ancient East and the fundamental pattern of the apocalyptic point of view.

3. For a full account of the details of the myth and ritual pattern of the ancient East the reader is referred to *Myth and Ritual*, already quoted in this Essay. Hence it will suffice here to say that the general pattern of the great seasonal rituals of Egypt and Babylon involved the dramatic representation of the death and resurrection of a god, the place of the god being taken by a king, a sacred combat in which a god was victorious over a hostile power, usually symbolized by a dragon; a triumphal procession, an enthronement, a sacred marriage,

Procession of Gods
(From Gressmann *T.u.B.* Pl. CLXXXV)

and, in Mesopotamia, the important ceremony of the fixing of destinies. In *Myth and Ritual* it was also suggested that much of this pattern existed in the ritual of the Hebrew people in the early stages of their religion (cf. Dr Aubrey R. Johnson in *The Labyrinth*). It also survived in their myths and their poetry. In this connexion it may be remarked that there is a striking witness to the close relation between the general form of Jewish apocalyptic and this ancient ritual pattern, in the fact that a number of passages which Gunkel and his followers classed as apocalyptic, and accordingly assigned to the Maccabean period, have been explained by Mowinckel[11] as liturgical survivals of the ritual of the enthronement of Jahveh at the early Hebrew New Year Festival.

It is true that among the Hebrews, perhaps owing to an impulse derived from Moses, and certainly by reason of the strong opposition of the prophets to the idea of the monarchy, the kingship lost the magical sanctity which it possessed among the Egyptians and in Mesopotamia. Nevertheless, as is shown by Dr Aubrey R. Johnson (*op. cit.*), surviving traces of the divinity that doth hedge about a king are to be found in the history of Israel. But in the main, as we have suggested above (p. 109), the prophets succeeded in eradicating almost completely from the religion and the literature of their people the characteristic features of the ancient pattern.

It is, however, impossible to exterminate a pattern which has its roots in the oldest tendencies of human nature, and it is one of the ironies of history that the successors of the prophets, the apocalyptists, should have been destined to perpetuate in a new form the main features of the ancient pattern. As the actual power of the Jews to control their own destinies grew less, the imperative sense of the need of some means of controlling the future grew stronger and found expression in the revival of ancient forms. The old magical drama with its power to determine the future reappeared as a drama, an idealized pattern, of the course of events leading up to the desired consummation.

The precise manner in which the pseudonymous authors of the various apocalyptic books depicted for the encouragement of their persecuted compatriots the closing drama of world-history differed according to the historical circumstances under which they were written. But there is a family resemblance between them all, they can with truth be said to be moulded after a common pattern.

[11] S. Mowinckel: *Psalmenstudien*, vol. II (1922), pp. 210-30.

Some, such as the author of IV Ezra, display a philosophic tendency to enquire more deeply into the causes of moral and physical evil, but practically all begin with a review of the past history of their people. The disasters of the history are depicted in symbolic form, always implying a secular struggle between the underlying forces of good and evil. In the mind of all the writers the end of the struggle is about to take place in their own day. Dr Charles has rightly emphasized the ethical character of Jewish Apocalyptic, but this literature did not spring from a desire to inculcate a standard of ethics. Their passion for the vindication of their national hopes led them to see the whole history in dramatic form. Hence the inevitable resurgence of those ancient forms which had embodied in the past the emotions and desires of earlier generations. The events of the culminating period of 'this age' of world history, as they conceived of it, fell naturally into the ancient pattern which had been shaped so long ago by similar desires and emotions.

The first stage of the apocalyptic drama consists of a period of tribulation, the great πειρασμός of the Gospels and the Apocalypse, during which the forces of evil appear to be triumphant. This has its counterpart in the period of search and mourning for the dead god, common to all the ancient rituals. Then, when evil seems victorious, the deliverer appears; the central figure of the king-god, banished by the prophets, returns in the apocalyptic pattern as the Messiah, the agent of the Most High in the shaping of the future, the victor in the final struggle against the powers of evil. It is hardly necessary to quote passages in the apocalyptic literature illustrating the conception of the Messiah and his activities, since we are not concerned here with various forms which that conception assumed in different stages of the growth of apocalyptic literature, but only with the main point that the Messiah is central, save for a very few exceptions in which historical conditions led to the formation of an apocalyptic picture in which there was no Messiah.

One important difference between Jewish and Christian Apocalyptic must be pointed out here. Save for the apparent exception of IV Ezra 7.29-30, Jewish Apocalyptic does not know a dying Messiah. The exception just mentioned is only apparent because the death of the Messiah there has no relation to the great apocalyptic crisis. But in Christian Apocalyptic this fundamental element in the ancient pattern returns. The death and resurrection of the Lamb ensure the final victory. This conception of the dying and rising god, banished from Jewish thought, had survived in the Mystery religions and becomes the clue of the whole drama in Christian Apocalyptic.

The dragon, the personification of those forces whose defeat had been dramatically re-enacted from year to year in the ancient seasonal festivals, emerged from his embalmment in Hebrew poetry and lived again in the lurid and fantastic shapes of the Apocalypse. The many forms of the powers of evil associated with the dragon take on the old monstrous forms which we have seen on the Babylonian seals connected with the ritual pattern.

After the final victory of the hero-god, the Lamb in Christian Apocalyptic, we have a triumphal procession after the fashion of the procession along the Sacred Way in the Babylonian New Year Festival, and the important ceremony of the fixing of destinies is represented in both Jewish and Christian Apocalyptic by the scene of the Great Assize when the destinies of mankind are finally determined.

Another important element, absent from Jewish Apocalyptic, save that the marriage of Israel to Jahveh appears as an element in the prophetic vision of the future, is found in Christian Apocalyptic, namely, the sacred marriage. The announcement of the marriage of the Lamb, and the description of the bride's adornment, form the climax of the Book of Revelation.

Thus it is difficult to avoid the conclusion that the general pattern of Jewish and Christian Apocalyptic, in spite of differences in detail, conforms in the most striking manner to the pattern of the ancient myth and ritual which had once embodied the hopes and desires of the inhabitants of the ancient East.

CHAPTER TEN

Archaeology and the Old Testament[1]

THE PRESENT SITUATION

IN 1938 Professor W. F. Albright contributed to the *Haverford Symposium* an opening article on 'The Present State of Syro-Palestinian Archaeology'. In 1951 he contributed to *The Old Testament and Modern Studies* the two opening articles, one entitled 'The Old Testament and the Archaeology of Palestine', and the other 'The Old Testament and the Archaeology of the Ancient East'. These articles by one of the most distinguished archaeologists of our time provide a useful measure of the advance which has been made during the last quarter of a century in the understanding of the Old Testament by the help of archaeology.

One of the most important indirect contributions has been the publication of a number of valuable books in which the results of recent archaeological research, using the term in the widest sense, have been summed up and made available both for the student and the general reader. It may be relevant to our subject to mention a few of the most outstanding of these. First, should be named the magnificent volume which came from the Princeton University Press under the editorship of Professor Pritchard entitled *Ancient Near Eastern Texts relating to the Old Testament*. This appeared in 1950 and supersedes the long valued *Texte und Bilde zum Alten Testament* of Gressmann and Ebeling. It contains more than double the number of texts, which is not surprising, since so many new collections of documents have come to light since the second edition of Gressmann was published in 1926. Only to mention the most noteworthy, we now have the Lachish Letters, the Ugaritic texts, letters of historical importance from the excavations at Mari, much new Hittite material, some fresh Akkadian texts from Professor Mallowan's ex-

---

[1] Paper read to the Palestine Exploration Fund, 1952.

cavations at Nimrud, too recent to be included in Pritchard, and most recent of all the much discussed scrolls from Wadi Qumran and Murabba'at. Also many old texts have been re-translated in the light of further knowledge about their textual problems, notably the Epic of Gilgamesh and the Creation Epic. Professor Kramer's researches have made available much new material which will make a revision of current interpretations of many Sumerian and Babylonian myths necessary.

Much new light has accrued in recent years on the impor-tant subject of the development of writing in its earliest stages, and on the still much debated problem of the invention of the alphabet. Two books of special importance on this subject may be mentioned here in the order of their appear-ance. In 1947 Dr David Diringer's monumental book *The Alphabet* appeared, embracing all that is known at present about the history of writing in every part of the habitable world. In the following year Professor G. R. Driver's Schweich Lectures for 1944 appeared under the modest title *Semitic Writing*, a book which contains an account of all the theories which have been proposed to explain the invention of the alphabet, together with an acute criticism of them and valu-able constructive suggestions towards the solution of a problem which still remains obscure.

In the important field of ancient law archaeology has con-tributed much during the last thirty years. Many previously unknown collections of laws have come to light and have been made available to students; and in addition to these new sources must be added the vast number of business documents, contracts, agreements, and other similar material, which have been translated and commented upon. This body of new material is of special importance in relation to Hebrew law, and much use has been made of it in recent studies. In this connexion M. Henri Cazelles' valuable study *Études sur le Code de l'Alliance* (1946) should be mentioned; but the most important contribution in this field has come from Professor Driver and his eminent colleague Sir John Miles. In 1935 they brought out the volume entitled *The Assyrian Laws*, to be followed in 1952 by *The Babylonian Laws*, containing the legal commentary on the Code of Hammurabi; a second volume containing the text and translation will appear shortly. In these two volumes the student of Hebrew law will find the fullest light hitherto available on the relation between the ancient Semitic corpus of law and custom and the various collections of Hebrew laws. Lastly mention should be made of Professor Albright's admirable Pelican volume entitled *The Archaeology of Palestine*, published in 1949, and providing a compendious and indispensable guide to the present state of knowledge about Palestinian archaeology and its relation to the Bible.

Turning now to the direct contribution of archaeology in recent years to biblical studies, since the whole field is far too large to cover in our limited space, let us select a few points upon which the light of archaeological research has been specially concentrated of late. Much new light has been thrown upon the patriarchal period, a period which used to be regarded as almost unknown territory, peopled by myths and legends or the tendentious inventions of post-exilic editors. The one glimpse into contemporary history, in Gen. 14, was dismissed as a late midrash. Now all that is changed. In the first place, the long gap in time between the entry of Abraham into Canaan and the descent of Jacob into Egypt, a gap which raised many difficult problems, has been reduced by about two and a half centuries. Professor Sidney Smith's monograph *Alalakh and Chronology*, based on the results of Sir Leonard Woolley's excavations at Tell el Atchana, has reduced the dates of the first Amorite dynasty of Babylon so far as to bring the date of Hammurabi down to 1792-50, and if the synchronism of Hammurabi with Abraham be still accepted, that gives us the approximate date for Abraham's entry into Canaan. But more important than this is the way in which recent archaeological research has thrown light on ethnic movements at the beginning of the second millennium B.C., illuminating the background against which the movements of Abraham and Jacob in Canaan must be seen. The mysterious Horites of the Old Testament, supposed by early commentators to be pre-historic troglodytic inhabitants of Canaan, are now an important ethnic group, the Hurrians, who ruled the kingdom known as Mitanni, and contended with the Hittites for several centuries for the mastery of the region lying to the east of the Taurus, between the Zagros Mountains and the Euphrates. With regard to them Professor Albright has said, 'One of the most fascinating achievements of our generation has been the reconstruction of the Hurrian language and religion from scattered tablets in different scripts and from different periods. Hurrian texts come from Amarna in Egypt, and from Boghazkoy in Cappadocia, from Ugarit in north-western Syria and from Mari on the middle Euphrates.' Harran, linked by early Hebrew tradition with the wanderings of Abraham, lay in the heart of the Mitanni empire, and various incidents in the Genesis stories of the patriarchs have been illuminated by the discovery of the Hurrian laws. Another closely related problem, that of the Habiru, has received a greatly enlarged significance by recent archaeological discoveries. The first result of the discovery of the Tell el-Amarna Letters was the rather too confident identification of the Habiru with the invading Hebrews. But subsequent discoveries revealed the presence of the mysterious Habiru in widely separated regions of the Middle East, making the earlier identification difficult if not impossible. We find the Habiru in Babylonian documents of the pre-Hammurabi period, and the new texts from Mari mention their activities during the reign of Zimri-Lim, the last king of Mari, and a contemporary of Hammurabi. In the Hittite records from Boghazkoy they are found in the service of the Hittites; the tablets from Arrapkha, in the Hurrian district, east of the Tigris, speak of people, who are described as Habiru, having sold themselves into slavery there; and if we accept the identification of the *'apiru* of Egyptian sources with the Habiru, they are found in Egypt as late as the time of Rameses IV in the twelfth century B.C. The bearing of the appellation Habiru on the position of Abraham the Hebrew in the history of the ancient Near East is well summed up by Professor Sidney Smith: 'It is no longer easy to doubt that the story of Abraham the Hebrew sums up the tribal history of a part of the Habiru if the circumstances of his life are considered broadly. A typical nomad, he is able to wander from one place to another; possessed of great flocks, he avoids the crowded industrial areas whose religion and civilization he regards with horror, though he thereby loses the adherence of an important section of his family, headed by Lot; a leader of men, capable of effective military action, he intervenes in great wars and is able to force his presence upon the local princes of Palestine, who dare not resist his demands.'[2] Much more might be said about the fresh light thrown by archaeology upon the patriarchal period, but to sum up briefly it may be said that Genesis has been conclusively shown to reflect faithfully the life and customs of Canaan and the movements of peoples in the first half of the second millennium B.C.

The next focal point to which we may turn is the period of the Exodus. Here the effect of fresh light from many archaeological sources has been in the main to show that the problems raised by the Hebrew tradition of that crucial event in their history are far more complicated than was realized by earlier commentators. First there is the problem of chronology. What was the date of the Hebrew descent into Egypt, what was the length of their sojourn there, and what was the date of their departure from Egypt? The attempt to apply the evidence of archaeology to throw light on these three connected questions has shown that they depend on the answer to another group of questions, namely: Did the whole of the Hebrew people come down into Egypt; if not, what part of them did enter Egypt, and was there more than one Exodus? A third group of questions cannot be separated from those already enumerated, namely, the length of the wilderness sojourn, was Canaan entered from more than one direction, and the date of the fall of Jericho? The mere statement of these problems which are now occupying the attention of scholars is enough to show that archaeology may often raise more questions than it is able to solve, but it has rendered a

[2] S. Smith, *Early History of Assyria* (Chatto & Windus, 1928), p. 192.

great service to biblical studies by showing that these questions must be asked and answered.

What concerns us now is to state briefly the general position occupied by scholarship with regard to these interrelated questions. It is necessary to remember that while excavation has provided factual evidence that must be accepted without question, yet, as Professor Rowley has pointed out, 'the interpretation of the evidence is a different matter. The same evidence is often very differently interpreted by different archaeologists, and even the same archaeologist may vary from time to time the conclusions he draws from it.'[3]

With regard to the first group of questions it may be said that while there is still a considerable amount of divergence among scholars concerning the date of the traditional descent into Egypt, that is, the descent of Jacob and his dependents, the majority at present favour a date about 1360 B.C., accepting a much briefer stay in Egypt than is given by the main line of Hebrew tradition, i.e. about four generations, which agrees with the Hebrew tradition preserved in Ex. 6.16-20, making Moses belong to the fourth generation from Levi. Thus the biblical Exodus would have occurred about 1230 B.C. But here the archaeological evidence relating to the second group of questions comes in to show that it is impossible to give any single answer to the first group which will satisfy all the facts presented by archaeology. In the first place the evidence from the Tell el-Amarna Letters showed invaders called Habiru entering Canaan during the reign of Amenophis IV. Hence, if the identification with some part of the Hebrew people stands, some Hebrews were in Canaan in the fourteenth century B.C. Then Professor Garstang's evidence from his excavation of Jericho convinced him and many other scholars that Jericho fell to Hebrew conquest about 1400 B.C. Third, we have the evidence of the well-known stele of Merneptah in which a victory over Israel is described in the words, 'Israel is desolated, his seed is not'. This would imply the presence of Israel in Canaan about 1220 B.C. Fourth, there

[3] H. H. Rowley, *From Joseph to Joshua* (Schweich Lectures, 1948), pp. 2-3.

is the problem of Ai which was shown by Mme Marquet-Krause's excavation of the site to have been destroyed and left in ruins from about 2000 to about 1200 B.C., and could not have been taken at the same time as Jericho. Last, there is the evidence of the stele of Seti I found at Beth-Shan, which mentions his capture of the city. The first year of Seti I is usually given as about 1305 B.C., and hence the stele is evidence for the presence of the Egyptian power in Canaan at a date when by the Tell el-Amarna and Jericho evidence the Hebrews were already in occupation of Canaan.

Thus again it becomes clear that no single and simple solution can harmonize all these conflicting data. In the first place the archaeological evidence seems to suggest that (*a*) there may have been more than one 'descent' of Hebrews into Egypt; a tradition of one such movement may be preserved in the story of Abraham's descent into Egypt in Gen. 12; (*b*) that a considerable portion of the early Hebrew settlers in Canaan never went down into Egypt, and that the conquest of Canaan began before any descent into Egypt took place. The Hebrew tradition of Jacob's conquest of Shechem preserved in Gen. 48.22 supports this view; (*c*) that more than one Exodus took place. The theory of two Exoduses has been recently put forward by Mr Rowton in a lecture delivered to the Palestine Exploration Fund, and has strong archaeological support; (*d*) that Canaan was entered from more than one direction, apart from the earlier settlements represented by the movements of Abraham and Jacob. The capture of Jericho was the result of the entry of one body of invading Hebrews from the east under Joshua, according to Hebrew tradition. On the other hand, the capture of Hebron by Caleb and of Debir by Othniel, and the campaign against the Canaanites in Arad, seem to represent a tradition of a Hebrew entry into Canaan from the south.

Professor Albright had already suggested the possibility of two Exoduses, first the Exodus of the Joseph tribes in 1400, and then the Exodus of the Levites under Moses early in the reign of Rameses II. But there are several difficulties raised by this theory, which have been cogently stated by Mr Rowton in a paper published in the 1952 April issue of the *Quarterly Statement of the Palestine Exploration Fund.*

In his recent Schweich Lectures Professor Rowley with characteristic thoroughness has collected everything that has been written about the problems of the Exodus. He accepts the Hebrew tradition of the entry into Canaan from two directions, acknowledging that archaeology has offered no evidence against it. But he rejects the theory of a double Exodus, and places the Exodus from Egypt under Moses in about 1230 B.C.

Mr Rowton's theory, the arguments for which will be found in the article mentioned above, is that there were two Exoduses, one of the Joseph tribes and one of the Levites, agreeing so far with Albright. But in his reconstruction of the history of the two movements he differs widely from the American scholar. In his view the Joseph tribes reached Canaan early in the thirteenth century B.C., and there, after the destruction of Bethel and Jericho, they founded what Mr Rowton, following Noth, calls the anphictyony of Israel. The Levites under the leadership of Moses came out of Egypt about 1170 B.C., but did not enter Canaan until a generation later, about 1125. Hence, on this view, Joshua was not responsible for the capture of Jericho, and Garstang's date for that event is rejected. An important piece of archaeological evidence supporting his theory is pointed out by Mr Rowton. It is that the pottery of Jericho corresponds with that of Beth-Shan IX and VIII, whereas that of Mersim C2 corresponds with that of Beth-Shan VII and VI, implying a gap of about a century. Mr Rowton acknowledges that the last word must lie with archaeology, and suggests that if excavation of the numerous sites connected with the Exoduses and the conquest of Canaan should reveal that at these sites Canaanite occupation came to an end in two distinct phases more than a century apart, then at least in broad outline his solution is likely to be correct.

This brings us to one point of considerable importance. That is the date of the destruction of Jericho. In the *Quarterly Statement of the Palestine Exploration Fund* for 1936 Professor Garstang wrote as follows, 'We may logically conclude that the fall of Jericho took place between 1400 B.C. and the accession of Akhenaton. No other conclusion will satisfy the archaeological evidence as a whole.' Now it has long been recognized that the weight of archaeological evidence as a whole places the main bulk of Israelite conquest of Canaan in the thirteenth century B.C. Hence the acceptance of Garstang's dating made it necessary to separate the capture of Jericho from the main conquest. But the archaeological evidence from Lachish and other sites which the Old Testament associates with the fall of Jericho places the capture of these places in the last quarter of the thirteenth century B.C. This patent difficulty made many scholars reluctant to accept the early date for the fall of Jericho. Now, however, there are signs that the evidence from Jericho may have to be reinterpreted, and in his latest book on the subject, *The Archaeology of Palestine* (1949), Professor Albright has come down to the early thirteenth century for the fall of Jericho. It is too early yet to say what the bearing of Miss Kenyon's fresh excavation of Jericho may be on the question of the date of the capture of the city, but it is to be hoped that it will remove some of the doubts which at present bedevil the whole question of Hebrew settlement in Canaan.

CHAPTER ELEVEN

The Early History of Writing[1]

O N the 29th of June 1910, at the consecration of Westminster Cathedral, a curious piece of ritual was performed called 'The Ceremony of the Alphabet', almost identical with a ceremony which had been witnessed by the London of a by-gone day at the dedication of Westminster Abbey in 1065. *The Times* of 29 June 1910 described the ceremony as follows:

'On the floor of the spacious nave, from the main entrance to the sanctuary, were painted in white two broad paths, which connected the corners diagonally opposite, and intersecting at the centre of the nave formed a huge figure X, or St Andrew's Cross. Where the lines converged was placed a faldstool; and here the Archbishop, still in cope and mitre, knelt in prayer, while the choir continued to sing the ancient plainsong of the "Sarum Antiphoner" . . . Meanwhile attendants were engaged in strewing the nave with ashes. This meant the laying of small heaps of the ashes, about two yards apart, along the lines of the St Andrew's Cross. Beside each heap of ashes was placed a piece of cardboard containing a letter of the alphabet—the Greek on one line and the Latin on the other. The Archbishop then went towards the main entrance, attended by the deacon and sub-deacon, and preceded by the Crucifix carried between lighted candles. Starting first from the left-hand corner Dr Bourne advanced along one path of the St Andrew's Cross, tracing with the end of his pastoral staff the letters of the Greek alphabet on the heaps of ashes; and returning again to the main entrance repeated the process on the other path, tracing this time on the heaps of ashes the letters of the Latin alphabet. This curious ceremony is variously interpreted as symbolizing the union of the Western and Eastern Churches, or the teaching of the rudiments of Christianity, and as a survival of the

[1] First published in *Antiquity*, 1937.

[153]

Roman augurs in laying their plans for the construction of a temple, or as the procedure of Roman surveyors in valuing land for fiscal purposes.'

The ceremony is a reminder that behind all the symbolism of the many religions of the world lies that most ancient and most potent symbol, the symbol of the spoken word. This paper attempts to deal briefly with some aspects of the early history of writing, that most significant of all human inventions which first gave permanence to the achievements of civilization.

We are still a long way from being in a position to make a comparative survey of all the early forms of writing known to archaeology. The Minoan linear and pictographic scripts have not yet yielded up their secret[2]; the proto-Elamite script is still undeciphered; and although astonishing progress has been made with the various scripts which come under the designation of Hittite, it is too soon yet to make a comparative study of the relation of these scripts to the early Egyptian and Sumerian scripts. There is also the new problem of the early Indian script awaiting solution. Hence in this paper we shall limit our enquiry to the beginnings of writing in Egypt and Sumer, with special reference to the new material which has been made available by the publication of Falkenstein's *Archäische Texte aus Uruk* (Harrassowitz, Leipzig, 1936).

The late Sir Grafton Elliot Smith's researches in the development of the brain have shown that the most significant step in the process by which man emerged from the level of the lower animals was the acquirement, by the visual area of the cortex, of a predominance over the areas connected with smell and other senses. The natural correlate of this increased significance of visual experience was the development of intelligible speech as the most convenient means of communicating experience. At the same time the co-ordination of visual and motor mechanisms which brought man's hand under the control of his eye with a delicacy of adjustment possessed by no other animal made possible another method

---

[2] This is no longer the case; cf. John Chadwick and Michael Ventris, 'Greek Records in the Minoan Script', *Antiquity* no. 108.

of recording visual experience. Man developed the power, not only of describing the world of sense-experience by intelligible sound-symbols, but also of portraying it in pictorial form. In the caves of Altamira and Cogul and in many other places are still to be seen fresh and vivid paintings and drawings which show that prehistoric man had developed a very high degree of skill in the representation of those animals which constituted his food supply. There is a general agreement among anthropologists that the motive for these drawings and paintings was not pleasure but desire. The fact that many of the drawings either mark the vital spot of the animal with red, or represent the animal as pierced with a weapon, suggests that the drawings had a magical purpose. They were intended to secure good hunting.

It is this power of pictorial representation which seems to provide the first step in the process which led to the invention of writing. There seems to be little doubt that the earliest elements of written speech both in the Nile Valley and in Mesopotamia were pictures of recognizable objects. But a possible alternative source for the beginnings of writing must be noticed. In his book *The Formation of the Alphabet*, Sir Flinders Petrie has collected a body of linear signs or marks on pottery, with regard to which he says: 'Further, the body of signs belongs to the early age, when drawing was of the rudest, and only mechanical abilities were developed in the art. Hence from the psychological point of view it is impossible to presuppose a pictorial source for them. They start at an age when rude marks satisfy the mind by symbolizing the intended meaning, and long before more exact copies of forms were thought needful.' It is a little difficult, in view of the archaeological evidence, to accept the suggestion that linear signs arise in a stage of culture when the power of pictorial representation is still rudimentary. The earliest appearance of anything resembling linear signs occurs in the painted pebbles of Mas d'Azil. But whether these may have been a linear script or not, they are certainly contemporaneous with a highly developed power of pictorial representation both in the flat and in the round.

It seems hardly open to doubt that, given a motive of sufficient interest, prehistoric man, long before the signaries under discussion could have come into existence, was capable of producing pictorial representations of the highest degree of skill.

It is also clear that in the early history of writing a process of detrition, so to speak, may be observed, by which pictures of objects were reduced to groups of linear signs bearing no resemblance to the original pictures. Hence, if Sir Flinders Petrie's theory is well founded, we should have, for Egypt at least, a double line of possible development, as the following words from his book already mentioned suggest: 'It is more likely than not that the mental attitude of thinking of signs phonetically occurred in the same age to the Egyptian with his pictorial hieroglyphs, and also to the dweller in Egypt—whoever he may have been—who used the linear signs.'

It does not seem possible at present to find any certain connexions between the main line of development of writing as seen in the Egyptian hieroglyphic system, and the linear signs referred to. We cannot tell whether they were true phonetic signs or merely marks of ownership. Perhaps when further light on the history of the so-called Sinaitic script is forthcoming they may be found to have had a part in the origination of this system of writing.

One more point of connexion between prehistoric art and early picture-writing may be mentioned. In the prehistoric cave-drawings there is a curious difference between the drawings of animals and the representations of human figures. The drawing of the latter is rudimentary and often resembles the rudimentary human figures on the early decorated Egyptian pottery. The drawing of the animals shows that it was not due to any lack of skill that the human figure was so crudely depicted. It seems rather to point to the earliest stage of symbolization, the reduction of the pictorial representation to its simplest terms. An alternative explanation may be found in the fear of maleficent magic.

We have then clear evidence of the very early development of pictorial representation and of its early conventionalization.

The general analogy of picture-writing among savage peoples points to pictorial representation as the earliest and simplest method of communicating ideas. We have also abundant evidence for the existence of a pictographic system of writing in use among the early Egyptians and the Sumerians. Hence we shall now go on to examine these early forms of writing to find out what light they throw upon the beginnings of the representation of sounds by visual symbols.

The moment in Egyptian history when we can observe the first emergence of writing as distinct from pictorial representation coincides with the beginnings of the united monarchy in Egypt. It is on the famous slate-palette of a king that, in the words of Dr Alan H. Gardiner,[3] 'we are able to observe the birth of hieroglyphics taking place, as it were, under our very eyes'. The king, whose Horus-name is usually read as Narmer, was possibly the second king of the first dynasty of the Old Kingdom. His palette, like so many other pictorial representations of the Pharaohs, celebrates the military achievements of the monarch. The greater part of the palette is occupied with a vigorous representation of Narmer in the act of striking down a vanquished enemy with his mace. There are seven hieroglyphs in different positions on the palette; two of them at the top form the Horus-name of the king, while five others whose phonetic equivalents are uncertain serve as labels to the different figures grouped round the king. But the group of particular interest is the one occupying the right-hand top corner of the palette. The following is Dr Alan Gardiner's description[4] of it:

The group in the right-hand top corner is of a much more puzzling character; an ordinary, simple picture . . . it is not. There is nothing, indeed, unpictorial about the representation of the god Horus under the image of a falcon, but the human hand by which he grasps a rope introduces an element of symbolism which is alien to purely pictorial art. This symbolical note is still further emphasized by the bodiless head of a foreigner growing out of a cylindrical object; but we have not much trouble in concluding that the foreigner is a prisoner, and that the cylindrical object is meant to indicate his

[3] *Journal of Egyptian Archaeology*, 1915, II, 72.   [4] *Ibid.*

land. The six stalks with flowers, on the contrary, would altogether elude our comprehension, were it not that their signification is at once apparent to anyone with a slight knowledge of hieroglyphics; the veriest beginner could hardly fail to recognize in them the common word 𓆼, *kho'*(*ḥ'*), meaning 'a thousand'. Now there is nothing in the outward appearance of 𓆼 to suggest the signification 'thousand', and the existence of a word 𓆼 𓃃, *ḥ'*, for a water-plant or some such botanical object makes it obvious that this is a typical case of phonetic transference; 𓆼 means a 'thousand' simply because the plant it depicts was called in Egyptian by a name closely resembling the Egyptian word for 'thousand'. The six-fold 𓆼 on the palette therefore signifies 'six thousand', and the sense of the whole complex group in which it occurs may be thus defined: 'Horus brings to the Pharaoh six thousand foreigners captured within their land.'

The *ensemble* which centres around the falcon-shaped Horus is supplementary, therefore, to the larger figures below it on the left, and serves to explain the circumstances under which the Pharaoh is enabled to immolate his foes. It would be wide of the mark, nevertheless, to describe this *ensemble* as an early example of writing; its size and importance prohibit that view, and moreover no particular order of words is suggested, nor yet any specific word except *kho'*, 'thousand'. On the other hand it cannot properly be ranked as a picture, since its method of expression is not that of imitative pictorial art, and since it incorporates one undeniable phonetic sign. It occupies a place, in fact, intermediate between picture and writing; it is neither the one nor the other, but possesses something in common with both. Now what to all intents and purposes is exactly the same subject is represented in magnificent sculptured relief on the walls of the funerary temple of Sahurē, where two rows of divinities are shown leading before the king two rows of prisoners with ropes tied to their arms and waists. But this sculptured scene is not complete in itself; its meaning is eked out by three lines of hieroglyphic inscription, of which the most relevant line reads as follows: '*Words recited: we have given to thee all the western and the eastern deserts, together with all the nomads and all the Beduin who are in every desert.*' Here we have the last step in the development towards which the group on the palette of Narmer unmistakably points: the differentiation of two complementary forms of expression, the one definitely pictorial, and the other definitely writing. The combination of hieroglyphic inscriptions and pictorial representations is extremely frequent on Egyptian monuments, and is accounted for by the common origin of both and by the fact that they have not yet drifted so far apart as to be incompatible side by side with one another. Hieroglyphic writing is, after all, merely a sequence of small pictures with special meanings attached to them; and, on the other hand, Egyptian pictorial art shows analogies with the methods of writing which are both striking and significant.

Here, then, we find the point at which the symbolic expression of ideas, which is writing, begins to diverge from the realistic representation of persons, things and actions.

It is important to note that this vitally significant advance is directly connected with a stage of social development. At a certain level of social progress there is not sufficient motive present to give rise to so complicated a social mechanism as written speech. It is possible, as we can see from a survey of present-day savage societies, for a language to reach a high degree of flexibility and a large vocabulary without any development of writing. But among the ancient Egyptians at the beginning of the Old Kingdom period certain elements in the social situation combined to produce a need which only the invention of writing could satisfy. We have already seen that in the first place the art of pictorial representation arose out of a need, the need of exercising a magical control over the food supply. Early in the Old Kingdom a new and urgent social motive appeared. The disposal of the dead assumed an importance which it has never possessed in any other civilization. The elaborate system of mummification began to develop, and among the many arts which it carried in its train the art of pictorial representation, with a magical significance, became an essential element of funerary ritual. The primary object of inscribing or writing down the words of the spells and incantations which formed part of the ritual of mummification was similarly a magical one. Preserved in the tomb, or about the person of the dead, the written word perpetuated the efficacy of the spoken word.

[159]

Furthermore, these funerary beliefs and practices centred in the person of the king, and the achievement of a united monarchy produced a social situation of which the invention of writing was the natural outcome. The palette of Narmer shows that the need was arising of a written record to supplement the pictorial representation of the king's exploits, and it is also possible that even here the magical value of the pictured scene and the written word had a place. On the reverse of the palette a scene is depicted in which a bull is goring a fallen enemy, and in the first book of Kings there is an interesting account of the way in which the leader of the court prophets assumes a bull-mask and dramatically enacts in a similar fashion the coming victory of the Israelite king over the Syrians. He is engaged in making victory, not merely in predicting it. It is extremely probable that the palette of Narmer served not only as a record of victory achieved but also as a magical means of securing it.[5]

Hence it may be suggested that among the Egyptians the invention or the emergence of the hieroglyphic system of writing is simply the extension of already existing cultural elements to a new social situation. This must be borne in mind when the question of the independent invention of writing in various parts of the ancient world is raised. The earliest texts from Sumer would appear to have no such character as that presented by such a document as the palette of Narmer. While they are connected with a temple and presuppose the organization of a small city-state, they are simply business memoranda, accounts, lists of cattle or articles of trade, of only temporary significance. Some of them, as Falkenstein points out, seem to have been bored through as a kind of cancellation. This would suggest that writing in early Sumerian culture had a more secular and utilitarian motive for its invention. The question of any possible relation between the Egyptian and Sumerian systems of writing will be dealt with later.

Before we go on to speak of the stages of development which appear in the early history of writing in the ancient

[5] Cf. above p. 107

East it is necessary to give a brief account of the beginning of writing in Sumer for which the archaic texts from Uruk (Erech) give us the material. It has long been known that the cuneiform script characteristic of Mesopotamia, whence it spread over large areas of the ancient East, was originally pictorial. Speaking of the well-known tablet from Kish in the Ashmolean Museum Mr C. J. Gadd says: 'The limestone "Pictographic Tablet" from Kish must be regarded for the present as representing the archetype of all Sumerian writing.' On this tablet are a number of signs representing objects, the human head, hand, foot and membrum virile, a hut with a man squatting in it, a sledge, and other signs not clearly determined. Very early tablets from Jemdet Nasr and Fara showed later stages of development in which the pictorial signs were in process of transformation into groups of wedges bearing little or no resemblance to the original forms. But the material from Uruk, consisting mainly of small clay tablets from layer ivb, in the judgment of competent authorities, takes us back to the earliest stage of writing in Sumer so far discovered. With the exception of the numerical signs all the signs on these tablets are pictographic, that is, they are representations of objects mostly recognizable, such as parts of the human body, heads of animals, birds, fishes, various kinds of plants, vessels, boats, tools, weapons, buildings, and so forth. Many of the signs can be identified with later cuneiform equivalents. The writing is, however, too well-developed for us to be able to regard the Uruk material as representing the earliest stage of writing in Mesopotamia. No small period of time must have been necessary for the writing to have reached the form in which it appears on these tablets. It is true that Dr Falkenstein considers them as the earliest written documents (cf. *Antiquity*, x, 137), but other competent authorities, such as Mr Sidney Smith and Mr Gadd, consider that earlier stages of writing must lie behind the ivb tablets from Uruk.

If we accept the date assigned to layer 1 at Uruk, namely, the period of Ur-Nanše, about ± 3000 B.C., and allow about 500 years for the development from ivb to 1, we get a date early in the fourth millennium, and possibly earlier than the palette of Narmer.

Hence, both in Egypt and in Sumer, we find a well-developed pictographic writing in use about the beginning of the fourth millennium, and in the light of our present knowledge it is possible to say that in both countries the development of writing follows a very similar course. We must now attempt a brief description of the stages of this development.

As soon as the need for the representation of continuous discourse arises it becomes evident that a number of the vital elements of speech are not capable of pictorial representation. Hence it becomes necessary to invent symbols to represent the sounds denoting pronouns, prepositions, adverbs, inflexions, and all such elements of speech as have no natural pictorial associations.

There are two ways in which this may be done. One such way is illustrated by Pitman's system of shorthand writing where we find an arbitrary allocation of linear signs to sounds; speed combined with ease of reading is here the only consideration. The system is arbitrary in the sense that it is not the result of a natural development of the relation between the signs and the sounds. We have already referred to the theory that the earliest script in Egypt was of this nature, an arbitrary selection of linear signs which never, so far as we know, had any pictorial value. It may be added that there is no evidence for the existence of such a form of script in Mesopotamia. But we do know with certainty that the various forms of script in use in Egypt, down to the purely cursive demotic, all go back to the hieroglyphic system. All writing in Egypt, until the intrusion of the Greek alphabet, is of one origin. Here we have the second way in which a script may arise, namely, by the extension and adaptation of the pictorial principle to the need of expressing non-pictorial elements of speech.

We find, then, that both in Egypt and in Sumer the picture constitutes the first element of the script, and in different ways remains an essential part of the system of writing in both countries. That is to say that both in Egyptian and Sumerian a large number of signs retain the function which they had as pictures; their primary function is to indicate an object, while their secondary function is to indicate the sound or word

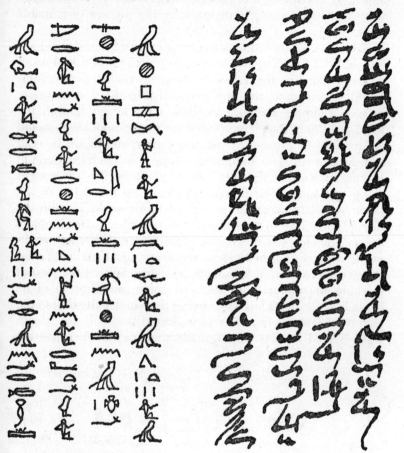

Extract from the story of Sinuhe, in Hieroglyphic and in Hieratic Script (after Bonnet, *Ägyptisches Schrifttum*, Leipzig, 1919).

which denotes that object in speech. Hence the pictorial origin of writing has left its mark on both the hieroglyphic and cuneiform systems in the form of a large body of signs which are known as *ideograms*, although the term is not entirely satisfactory. It is perhaps simpler to speak of such signs as *word-signs*. For instance, in Egyptian, the ideogram or word-sign for 'house' is the sign ⌐⌐, which represents the word *pr*, and is the picture of the groundplan of a house. In Sumerian the word *sag*, 'head', is denoted by the picture of a man's head.

Now it is obvious that ideograms or word-signs alone are incapable of fulfilling the necessary functions of a system of writing, namely, the representation in visible form of intelligible discourse, the movement of thought. For instance, in such a simple sentence as 'this is the king's house', the juxtaposition of the picture signs for 'house' and 'king' would fail to yield that meaning unambiguously, and might be read in several ways. The history of writing, both in Sumer and in Egypt, shows that the solution of this difficulty was sought along two lines. The first was to increase the detail of the picture-sign, to make the picture do more work. Thus in the hieroglyphic system the basic picture of a man is used in many ways. The sign list in Dr Alan Gardiner's *Egyptian Grammar* gives no less than 53 signs representing a man in different states or activities. The Sumerian scribes devised the plan of marking the picture-sign to show some modification of its original meaning. Thus by drawing lines under the chin of the picture of a man's head it was indicated that only the mouth was referred to, and the sign *sag* was transformed into the

SAG........*development of the sign from 3500–700 B.C.*

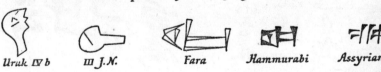

Uruk IV b   III J.N.   Fara   Hammurabi   Assyrian

sign *ka*. The result of such a tendency was inevitably a great increase in the number of pictorial signs employed. The sign list in Dr Gardiner's *Grammar*, representing Middle Egyptian usage, contains 732 signs, while the number of signs employed in the period represented by the early documents from Uruk is estimated at 2000. Apart from the cumbrous nature of such a system its limitations are obvious. No increase in detail could adequately represent all the possible extensions of meaning implicit in a picture-sign, nor could it ever succeed in denoting all the relations of the words in a sentence.

The alternative solution, which was to mark out the ultimate line of development for writing, was to make the picture-signs represent sounds without regard to their meaning. This process was possibly suggested, at the outset, by the existence in both Egyptian and Sumerian of homonyms, that is, of words with the same sound but of different meanings. According to Dr Falkenstein the earliest example of this method of extending the range of the pictorial signs comes from the Jemdet Nasr tablets and is the name *en-lil-ti*, meaning 'Enlil causes to live'. The word-sign *ti* is the picture of an arrow, according to Dr Falkenstein, and is the Sumerian word for that object. In the proper name referred to, the pictorial sign for an arrow had been transferred to the Sumerian word of the same sound meaning 'life', a word which it would be very difficult to represent pictorially. Similarly, in Egyptian we find the familiar sign for the scarabaeus (*hpr*) transferred to the homonym *hpr* meaning 'to be, to exist'.

While this device increases the range of expression of the pictorial signs it also increases their ambiguity, and its use is limited by the comparatively small number of homonyms.

But this use of homonyms to increase the range of utility of a single sign, pointed the way to the main line of development along which early writing was destined to progress, namely, the divorce of sound from meaning. The fact that the Sumerian vocabulary was mainly monosyllabic aided the process, and early in the third millennium we find three well-developed tendencies:

1. the use of the same word-sign for words similar in sound but not in meaning, and the closely related development of syllabic sounds.
2. the introduction of what are called Determinatives.

3. the arrangement of the signs within a compartment of a
tablet in the order in which the words would have
been read or spoken.

The effect of the development of syllabic signs is seen in
the progressive reduction of the number of signs in current
use. The 2000 signs in use in the period of Uruk ivb have
dwindled to 800 in the period of the Fara texts, while by the
time of Urukagina (*c.* 2900 B.C.) another 200 signs in use in
the Fara texts have disappeared. A striking example of this
process is afforded by the story of the sign for UDU, the
Sumerian word for 'sheep'. It has already been pointed out
that these early tablets are mainly temple documents, lists of
offerings and so forth, hence it is not surprising that the sign
for 'sheep' should be of frequent occurrence. Now in the
material from layer ivb there are no less than 31 variations of
the sign UDU, corresponding no doubt to the many varieties
of sheep and goats used in the temple for ritual purposes. But
in layer iii only 3 signs for 'sheep' remain, and in layer i there
are only 2 left. Here as Falkenstein remarks there has evidently been a deliberate rejection of an almost unlimited
tendency to differentiation.

The use of Determinatives is a device intended to remove
ambiguities, and appears at an early stage in the development
of both the Sumerian and Egyptian systems of writing. It
consists in the use of certain signs denoting classes of persons
or things, such signs being placed before or after the sign to
be determined. Probably the earliest of such signs is the sign
for DINGIR, god, which is prefixed to the names of the gods.
The sign GIŠ, wood, is placed before the names of things
made wholly or partly of wood. Thus the word-sign for
'plough', originally the picture of a plough, and capable of
meaning either a plough or a ploughman, by the use of
determinative signs can have its meaning limited or determined. With the sign GIŠ prefixed it means a plough, but
with the sign LU, man, prefixed, it can only mean a ploughman. Two other very common determinatives are the signs
KUR and KI, used respectively to mark the names of countries
and cities, KUR coming before the sign which it determines,

and KI after its sign. The traditional rules governing the use and position of the determinatives seem to have been established at a very early date.

The development of syllabic signs made it possible to express in writing those grammatical elements of speech, such as case endings, pronominal affixes and suffixes, prepositions, adverbs and conjunctions, which by their nature cannot be expressed pictorially. As far as our knowledge goes at present, the first of the syllabic signs to be used in this way was the plural sign.

Another important use of the syllabic signs as an aid towards clearness of meaning is their use as 'phonetic complements', a use found at an early date in both the Egyptian and the Sumerian systems. This can best be explained by an example.

One of the ambiguities which had to be dealt with by the people who shaped the Sumerian system of writing was the fact that many of the Sumerian word-signs were polyphons, that is, they had more than one phonetic value, carrying more than one meaning. This difficulty arose from the pictorial origin of the script. For example, the sign DU, whose original pictorial form was the human foot, might stand for the various activities connected with the use of the feet, and the words describing such activities would naturally have different phonetic values. Thus the sign DU came to stand for the words *gin*, to go, *gub*, to stand, and *tum*, to bring. By writing the syllabic signs *-na*, *-ba*, and *-ma*, respectively, after the sign DU, the scribe indicated which value was to be given to it. Thus the sign DU with the syllabic sign *na* written after it would be read *gin-a*, going, and similarly with the other words named.

The third tendency mentioned above, namely the arrangement of the signs within a compartment of a tablet in their proper, that is, their spoken order, completed the early stage of the internal development of Sumerian writing. On the earliest tablets there are no compartments marked, and the few signs which such tablets contain are arranged quite arbitrarily. When compartments begin to appear the signs which they contain show no traces of arrangement. This is no doubt due to the fact that these early documents were simply memoranda of merely temporary importance relating to temple business. They were quite intelligible to the people who wrote them, but were not intended to have any permanent value. When however it became a matter of interest to the rulers of cities like Lagash, for instance, to preserve records of their achievements, such a rough and ready way of making occasional notes gave place to an orderly arrangement of the signs in successive lines within the compartments of the tablet. This process seems to have been complete by the time of Eannatum (*c.* 3000).

Hence, by the end of the fourth millennium, the Sumerian system of writing consisted of a syllabary, or sign-list, containing about 500-600 signs. About 100 of these were phonetic signs representing the vowels a, e, i, o, and u, and the various combinations of these vowels with the consonantal sounds used by the Sumerians, but, unlike the Egyptians, the Sumerians had not devised any method of representing simple consonantal sounds, that is, they had not reached, nor did they ever reach, the final stage in the development of writing, the creation of an alphabet. It is interesting to observe that although the Egyptians had, at a very early date, discovered the alphabetic principle of writing, they never went on to take the logical step of discarding the cumbersome machinery of ideograms, determinatives, and phonetic complements, but to the end of their civilization continued to use the alphabetic method of writing simply as an adjunct to the rest of their ancient traditional system.

The history of the alphabet, however, is another story which would require much more space than we have at our disposal.

So far we have been concerned entirely with the internal development of the Sumerian system of writing. But there are various important changes in the external appearance of the script of which a brief account must be given.

We have already seen that the earliest forms of the sign used both by the Sumerians and the Egyptians was completely pictorial, but the external development of the signs as we watch it from the early tablets of Uruk up to the elegant script of the Assyrian scribes follows in Mesopotamia an entirely different course from that which it took in Egypt. This is mainly due to the fact that while in Egypt from very early times the papyrus reed furnished an inexhaustible supply of excellent writing material, the only generally available writing material in Mesopotamia was clay.

The early tablets from Uruk show that the signs were drawn on the clay in strokes of uniform thickness with a reed stylus. Falkenstein remarks with reference to the stylus, 'judging from the fineness of the lines in some of the tablets, an almost knife-sharp reed must have been used'. But it must have been a slow and difficult business to draw curved lines on wet clay, and by the time we reach the period of the Fara tablets the scribes had begun to cut the ends of their reed pens in a fairly wide-angled wedge, and instead of drawing their pictures in lines, curved or straight, they were beginning to make them by pressing the wedge-shaped end of the stylus into the clay and forming the required design by means of a group of wedges of different sizes and thickness.

The process is best illustrated by observing the change which has taken place in such a characteristic sign as SAG, representing the head of a man. In Uruk ivb the head is fully drawn, with eye, nose and mouth; in Uruk iii and in Jemdet Nasr it is still drawn, but in a greatly simplified form; in Fara we find a design composed of a group of seven wedges, in which it would be hard to recognize anything resembling a human head; finally we have the sign in the compact form which it received from the Assyrian scribes. It is from the appearance which the script presents in this stage of its development that it has received its name 'cuneiform' (Latin, *cuneus*, a wedge).

But there is another curious phenomenon to be noticed in the external development of the Sumerian script. It may be seen in the story of the sign SAG, mentioned above. When we first meet the sign, as for example on the Kish tablet, the sign is drawn in its normal position, i.e. with the head upright, and facing to the right. But when we come to layer III, or Jemdet Nasr, the sign appears lying on its back, with the face pointing upward, and we see that all the other signs have suffered the same change. The reason for this curious change seems to be that the early tablets which were small enough to be held comfortably in the palm of the hand, were held by the scribe in the left hand at an angle of about 45°, and the signs were written on the tablet as if it were horizontal.

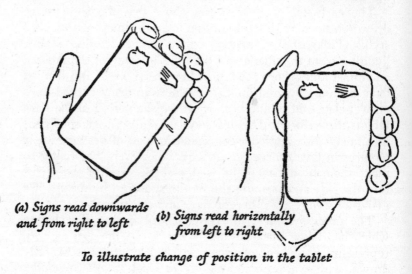

(a) Signs read downwards and from right to left   *(b) Signs read horizontally from left to right*

To illustrate change of position in the tablet

With an increase in the size of the tablets this position became inconvenient and the tablet was turned in a counter-clockwise direction till it was perpendicular. But as the turn was only one of 45° the signs were written in the same way as before, and hence, when the tablet was read in the perpendicular position, the signs would appear to be lying in a horizontal position face upward. By the time the change took place, possibly after the period of the Fara tablets, the form of the signs had so far departed from their original pictorial character that they were no longer felt to be in an unnatural position.

This explanation is supported by the fact that in the case

[170]

of inscriptions on monuments of stone or metal, where such a change of position was not practicable, the old position of the signs persisted. For example, on the stele of Hammurabi, the signs are engraved in the old position. Shortly after this date, i.e. about 2000 B.C.,[6] the practice in the case of monumental inscriptions came into line with that which had already long been in operation in the case of clay tablets.

Another important fact in connexion with the history of the Sumerian system of writing calls for notice. It is that as the result of the Semitic conquest of Mesopotamia, the Sumerian script was taken over by the invaders and adapted to the writing of a language whose sounds and vocabulary were totally different from the language which the script was invented to express. While this change had no effect on the nature of the script itself, it had very disturbing effects on the use of the script, since to the values which any Sumerian sign possessed, as a word-sign or a syllabic sign, there were now added Semitic values as well. Moreover, Sumerian continued to be used as the language of religion, for ritual purposes, much as Latin survived through the Middle Ages as the language of the Mass. Hence it had to be studied by the priests, and the large number of lexical and bi-lingual tablets discovered by excavators shows that the difficulties which these ancient texts present to the modern scholar also existed in some measure for the Babylonian and Assyrian scribes.

But in spite of these difficulties the cuneiform script acquired a place in the ancient Near East which its most important rival, the Egyptian hieroglyphic script, never attained. The Tell el-Amarna Letters show that the cuneiform script was used as the medium of diplomatic intercourse between Egyptian pharaohs, Hittite kings, Mitannite princes, and Canaanite chiefs in the middle of the second millennium B.C. It was used at an earlier date as a means of writing the Hittite, Hurrian, and other kindred dialects, languages which were totally different from either Sumerian or Akkadian. It was used as late as the time of Darius Hystaspis to inscribe

[6] The date of Hammurabi has now been brought down to *circa*. 1750. See above, p. 146.

in Susian on the Rock of Behistun the record of the victories of the Great King, and continued to be used on tablets down to the end of the pre-Christian era. This is a remarkable practical achievement for a system of writing which had never reached the final stage of development in which all the simple sounds, the vowels and consonants, used by any speech, are each represented by a separate sign, that is to say, the purely alphabetic stage of writing.

As we have already said, there is not space here to tell the story of the alphabet, but this much may be said in conclusion. By the middle of the second millennium the need felt by traders and merchants of the Mediterranean seaboard for a script that was simpler to read and easier to write had led to several experiments in the direction of an alphabet, but various causes combined to give the script commonly known as the Phenician script, the earliest example of which so far as we know at present comes from Byblos[7] in the fourteenth century B.C., the pre-eminence over its rivals and this form of writing ultimately ousted all others in the Near East and in the East, and became the ancestor of all our western alphabets.[8]

[7] The reference is of course to the well-known inscription on the sarcophagus of Abiram, King of Tyre, recognized as the earliest example of the so-called 'Phenician' script, and has nothing to do with the undeciphered inscription referred to by Dr Alan Gardiner in his letter to *The Times* of 16 July 1937.

[8] Reference may be made to Dr David Diringer's authoritative book *The Alphabet* (Hutchinson, 1948).

CHAPTER TWELVE

Myth and Ritual Reconsidered[1]

IT is nearly a quarter of a century since the lectures were delivered which were subsequently published as a symposium under the well-known, or perhaps I should say notorious, title of *Myth and Ritual*. The sub-title showed that the purpose of the book was mainly directed towards the religion of Israel, a fact which some of its critics have not always remembered.

I do not know whether the term 'patternism' was a product of the controversies aroused by the book in question, but it has become in recent years what the term 'diffusionism' was thirty years ago. It is a major heresy whose stronghold is now to be found in the Scandinavian universities, and whose exponents number amongst them some of the ablest of modern Old Testament scholars. Kind things have been said about me by the Scandinavian school, much kinder than I deserve, and I wish I could respond by a whole-hearted defence of patternism. I admire their work and have found much to learn from them, but my 'patternism' is limited in several important respects, as I shall try to make clear in this paper. The two main objects in view are, first to reply to some of the criticisms in the writings of Professor H. Frankfort, and some others of what is assumed to be the patternist position; secondly to say what modifications my own position has undergone during the long period of time that has elapsed since the publication of *Myth and Ritual*.

In the Frazer Lecture for 1950 Professor Frankfort delivered a resounding attack against what he conceived to be the patternist position, and in particular against the book *Myth and Ritual* and my own contribution to it in the first essay. The two heresies which formed the special object of attack were, first, the view, based on Frazer, that differences

[1] Paper read to the Oriental Society of the University of Manchester, 1954.

are specific and similarities generic, and, second, the claim that one definite pattern underlies most of the religions of the ancient Near East. With regard to the first point Professor Frankfort says: 'the belief that differences are specific and similarities generic vitiates one's very approach to the evidence.' This somewhat pontifical utterance is open to question. From the point of view both of logic and of scientific method the principle holds good that similarities are generic and differences specific, and the fact that similarities may be overemphasized or improperly defined does not invalidate the fundamental rule. The gravamen of Professor Frankfort's charge is that *Myth and Ritual* has over-emphasized the similarities and ignored the differences to be found in the religions of Egypt and Babylon respectively. While we have every cause to be grateful to Professor Frankfort for his brilliant exposition of the important differences between the religions of Egypt and Babylon in his book *Kingship and the Gods*, yet it must be pointed out that the declared object of *Myth and Ritual* was to draw attention to the existence of certain significant similarities between those two great religious systems. I might even put it a little more strongly and say that the contributors to that book sought to establish the fact that such similarities existed from their own first-hand knowledge of the sources. With no disrespect to Professor Frankfort, I cannot recognize his authority as superior to that of Professor Blackman and Mr Gadd, each of whom has adduced evidence from his own special field of study for the existence of the similarities of which we have spoken. I can speak for myself, and I am sure for the distinguished contributors mentioned above, when I say that the assertion of the existence of similarities was never intended to imply a denial of the existence of very important differences; indeed the essays themselves bear witness to the differences with no uncertain voice.

Next, with regard to the use of the term 'pattern', Professor Frankfort, while allowing the anthropologists to speak of culture patterns as a descriptive term for certain distinctive characteristics of particular primitive cultures, will not allow

me to use it to describe the similarities which the scholars
contributing to *Myth and Ritual* believed that they found in
the religious beliefs and practices of Babylon, Egypt, and
Canaan early in the second millennium B.C. I cannot accept
the restriction. The term is very widely used to-day in many
branches of science. The modern development of psychology
known as Gestalt psychology has shown the tendency of the
human mind to produce patterns of thought and action, and it
is no misuse of the term to apply it to a well-defined body of
beliefs and practices which appear among agricultural societies
in the ancient Near East at a very early date, probably prior
to the process of urbanization. That the Scandinavian school
has developed the Mesopotamian kingship pattern to an un-
warrantable degree, is no ground for denying the existence
of the pattern, any more than the extreme pan-Egyptianism
of Perry and Elliott-Smith was a ground for denying the
existence and importance of that diffusionism which it is their
merit to have so convincingly demonstrated that, as someone
has said, we are all diffusionists to-day.

I willingly admit that Egypt developed her religious system along lines which diverged so widely from Mesopotamia
that the differences are more apparent than the similarities by
the end of the second millennium B.C. But Osiris is a culture
hero, possibly, as some scholars suggest, coming to Egypt
from Asia, bringing with him the knowledge of cereals and
the beginnings of agriculture. His myth, with his ritual dismemberment, the conflict with Set, the search of Isis, and his
restoration to life by magical rituals, has similarities with the
early Mesopotamian agricultural myth and ritual which it is
difficult to ignore or disprove. Here mention may be made of
Professor Sidney Smith's discussion, in his book *The Early
History of Assyria*, of a possible relation between the *ṭaṭ*-tree
ritual of Osiris and the Assyrian tree ritual frequently represented on Assyrian reliefs. Note also the name Usir or Usirsir
for Tammuz in the Liturgies.

One more item in the charge against my 'patternism' may
be briefly dealt with. Professor Frankfort, having denied its
right to exist, accuses it of 'rigidity', and claims that it has

[175]

been arbitrarily imposed upon other religious systems, and especially upon Israel, where he uses the word 'recklessness'. Now, in the first place, the 'pattern' was never intended to be rigid, even if others have tended to make it so. Its character was wholly provisional, subject to modification in the light of further knowledge. It was, for me, nothing more than the enumeration of certain cult phenomena observed to occur together at certain important points of the religious year. That they were imposed 'recklessly' upon the religion of Israel is Professor Frankfort's most serious charge, and, I believe, underlies his whole attack on the *Myth and Ritual* position. Hence it is to this issue that the rest of this paper will be devoted.

But there are a few points to be dealt with briefly before we turn to this central question. First, may I remark that the guilty book was published a long time ago. The Ras Shamra texts were only just beginning to be available for study, and some of the things I said about them then would not hold good to-day. But I think most scholars would agree that the weight of their evidence, now that we are in a position to evaluate it, strongly supports the position outlined in my essay on the 'Myth and Ritual Pattern in Canaan'. Second, I have no hesitation in admitting that some of the things said in the first essay about divine kingship in Mesopotamia need to be re-stated. The sense in which Mesopotamian kings of the third millenium B.C. can be called divine needs to be severely limited, both in time and in the extent of its application, as Professor Fish has so admirably demonstrated in his paper on *Some Aspects of Kingship in the Sumerian City and Kingdom of Ur*. I should not now use the expression 'king-god' for Mesopotamian kings, although I might point out that I did make it clear from the first that by the term 'god' I meant an individual who was regarded by the community as the focus and embodiment of the magical powers which were necessary for its well-being. But I gladly accept Professor Fish's statement regarding the phrases used about the kings of Ur III as holding good, in all probability, for Mesopotamian kings in general, that 'all such titles and the beliefs

associated with them gave to society a sanctified order personified in the king beloved by the gods'. Perhaps the term
'sacral kingship' might be more acceptable, but, in any case
I have so far found no reason to change my views about the
central position of the king in relation to the cult, whether in
Egypt, Mesopotamia, or Canaan.

The third and last point about which something must be
said before passing on to the question of the religion of Israel
concerns the ritual myth. The existence of myths of this
character has been called in question, but I still remain convinced of the reality and importance of this type of myth. I
may be allowed to quote from a paper entitled 'Myth, Ritual
and History' (see Chapter III in this volume) given before the British Association in 1938: 'I have no intention of
putting forward the view that all myths are ritual in origin,
and there can be no doubt that many early myths from our
culture area are aetiological myths. But such study as I have
been able to make of the myths of the earliest civilizations of
which we have any documentary evidence seems to suggest
that the ritual myth appeared earlier than the aetiological
myth. It would be rash to dogmatize on the point, but I
cannot help feeling that the ritual myth which is magical in
character, and inseparable from the ritual which is directed
to certain fundamental needs of an early society, whether
pastoral, agricultural, or urban, is older than the aetiological
myth which has no magical potency, and does not seem to
satisfy any more fundamental need than curiosity. From the
point of view of a functional anthropology the ritual myth
would seem to be more important and likely to appear earlier
than the aetiological myth.' In the paper referred to I have
taken three basic myths, the myth of Tammuz and Ishtar, the
Creation myth, and the Deluge myth to support the view that
what may appear at first sight to be an aetiological myth is
capable of explanation at a deeper level as an authentic ritual
myth.

The much-vexed question of the influence of the ritual
pattern on the religion of Israel involves the prior question of
the nature of Canaanite religion at the time of Hebrew settle-

ment in Canaan. The interpretation of the Ras Shamra texts has now yielded sufficiently assured results, in spite of much that remains obscure, to enable us to see the broad lines of a well-established pattern of fertility rituals associated with myths describing the actions of Baal, Anat, and other figures in the Ugaritic pantheon. A number of shorter texts show the important part played by the king in the rituals. In the Baal-Anat cycle there clearly occurs the myth of the killing of Baal by Mot, the subsequent mourning of the land and its vegetation, and the revivification of Baal accompanied by the rejoicing of nature. In his introduction to his valuable translation of the Ras Shamra poetic and prose texts, Professor C. H. Gordon claims, probably correctly, that the death and resurrection of Baal are not an annual event, but are connected with a seven year cycle of alternating drought and fertility. Be this as it may, there are many elements in the Baal-Anat cycle, such as Baal's conquest of the Sea by means of magical weapons, the slaying of the seven-headed dragon, the enthronement of Baal, and the building of a temple for him, which bear striking resemblance to features of the Babylonian Creation Epic, although the American commentators in general seem determined to concentrate on differences and to ignore resemblances. But in any case the texts give us, in one important centre of Canaanite culture in the middle of the second millennium B.C., a picture of an agricultural civilization with a priesthood, a sacrificial system whose terminology corresponds in many respects with the technical terms in the Old Testament, a pantheon containing most of the names familiar to us in the Old Testament, and a number of what may, I think, be rightly called ritual myths.

This, then, was the type of cult prevailing in Canaan when the Hebrews began to settle there. It is no longer possible to think of the Hebrews as bringing with them a purely nomadic type of religion and social organization. That element in the early stage of settlement represented by Abraham and his clan had, according to Hebrew tradition, lived for two or more generations, in Mesopotamian civilization, in an agricultural and urban milieu. The tradition preserved in Joshua

24.2 says, 'Your fathers dwelt of old time beyond the River, even Terah, the father of Abraham, and the father of Nahor, and they served other gods.' The early Aramaean strain, represented by the saga of Jacob, may well have borne a more nomadic character, as suggested by the Deuteronomic phrase 'a wandering (or nomadic) Aramaean was my father' (26.5), but the tradition preserved in Gen. 35.2-4 suggests that the Aramaean element brought ancestral gods into Canaan. From the mixture of these two stocks sprang the clans and tribes who formed the beginnings of Hebrew settlement in Canaan. From these a small part, according to Hebrew tradition 70 souls, settled in Egypt because of famine in Canaan, increased in number, and ultimately experienced the deliverance through Moses, and received from him the religion of Jahveh. The form of the Hebrew tradition makes it a possibility that some part of what was to be Israel entered Canaan from the south, while another part, perhaps the Ephraim tribes, entered from the east under the leadership of Joshua. The problem of how Jahvism became the religion of the whole of Israel has been ably dealt with by Professor Rowley in his Schweich Lectures, *From Joseph to Joshua*, and need not be discussed here. But what seems to emerge from Hebrew tradition is a picture of a far from homogeneous settlement, gradually adjusting itself to the agricultural civilization of its new home. The Deuteronomic editing of the book of Judges conceives of the religious conditions of that obscure period as a series of national apostasies from an original pure Jahvism, bringing in their wake chastisements, repentance, and deliverance. It is difficult to regard this as an historical account of what was taking place during this period. There was as yet no national consciousness, as the Song of Deborah shows. In his Schweich Lectures for 1925 the late Professor S. A. Cook showed that the new settlers took over the existing local shrines and utilized them for their own cult. The story of Micah is an instructive sample of what was probably taking place in many other parts of Canaan at this time. The seasons and operations of agriculture were inseparably bound up with religion, and we have seen in the Ras Shamra texts what the pattern of that religion was like. Hence it is difficult to avoid the conclusion that during this period of two or three centuries before the establishment of the monarchy and the growth of a national consciousness the Israelites were assimilating such elements of the existing ritual pattern as seemed necessary for the success of their agricultural operations. We know from Hosea that for Israel, at least for northern Israel, Jahveh was a Baal, and the whole polemic of the eighth century prophets against the state of the national religion of their time is the strongest evidence for the existence of many features of the Canaanite ritual pattern in the cult of Jahveh. Here I should like to say that I am fully persuaded that God chose Israel to be the vehicle of his revelation of himself, just as I believe with equal assurance that the Scriptures are the Word of God; but just as I do not believe that God has miraculously preserved the Scriptures from all human sources of error inseparable from his use of human instruments, so I do not believe that he similarly preserved Israel from all the chances of contamination from the cultic patterns of its environment. I think it is a kind of mistaken fundamentalism to deny or minimize the evidence of the existence in the early period of Hebrew religion of many elements derived from the contemporary Canaanite pattern. At the risk of being tedious I must recall the most important of these elements. First, there is the place and importance of the king in the cult. I am glad to learn that Professor A. R. Johnson has not abandoned the position laid down by him in his essay on the place of the king in the Jerusalem cult, published in the collection of essays entitled *The Labyrinth* in 1935. So far as I know no one has satisfactorily rebutted the detailed demonstration of the sacral and central character of the king in the Jerusalem cultus. While Mowinckel's arguments for the ritual character of a number of psalms as used in a New Year ceremony of the enthronement of Jahveh have been somewhat weakened of late, yet it still remains beyond dispute that many of the psalms were originally composed for liturgical use on such an occasion. I am not sure that Professor Snaith has satisfactorily proved that some of the enthronement psalms are not pre-exilic, but cannot embark on a discussion of this point here

Then there is the element of the ritual combat. No one has attempted to deny the existence of numerous passages in the poetic literature of the Old Testament which refer to Jahveh's conquest of a dragon, or of the Sea personified, often in language closely resembling that of the Ras Shamra texts. But these are all explained as literary survivals, and it is strenuously denied that there ever was at any time in the history of Israel as part of the New Year ceremonies, either in the spring or autumn, a ritual enactment of the slaying of the dragon. It is perfectly true, as Professor Frankfort and others have argued, that we have no account of, or reference to, any such rituals in the Old Testament, but that holds good for all the early cult activities of the early period of Hebrew religion. We do not know what the Hebrew immigrants did in the Canaanite temples which they took over, nor what elements of the local pattern they adopted to secure the success of their agricultural operations, with Jahveh taking the place of the local Baal and assuming his title. But if we admit that they did take over such elements, then it is reasonable to believe that they would have taken over those which were most essential. Of these the seasonal re-enactment of the triumph of the god over hostile powers was clearly one. An argument whose weight is not always recognized is the persistence of such elements as the ritual combat and the sacred marriage on into Jewish and Christian Apocalyptic. If these images of the divine action had never been anything but literary survivals, without living roots in the religious consciousness of the people, their persistence is hard to explain; but if they had once formed part of religious experience, as cultic acts are intended to do, then we can understand how, having passed through the transforming crucible of the prophetic experience of God in history, they survived, and still survive, as the most moving images of the divine triumph of redeeming love. What I have said about the ritual combat can be applied, *mutatis mutandis*, to that other central element in the pattern, the sacred marriage. But here the traces of the existence of such a feature in the ritual are, as I consider, undeniably present in the institution of sacred prostitution. Wherever it is found, it is always the concomitant of the sacred marriage as part of the seasonal ritual. The purpose of the sacred marriage is clear from all texts: it is intended to promote all the powers of fertility in man, and beast, and soil. Sacred prostitution is intended to extend and multiply the potency belonging to the sacred marriage. Its existence in Israel is amply attested in the Old Testament, and I need not spend time in proving it here. It is naturally repugnant to most people to entertain the suggestion that Jahveh could ever have been thought of as possessing a female consort like all the Baals of Canaan, and not a few scholars have rejected the idea that the Anat-Jahu of the Elephantine Papyri was regarded by the Jews of that settlement as Jahveh's consort. I am not afraid of the idea myself, and I think that Chapter 2 of Hosea points strongly in the direction of such a possibility. In their book *Culture and Conscience*, Professors Graham and May have suggested that the sign of Immanuel in Isa. 7, is connected with the ritual of the sacred marriage, but I am not inclined to accept the suggestion.

It is not necessary to pursue the subject further and to discuss all the elements of the pattern which have left traces of their existence in the early religion of Israel. But before bringing this paper to a close I should like to say something about certain respects in which my position with regard to the development of the religion of Israel has changed in recent years.

Twenty years or so ago, I was inclined to see in the eighth century prophets the true founders of the religion of Israel. I thought that Abraham was too misty a figure of saga to have any real significance for the history of Israel's religion, and that, while I accepted Moses as an historical figure, so much legendary material had accumulated round him, and so much of the legislation ascribed to him was clearly either of a later date, or dependent on an earlier common stock of Semitic law and custom, that I discounted his importance for the founding of the corporate religion of what was ultimately to be Israel. In this I now believe I was mistaken. In the first place, the more I admitted the existence of those elements in the early development of Israel's religion of which I have already spoken, the more it became necessary to account for the fact that Israel's history did not peter out like that of the other small nations around her, but became the vehicle of the unique revelation of God. The emergence of the eighth century prophets was a religious phenomenon which itself called for an explanation. So I came to see in the tradition of the double call and choice of Israel in Abraham and in Moses an authentic tradition of a profound religious experience. In Abraham God found a response of faith which made the patriarch the 'father of all them that believe', and won for him the title 'Abraham my friend'. In the flame of fire in the bush Moses encountered the same God who had called Abraham, and had an experience of God which fitted him to be the agent of the divine activity of redemption. Although it may be that the amazing experience recorded in Ex. 33 and 34 has been coloured by the later experience of a prophetic editor, yet the narrator was right in seeing that the God whom he knew was the same God who revealed all his goodness to Moses at that crisis in Israel's history. So it seemed to me that one had to acknowledge that at the beginning, in the experience of Abraham and Moses, a flame was kindled which was never to be extinguished. Even when Baalism seemed to be almost triumphant, and Elijah wailed 'I, I only am left', Jahveh could tell him, 'Yet have I left me seven thousand in Israel, all the knees which have not bowed unto Baal'. When the prophets of the eighth and succeeding centuries appeared on the scene, challenging the whole established order of the cult as unworthy of the God they had encountered, and transforming the elements of the ritual pattern, the ritual combat, the sacred marriage, and other familiar features of the cult into images of a divine reality, the triumph of Jahveh over the powers of evil, Jahveh's betrothal of Israel to himself, and the shining figure of the Messianic king, they rightly claimed to be, not innovators, but in the great tradition that went back to Moses and Abraham. I feel that I ought to apologize for being so personal, but what I have now said represents the 'reconsidered' element in my title.

CHAPTER THIRTEEN

A Century of Biblical Archaeology in Palestine[1]

IN 1838 an American teacher of Hebrew named Edward Robinson came to Palestine, Bible in hand, with the purpose of identifying the sites of places mentioned in the Bible. Together with his friend Eli Smith he was successful in identifying a large number of biblical sites for the first time. The result of his researches was published uncompleted in 1865, after his death in 1863. In the same year that saw the publication of Robinson's *Physical Geography of the Holy Land*, the Palestine Exploration Fund was founded under distinguished patronage. It is probably true to say that Robinson's pioneer work provided the initial stimulus for its founding, and for the somewhat ambitious programme which was the Fund's first venture in the field of scientific archaeology.

Those responsible for this initial enterprise had realized that surface exploration such as Robinson's, successful as it had proved, must be continued, but that excavation was necessary to confirm the identifications reached by the surface method. At this point the story of the scientific excavation of the Holy Land begins. As we are dealing only with excavation, we must pass over one important feature of the Fund's first programme, namely, the carrying out of a scientific survey of Palestine. The great undertaking was brilliantly executed by a series of Royal Engineer officers, among whom may be named Sir Charles Wilson, C. R. Conder, Lord Kitchener, and Sir Charles Warren. Valuable work in the survey of the Negeb was done by two young men whose names were destined to become famous in different ways, Sir Leonard Woolley and T. E. Lawrence. Nor should the name of Sir Charles Arden-Close be passed over in this connexion.

[1] Contributed to the *Catalogue* of the Exhibition of the Land of the Bible at the British Museum.

But the first object of the Fund's attack was naturally the Holy City itself. Here the difficulties were very great, but in spite of the superstition of the inhabitants and the hostility of the Turkish authorities Sir Charles Warren began the excavation of the Temple walls and other points in the city in 1867, and laid the foundation for all the subsequent labours of archaeologists who in the years to come sought to solve the many problems which Jerusalem presented, many of which still remain unsolved. It is perhaps not out of place here to mention that the inside cover of the Fund's journal, the *Quarterly Statement of the Palestine Exploration Fund,* still commemorates in a quaint illustration Warren's first exploratory tunnel and shaft driven down outside the wall of the Haram esh-Sherif. The most striking result of Warren's excavational activities in the Holy City was his discovery of the subterranean watercourse made by the ancient Jebusite inhabitants and used by Joab and his men to effect the capture of the city, as related in II Sam. 5.6-8.

It should be remarked that at this stage of British archaeological activities the significance of the artificial mounds called 'tells' had not yet been grasped, Semitic epigraphy was still in its infancy, and the vital importance of pottery as a criterion for dating was still unrealized, while scientific stratigraphy was wholly unknown.

In 1890 a genius appeared on the archaeological scene whose work was to revolutionize archaeological technique and lay the sure foundations of the brilliant achievements of the next fifty years. This was Sir Flinders Petrie. Before his first excavation in Palestine he had served his apprenticeship for ten years in Egypt, a field with which his name is principally connected and where his most important discoveries were made. Petrie's first Palestinian site was the mound of Tell el-Hesi, in S.W. Palestine, thought at first to be the site of biblical Lachish. Here he applied scientific stratigraphic methods, introduced the hitherto unemployed practice of recording the position of every potsherd in the particular stratum in which it was found, and thus established the principle that different excavational layers or strata were charac-

terized by different types of pottery. The result of Petrie's
methods, though doubted at first by his contemporaries, was
the laying of sound foundations for a scientific chronology of
the ancient Near East. The chronology of the early excavators
had been somewhat undependable, to say the least, and the
accurate delimitation of the various archaeological periods,
Neolithic, Early, Middle, and Late Bronze Ages was as yet
unaccomplished; but on the lines laid down by Petrie, together with the help provided by a comparison with the
results of Egyptian and Mesopotamian excavation, archaeologists began to reach some agreement on the dating of sites
and biblical events.

The years which intervened between Petrie's excavation
of Tell el-Hesi and the outbreak of the first World War were
rich in archaeological activity, and other countries entered
the field of Palestinian excavation with fertile results. As our
concern is with British archaeology we cannot do more than
mention the admirable work of the Dominican School at
Jerusalem, coupled with the names of Vincent and de Vaux;
the early work of Sellin at Megiddo, and later with Watzinger
at Jericho; the magnificent work of Clermont-Ganneau in the
pre-excavational period, and later the valuable exploration of
Palestinian caves by René Neuville. The Americans also were
early in the field, bringing their enthusiasm and ample pecu-
niary resources. In their roll of honour the names of Reisner,
Bliss, Fisher, and Albright, only to mention a few, claim our
attention.

But to return to the activities of British archaeologists;
while work was being continued in Jerusalem under Bliss and
Dickie, R. A. S. Macalister carried out the excavation of
Gezer from 1902-9. The publication of his results marked a
distinct stage in the development of archaeological technique,
and is still a valuable storehouse of material, but all his
datings have had to be revised in the light of fuller knowledge.
It may be remarked that his most spectacular discovery, a
tablet in early Hebrew script giving a list of farming operations for each month in the year, and generally known as the
Gezer Calendar, was dated four or five centuries later than

the date which archaeologists now assign to it, viz. about the time of David. This error was due to inaccurate pottery dating. The next site chosen by the Palestine Exploration Fund for excavation was Beth-Shemesh. Here the work was under the direction of Duncan Mackenzie, and yielded some valuable tomb-groups. Then came the first World War which brought all archaeological activity to a standstill.

With the end of the war came the end of Turkish domination in the Near East, and the beginning of the British mandate in Palestine. The next twenty years saw an unparalleled increase in archaeological activity everywhere, and not least in Palestine. The first result of the assumption of responsibility for Palestine was the establishment of a Department of Antiquities in 1920. Its duty was to supervise and record all excavational activities in Palestine, and during the twenty years of its existence its annual reports, drawn up by a series of expert directors, provided a most valuable record of all archaeological discoveries made in Palestine during the period of intense activity between the two wars. Professor John Garstang, a scholar and archaeologist of great experience, was the first director. He also became director of the new British School of Archaeology in Jerusalem, which was founded in the same year. In 1926 pressure of work made it necessary to separate the two organizations and appoint a separate director for each. Under the joint auspices of the Palestine Exploration Fund and the School, Professor Garstang excavated the site of the ancient Philistine city of Askelon, but owing to lack of funds and other causes the excavation was not carried deep enough to throw that new light on Philistine civilization which had been hoped for.

During this fruitful period a new field of discovery was opened up. Hitherto nothing was known about the prehistoric period in Palestine. In 1925 F. Turville-Petre excavated two caves in northern Galilee and found the first remains of pre-historic man in Palestine. The work was continued by Miss Dorothy Garrod from 1928 to 1934 and resulted in the discovery of a number of complete skeletons of fossil men, and the establishment of a new pre-historic culture, named the Natufian.

In Jerusalem, between 1923 and 1928, Macalister, Garrow Duncan, and J. W. Crowfoot carried out a succession of important excavations on the Ophel hill, the site of 'the City of David'. Mr Crowfoot has given a detailed account of the results of the work done at Ophel in the July-October issue of the *Quarterly Statement of the Palestine Exploration Fund* for 1945. In 1929 Professor Garstang took up the work at Jericho which the Germans had begun, and in a series of campaigns established the chronology of the successive cities which had occupied the mound of Jericho. His most spectacular result, which attracted much public attention and created a lively controversy among archaeologists, was his dating of the fall of Jericho under Joshua's assault to about 1400 B.C., a date which placed the entry of the Hebrews into Canaan about two hundred years earlier than the commonly accepted date under Merneptah. Excavation showed that sections of the city wall had been violently disturbed, as if by an earthquake, and this was connected by many scholars with the biblical account of the collapse of the walls of Jericho at the blast of the Hebrew trumpets. In 1952 Dr Kathleen M. Kenyon resumed the excavation of Jericho at the point where Garstang had left it in 1936, and has already produced results which may make a revision of earlier findings necessary.

Here, too, should be mentioned the British share in the American enterprise of the excavation of the biblical site of Beth-shan. It was begun in 1921 under the directorship of Dr Fisher, and continued until 1931 under the successive direction of Mr Alan Rowe and Mr G. M. Fitzgerald. It has been described as a model excavation, and its results were magnificently published. Few Palestinian sites have yielded more valuable material.

About the same time as the end of the excavation of Beth-shan, Mr J. W. Crowfoot took up the excavation of Samaria where Reisner had left it. He established the chronology of Samaria on a sound basis and corrected many of the earlier findings, notably those relating to the round towers which had been dated five centuries too early. More inscribed ostraca were found in addition to the seventy which Reisner had discovered, and special interest was aroused by the discovery of a remarkable collection of ivory carvings which could be dated with certainty to the period of the Omri dynasty, and illustrate the reference to 'beds of ivory' in Amos 6.4.

In 1932 the excavation of Tell ed-Duweir was begun, financed by the Burrows-Wellcome Museum and Sir Charles Marston. It was under the leadership of the late Mr J. M. Starkey, a brilliant field archaeologist who was murdered by Arab bandits in 1938. Early results made it probable, and later discoveries made it certain, that this and not Tell el-Hesi was the true site of biblical Lachish. The most sensational discovery, if not the most important from the archaeological point of view, was the finding in the guard-room of the city-gate of a number of inscribed potsherds, now known as the Lachish Ostraca. These proved to be letters which passed between the military governor of Lachish and the commandant of a neighbouring military post. Their contents showed them to be concerned with events and persons belonging to the last period of the Hebrew monarchy, during the invasion of Judah by Nebuchadrezzar. The excavation of Lachish was broken off by the second World War, and now its continuation lies in the hands of the new state of Israel, which has already begun archaeological activities with great zest and skill. The results have been published by Mr Starkey's colleagues, Miss Tufnell and Mr Lankester Harding, in three magnificent volumes which form a fitting memorial of his achievements. The important inscriptional material from Lachish has been ably dealt with by Dr David Diringer.

We have already spoken of the preliminary survey of the Negeb by Woolley and Lawrence in 1913; this little-known region in the south of Judah was again explored from 1933-8 by H. Dunscome Colt and Colin Baly. The towns of Sbeita, Khalasah, and Auja el-Hafir were subjected to a careful archaeological examination, and the most important result was the discovery at the last-named place of a quantity of Greek and Arabic papyri of the sixth and seventh centuries A.D.

This brief survey may be closed by a mention of the valuable work done by Mr Lankester Harding, Mr Starkey's colleague at Lachish, and now the Director of Antiquities in the Hashemite Kingdom of Jordan. As a result of the sensational discovery of what are now generally known as The Dead Sea Scrolls, the attention of archaeologists was directed to the numerous caves in the neighbourhood of the Dead Sea. Together with Father De Vaux, Mr Lankester Harding has explored and excavated a large number of caves and sites in that region, with striking results. Perhaps the most sensational has been the discovery of a letter which appears to be an autograph letter of the famous leader of the last Jewish revolt against Rome, usually known as Bar-Cochba. A more important result of these explorations has been to reveal the existence in these remote and desolate regions of various communities of Jewish sects in the first century B.C., and the first two centuries A.D. The contents of their scrolls, now being made available to students, have already thrown much new light on that obscure period of Jewish history.

CHAPTER FOURTEEN

What has Christianity Inherited from Judaism?[1]

WHEN Paul said to the Galatian Church, 'But the Jerusalem above is free, which is our mother', he was stating a fact of history and of spiritual experience. In the deepest sense Christianity sprang from the womb of Judaism, and the birth was accompanied by birth-pangs whose effects might well be symbolized by the rending of the veil of the Jewish Temple. Francis Thompson has written:

> Till Time, the hidden root of Change, updries,
> Are Birth and Death inseparable on earth;
> For they are twain yet one, and Death is Birth.

When Judaism blindly rejected its one hope and slew its Messiah, from that death a new thing came to birth, in Paul's phrase 'a new creation'. But, underneath all the wonder of the new creation lay the inescapable fact of a relationship that could not be denied or ignored. The relationship carried with it an inheritance, and it is the purpose of this paper to consider some aspects of this inheritance.

In the first days of the new movement it was hardly conscious of its own newness. All its original members were Jews, and the majority of them Galilean Jews. To their fellow-countrymen they appeared an heretical Jewish sect. In his address before Felix, Paul said: 'But I admit this to you, that according to the Way, which they call a party, so worship I my fathers' God, believing in all which is written in the Law and the Prophets, having a hope towards God, which they also accept themselves, that there is to be a resurrection both of just and unjust' (Acts 24.14-15, Lake and Cadbury's tr.).

[1] Paper read to The Modern Churchmen's Union, 1950. First published in *The Modern Churchman*.

We cannot be certain that Paul's exact words on this occasion have been preserved, but the speech which the author of Acts has put into his mouth is at least good evidence for the way in which the adherents of the new movement saw themselves reflected in the minds of their compatriots. They worshipped the same God, they accepted the authority of the same Scriptures, they were regular in attendance at the Temple, observed the ancestral feasts and fasts, and were sustained by the same hope of a resurrection and the establishment of the Kingdom of God on earth. Hence when the admission of the Gentiles into the new community, and the irresistible logic of the new life whose newness they were slow in realizing, brought about unforeseen changes in the pattern of their beliefs and practices, it was inevitable that much of the Jewish heritage should remain and become an integral part of the life of the Christian Church. How much of this heritage is essential to the very existence of Christianity, not to be discarded without fatal loss, and how much must be regarded as a *damnosa hereditas*, is the question which this paper attempts to discuss.

But there is a preliminary point of considerable importance and considerable difficulty which must first be examined. It is the question of what and how much the early Church received directly from Jesus. There is an influential movement of theological thought, very vigorous on the Continent, and not unrepresented in this country, which wholly rejects the life, personality, and teaching of the earthly Christ as in any way relevant to Catholic Christianity. This is partly, as Professor Donald Baillie has pointed out,[2] the result of a healthy swing of the pendulum away from what might almost be called the cult of the historical Jesus, and partly the result of an undue emphasis on the somewhat uncertain findings of modern 'form-criticism'. But there are signs that this movement has spent itself, and a renewed and welcome insistence is to be found in several recent books that it is vital for Christianity to hold fast to the fact that there is an essential nexus between the life of the risen and glorified Lord and the

[2] *God was in Christ* (Faber, 1948), pp. 34 f.

earthly life of Jesus of Nazareth, the life in which the Incarnate Word took flesh.

Hence we must not allow ourselves to be debarred from enquiring how far the teaching and experience of Jesus served as a vehicle for the transmission of essential elements in the Jewish heritage. In admitting the possibility of such transmission, however, perhaps two reservations should be made. First, the transmission may not always have been intentional: that is to say, Jesus may not have intended that some of his sayings or replies to questions were to have permanent and universal binding validity, even though the Church subsequently attached such validity to them. This reservation also includes the factor of his human limitations in knowledge; so that while he may have seemed to accept the Davidic authorship of the Psalms, or the Mosaic authorship of the Pentateuch, and the early Church may have claimed his authority for such ascription of authorship, such transmission of Jewish tradition need not carry binding authority for us to-day. The second reservation is that much of what was thus transmitted was also transformed. We have to do, not with such a process of transmission as we find in rabbinical discussion and interpretation of the *Torah*, where authority mainly rests on tradition, but with the transmission of elements in Jesus' Jewish heritage which had been transformed by passing through his experience. One of the most important aspects of the Jewish heritage was its wealth of images, or symbols— water, blood, fire, wine, sonship, kingship, and so forth. In the mind of Jesus, saturated with the images of the Old Testament, and in his living experience, all this underwent a vital transformation and was thus transmitted to the early Church. It may be relevant to quote here a passage from Dr Farrer's recent book, *A Rebirth of Images*: 'If it is unreasonable to deny that the primary rebirth of images took place in the thought and action of Christ, it is equally unreasonable to suppose that it was so simply accomplished in him once and for all, as to require nothing but tranquil appropriation on the part of his disciples. The decisive act of transformation had taken place in him, but the whole furniture of images had

N

to be touched and leavened by it, all had to be reborn with Christ.' And again: 'Since, then, we must regard the Christian revolution as essentially a transformation of images, it is not reasonable to leave Christ himself out of the transforming work.' (*Op. cit.*, p. 15.)

This is undoubtedly the most important aspect of the direct transmission of the vital and enduring elements of the Hebrew-Jewish heritage to the Christian Church. But before we begin to discuss in greater detail some of the most important elements which the Church owes to its Hebrew-Jewish heritage, it may be helpful to take a brief survey of the general background and development of this heritage.

It may, very roughly, be considered as falling into three stages. First, it seems fairly certain that, whatever degree of importance may be attached to the early tradition of the Mosaic covenant at Sinai between Jahveh and Israel, during the period of settlement in Canaan and the early monarchy the religion of Israel was in the main assimilated to the general type of agricultural religion which held sway in Canaan, Syria, and Mesopotamia. The broad type of the ritual pattern which characterized this stage of Hebrew religion has been described in the volume entitled *Myth and Ritual*, and need not be repeated here. It had its priesthood, its sacrificial rituals, its cultic prophets, its great seasonal festivals, its sacral kingship, and all the elements which were considered necessary for the continued well-being of the community. It created a wealth of images which passed into the permanent heritage of Hebrew religion.

Secondly, about the middle of the eighth century B.C., there arose a class of persons for whom no parallel can be found in the religious development of any other people. They claimed to have had a direct experience of God, unmediated by the ritual forms of their time. On the strength of this experience they presented to Israel a new conception of God, a personal God, with a moral character, whose power and authority were not limited by local boundaries, and whose purposes gave a meaning to history. The effect of their activities during a period of about three hundred years was the complete transformation and spiritualization of the main elements of the ancient ritual pattern. The priesthood and the sacrificial system remained and continued to function until the destruction of Jerusalem brought them to an end, but the whole idea of the relation between God and man which they expressed had been transformed, together with all the images associated with them. The Epistle to the Hebrews, of which more will be said later, is a witness to the profound influence which this part of the Jewish heritage exercised upon the early Church.

Thirdly, when the prophetic movement appeared to have spent itself and a state of things was reached which is expressed in a late post-exilic psalm, 'We see not our signs: there is no more any prophet: neither is there any among us that knoweth how long' (Ps. 74.9), another class of persons arose to whom the name of traditionalists might be given. By their labours the literature and traditions of Israel were collected and given an authoritative form. They set the laws of Israel in an historical framework designed to show that God had revealed himself to and through Israel, and that the whole of human history from the Creation down to their own time showed the unfolding of a divine purpose whose climax had not yet been reached but which was nevertheless certain. As the hope of a political revival grew faint they turned with increasing devotion to that possession which no turns of political fortune could take from them, the Torah, eternal as God himself. To them is due the conception of the authority of the written word, replacing the authority of the prophetic oracle, 'thus saith the Lord'. From this was born the vast system of Jewish hermeneutics, of which, though it was still in its infancy, Jesus was forced to say, 'Ye make the word of God of none effect through your tradition' (Matt. 15.6).

During the development of this third stage of the religion of Israel, and particularly during the last two centuries B.C. and the first century A.D., two tendencies appeared which call for note in connexion with our enquiry. The first was the growth of a new attitude toward the destiny of Israel and the hope of the Kingdom of God which found expression in a new form of literature, generally known as Apocalyptic, of which the Book of Daniel is the principal representative in the Old Testament. While the apocalyptic writers developed the prophetic interpretation of history as the sphere of divine activity, they may be said to have traditionalized it by forcing history into a deterministic scheme of periods, fixed beforehand by God, and revealed in visions to the seer whose personality is veiled behind a pseudonym. One very important aspect of Apocalyptic, and one which specially concerns us here, is the concentration of all the accumulated wealth of Hebrew and Jewish symbolism into its picture of God's final activity bringing in the consummation of history.

Side by side with this development a parallel tendency appeared, due no doubt to Greek influence, and specially associated with the name of Philo of Alexandria. In his work the difficulties which the traditional view of the Scriptures literally interpreted was already causing, were met by an extreme development of the allegorical method of interpretation. The Rabbis were familiar with the method and often used it, but Philo transformed the whole of Hebrew history in its minutest details into an intricate and subtle system of symbols, representing the interplay of spiritual powers, good and evil, shaping the course of human destiny. The influence of his thought on early Christian theology, especially on the school of Alexandria, was very great.

We have, then, derived from these three stages of development, the following main elements of the Hebrew-Jewish heritage whose influence, direct or indirect, upon the origin and development of Christianity must be considered:

(i) Certain fundamental apprehensions and intuitions which underlie the ritual activities carried out by the community or by sacral persons on behalf of the community. In these are expressed by means of images various ways of apprehending the relation between man and that to which he gives the name of God, a name which, at this stage, is simply a convenient term covering all kinds of manifestations of life and power which man seeks to control, appease, or enter into some kind of satisfactory relation with. The difficulty with which some of these ritual practices were eradicated or transformed, in spite of the long-continued prophetic protest, might well be taken as an indication that they represented some profound if unconscious and mistakenly expressed sense of man's place in the Universe. It is noteworthy that in the only great New Testament apocalyptic book, all the vital images characteristic of this stage of religious development—creation, kingship, the sacrificial victim, the dragon-combat—the sacred marriage—appear transformed, glorious, and eternal.[3]

(ii) The most important and creative element in our Hebrew-Jewish heritage takes its rise in the period of the prophetic protest, that is, from the middle of the eighth century to the end of the sixth century B.C. The existence of the prophet as a cultural phenomenon, and the psychological characteristics of ecstatic prophecy, are far older than the beginnings of Hebrew history, but with the prophets of Israel something new appeared, something which had power to transform the images of which we have spoken above, and to purge a religion, which was in their time largely an agricultural fertility cult, of most of its grosser features. This new thing was a conception of a holy and righteous God, full of mercy and long-suffering, a forgiving God, the Father of his people, unchangeable in faithfulness. This conception of God passed directly from Judaism into Christianity, in the first place through the experience of Jesus, and secondly through the faith and experience of the early Christian community. Inseparable from this was the conviction that the whole of human history was under the control of God, that nothing happened by chance, and that every event was part of a divine purpose whose consummation was both certain and near at hand. This view of the meaning of history also passed over from Judaism into Christianity, determining the nature of early Christian eschatology, of which more will be said later. A third important contribution from this stage was the appearance in the early Church of the prophetic gift upon

[3] Cf. Ch. IX in this volume, pp. 142 ff.

whose value for the life of the Christian community Paul laid so much stress.

(iii) The third stage of the development of the religion of Israel made its own characteristic contribution to the new movement. When Paul asked, 'Of what use is it, then, to be a Jew?' he answered his own question by saying, 'chiefly because the Jews had the words of God entrusted to them'.[4] The work of the post-exilic scholars had made the Jews the people of a book. In addition to giving Hebrew tradition its final and authoritative form, the scholars of the third century B.C. had made the book available to Hellenistic Jews in the form of the Greek version of the Old Testament known as the Septuagint, a gift which they afterwards bitterly regretted. This Greek version, which contained a number of books which Palestinian rabbinical schools had never admitted into the category of books which 'defiled the hands', became at once the sacred book of the new community. Indeed, some of the early apologists, e.g. Barnabas, denied to the Jews any right to their own book. The collections of proof-texts, known as Testimonia, of which the best-known is Cyprian's Testimonia, show us how the early Church used the book. In the first place the Old Testament was ransacked for texts which might prove that anything relating to Jesus was already foretold in it; in the second place texts were similarly selected, by no means a difficult task, to prove that the Jews had always been rebels and apostates, by the showing of their own prophets, and had forfeited all right to the covenant and the promises of God. In direct connexion with this inheritance of the sacred book must be mentioned the modes of its interpretation. Three aspects of this element of the Jewish heritage call for special note. First there is the way in which Jesus used the Old Testament. In the main this is wholly his own. Very rarely he employs the rabbinical method, as an example of which, perhaps, may be adduced his use of Ps. 110 in dealing with the Pharisees' belief that the Messiah must be the Son of David. But in general his interpretation of the Old Testament, and his application of it to his own problems, is new, pro-

---

[4] Rom. 3.1 (R. Knox's tr.).

foundly spiritual, and free from insistence on the authority of the letter of scripture. Second, in the case of Paul, while, as we might expect from his rabbinical training, he often makes use of rabbinical methods of exegesis, yet much more often it is the mind of Jesus which we can discern in his use of the Old Testament. Third, the allegorical method, inherited mainly from Philo, and occasionally used by Paul, was widely used by the early Fathers and became an accepted method of interpretation. Origen, in his well-known classification of Christians into somatic, psychic, and pneumatic types, regards the psychic type who resort to the allegorical meaning of scripture, as being on a higher plane than the somatic who rely only on the literal and historical meaning of scripture, but below the pneumatic whose interpretation is entirely spiritual. In addition to the sacred book and the methods of its exegesis, the Church received from its Jewish heritage one element of very doubtful value, namely, the doctrine of verbal inspiration of the scriptures. It was largely due to the influence of the famous Rabbi Akiba in the beginning of the second century A.D. that this belief came to dominate the rabbinical interpretation of the Torah. Akiba held that 'in a book of divine revelation no smallest peculiarity of expression or even of spelling is accidental or devoid of significance, and evolved certain new hermeneutic rules for the discovery of the meaning thus suggested by the letter' (G. F. Moore, *Judaism*, i, 88). In spite of Paul's warning, 'the letter killeth', this disastrous element of the Jewish inheritance entered early into the Church's interpretation of scripture, and has never wholly disappeared.

The last inheritance from this third stage of development of Israel's religion to be dealt with here is the most controversial and in some respects the most important. It is the eschatological, and in the narrower sense, the apocalyptic, view of human destiny. Concerning the derivation of the early Church's eschatology there can be no question. It is one of the most characteristic features of the Jewish legacy. With regard to its importance, a quotation from Professor Butterfield's recent book, *Christianity and History*, is relevant: 'So

far as I can see, the apocalyptic thought that emerged before
the opening of the Christian era, and the turn to the kind of
speculation which we call eschatological, are in a certain sense
a continuation of the same story—a further phase of the search
for an interpretation of history which would embrace catastrophe itself and transcend the immediate spectacle of tragedy.
Altogether we have here the greatest and most deliberate
attempts ever made to wrestle with destiny and interpret
history and discover meaning in the human drama; above all,
to grapple with the moral difficulties that history presents to
the religious mind. The revelation appears not always to have
been granted to the ancient Hebrews until there had been a
great struggle to achieve the truth.' (*Op. cit.*, p. 2.)

The subject is much too large to be dealt with adequately
within the limits of a short paper, and only a few of the main
issues involved can be touched on here. The first question,
concerning which there is a considerable difference of opinion
still even among ourselves, is, what was the nature of Jesus'
eschatology? The school of thought represented by that well-
known book, *The Lord of Thought*, has still many adherents. I
think it is not unfair to say that in the main it rejects practically
all the apocalyptic sayings of Jesus as unauthentic, representing rather the mind of the early Church than the mind of Jesus.
As against this may be cited the judicious words of the late
Canon Streeter: after admitting that the Gospel evidence
shows that a tendency was at work at a very early date in the
Church to emphasize and even create sayings of our Lord of
the catastrophic apocalyptic type, he goes on to say: 'The
argument, however, must not be pushed to the length of
entirely eliminating the Apocalyptic element from the authentic teaching of our Lord. The beliefs of the early Church may
have modified and did modify the records of His utterances,
but it is too great a paradox to maintain that what was so
central in the belief of the primitive Church was not present,
at least in germ, in what the Master taught.' (*Studies in the
Synoptic Problem*, p. 433.)

Hence, without embarking on a discussion of how much of
the apocalyptic material in the Synoptic Gospels may be ac-

cepted as the authentic teaching of Jesus, a general acceptance of the following points may perhaps be assumed:

(a) While accepting the Kingdom of God as a present and eternal reality, Jesus also envisaged it as a decisive event in the immediate future to be brought about by the act of God.

(b) Jesus attached apocalyptic significance to the title Son of Man, carrying Messianic implications.[5] He regarded the 'coming of the Son of Man' as inseparably connected with the coming of the Kingdom. It is impossible to reject the authenticity of the final declaration before the High Priest (Mark 15.62).

(c) Jesus was brought by his experience to accept and declare a wholly new and revolutionary element in Jewish Apocalyptic—the will of God that the Messiah should die and rise again.

These fundamental elements in an eschatology which was wholly Jewish in character, together with the central fact that Messiah had actually died and risen again, passed into the heritage of the early Church, there to acquire changing forms and shifting emphasis with the lapse of time, and it is not the task of this paper to follow these changes. But it may at least be said that from Jewish eschatology, transformed in the mind and by the experience of Jesus, Christianity has inherited a moral interpretation of history and of human destiny, a sense of the profound moral crisis arising from the antinomy between the 'present age' and the 'age to come', and a conviction that God will not rest until the antinomy has been resolved and creation has been redeemed.

The form in which the Church received and has continued to hold the belief in resurrection was, and has remained, Jewish. The late Professor H. Wheeler Robinson has well remarked, in this connexion: 'It is a life on earth, however new its conditions, and it is a resurrection-life, involving the

---

[5] This must not be taken as excluding other implications of the title: cf. S. H. Hooke, *The Kingdom of God in the Experience of Jesus* (Duckworth, 1949), pp. 59-63.

restoration of the dead body. This form of belief is seen to
have been inevitable, once we have grasped the Hebrew idea
of personality; a resurrection of the body was the only form
of triumph over death which Hebrew psychology could con-
ceive for those actually dead. Even St. Paul shrinks from the
thought of bodiless existence.' (*Inspiration and Revelation in
the Old Testament*, p. 101-2.)

The Greek doctrine of immortality, which finds its first
Jewish expression in the Wisdom of Solomon, and which conceives of an immortality of the soul apart from the body, does
not occur in the New Testament, nor in the Creeds. Even the
Alexandrian Fathers appear to assume the identity of the
'spiritual body' spoken of by St Paul with the earthly body,
without, however, explaining the nature of the identity. The
permanent value of this element of the Jewish heritage is, to
say the least, open to question, and the Fourth Gospel seems
to represent an attempt to reinterpret early Christian eschatology, and especially the Parousia expectation, in such a way
as to remove some of its less desirable aspects.

Before bringing this very inadequate paper to a close,
something must be said about the bearing of the Epistle to
the Hebrews on our subject. We have already referred to the
great transformation of images which took place through the
experience and action of Jesus and was inherited by the early
Church. The Epistle to the Hebrews is a notable example of
this process at work. Under the Jewish economy, while the
prophet represented the possibility of an immediate relation
with God, based on personal experience and unmediated by
ritual, the institution of the priesthood and the existence of
an elaborate system of sacrificial ritual represented another
conception of the way in which the relations between the
community and God must be maintained. The author of the
great treatise to which we have referred undertook to present
a majestic argument in which was set forth the completeness
with which the transformation of images had been accomplished in Christ. He was the one true priest whose inter-
cessory and sacrificial work was eternally valid; he was the
one true victim whose offering could never be repeated, and

by whom the work of redemption and atonement had been accomplished once and for all. All the details of the tabernacle, the priesthood, and the sacrifices, were shown to have been the shadows of the perfect heavenly order which had been established in and by Christ. But, largely no doubt through the influence of this treatise, the conception of the Christian ministry and of the sacraments of the Church came to be dominated by this element of the Jewish heritage. Paul's charismatic ministry was replaced by a sacrificing priesthood, and the primitive eucharist became a sacrificial ritual, a dramatic re-enactment of the one Sacrifice, once offered; even the garments of the officiating priests were no doubt intended to represent the garments of the Jewish High Priest, although their form in later times came to be derived from other and non-Jewish sources.

This element of the Jewish heritage, deeply embedded as it is in Christian tradition, is nevertheless one concerning whose value widely differing opinions have been and still are held among Christians, perpetuating the age-long controversy between priest and prophet, a controversy which might be regarded as yet another element of the Hebrew-Jewish heritage. Time will not allow of further discussion of many other points arising from this fertile subject, but it may not be unprofitable to conclude with St Paul's words of warning to us Gentiles: 'Remember, in thy mood of boastfulness, that thou owest life to the root, not the root to thee. Branches were cut away, thou wilt tell me, so that I might be grafted in. True enough, but it was for want of faith that they were cut away, and it is only faith that keeps thee where thou art; thou hast no reason for pride, rather for fear; God was unforgiving with the branches that were native to the tree, what if he should find occasion to be unforgiving with thee too?' (Rom. 11.18-21, R. Knox's tr.)

CHAPTER FIFTEEN

The Theory and Practice of Substitution[1]

THE reason for the choice of this particular element of
ancient religious practice for discussion is that it pro-
vides an instructive example of that process of transformation of images which is such a striking characteristic of the development of Hebrew religion. We can trace the
ritual of substitution from its roots in the great complex of
Babylonian and Assyrian religion, through its early Hebrew
forms, up to the profound spiritual conceptions which underlie
the prophetic picture of the Suffering Servant. Nor is such an
enquiry a mere matter of antiquarian interest. In his book
Revelation and the Modern World, Father Lionel Thornton
has said, 'Since every image has its place in the revelation,
nothing is left behind in the passage of thought' (p. 257), and
again, 'Accordingly, whereas scriptural images are employed
selectively both by the inspired authors and by their successors in traditional exegesis, in accordance with the
pressure of circumstances, yet in the passage of thought
nothing in the form of revelation becomes permanently
irrelevant.'

When we come to examine the early forms of this ritual
and its relation to the larger complex of which it is a part, we
recognize that certain fundamental apprehensions and intuitions underlie the ritual activities carried out by the community or by representative persons on behalf of the community. In these are expressed by means of images various
ways of apprehending the relation between man and that to
which he gives the name of God, a name which, at this stage,
is simply a convenient term covering all kinds of manifestations of life and power which man seeks to control, appease,
or with which he desires to enter into some kind of satisfactory relation. The difficulty with which some of these ritual

[1] Presidential Address to the Society for Old Testament Studies,
1951. First published in *Vetus Testamentum*.

practices were eradicated or transformed, in spite of the long-continued prophetic protest, might well be taken as an indication that they represented some profound if unconscious and mistakenly expressed sense of man's place in the Universe. The late Principal Wheeler Robinson has said, 'When we wish to evaluate some ancient conception we do well to consider what those who held it were seeking to express, besides the degree of accuracy to which their explanation of it could attain.' (*Inspiration and Revelation in the Old Testament*, p. 191.)

It is noteworthy that in the one great New Testament Apocalyptic book all the vital images characteristic of this stage of religious development—creation, kingship, the sacrificial victim, the dragon-combat, the sacred marriage—appear transformed, glorious and eternal.

Underlying the various forms which the practice of substitution assumes in early Semitic religion is the principle of exchange, and this again rests upon certain characteristic Semitic forms of thought. First, there is the belief in the psychical nature of inanimate objects, a conception which is expressed by H. Frankfort[2] in the suggestion that in this early stage of thought there exists an 'I and Thou' relation between man and the material objects of his environment; or in Wheeler Robinson's words, 'the material objects of Nature were conceived as having a psychical life of their own, making them capable on occasion of more special manifestations of life' (*op. cit.*, pp. 12f). Second, there is the assumption that the part may stand for the whole, a conception which plays a large part in exorcism rituals, or in their reverse in the various practices of witchcraft. Third, there is the idea of representation or equivalence, that is to say, the idea that an image of clay, wood or other material may represent or take the place of a person in certain situations; the same conception includes the use of animals in substitution rituals. Last, there is the very important conception of corporate personality which plays a large part in some of the later developments of the theory and practice of substitution.

[2] H. Frankfort, *The Intellectual Adventure of Ancient Man*, p. 6.

We shall turn now to examine the situations which, in early Semitic religion, seemed to demand some form of substitution; then the forms which the substitute might assume; and third, the consequences of the ritual, that which it sought to effect.

The most spectacular form of substitution, of which we know a good deal from the state correspondence of the Assyrian kings, is the *šar-puḫi*, the substitute-king. With regard to this form of substitution Frankfort, in his book *Kingship and the Gods* (p. 262), has said, 'When the threat of danger assumed unusual proportions, a substitute was installed in the hope that the royal person might be saved'. The kind of threat depicted in the above-mentioned correspondence is usually when the omens are interpreted by the priests as unfavourable to the king; one of the most threatening situations was caused by an eclipse, though certain conjunctions of the heavenly bodies might also portend danger to the person of the king. The form of ritual practised in such a situation was the selection by the priests of a substitute-king who might be a noble or a commoner. This person was invested with the royal insignia and authority, and was required to fulfil all the religious duties of the king, exposing himself to the supernatural dangers which threatened the king at this critical time. The substitute exercised his functions for a period of a hundred days, during which time the king and the royal princes, who were also involved in the danger, were confined to the palace. The texts show that the priests expected that during this period the substitute would die. The usual form *ula ana šimte lillik* or *ittalak*, has been interpreted to mean that the substitute would be ritually killed, either during or at the end of the prescribed period, but Labat, in a recent article in *Revue d'Assyrialogie*,[3] has shown conclusively that in Akkadian the formula has always the meaning 'to die a natural death'. Hence, while the priests expected and probably hoped that the substitute would 'meet his destiny', i.e., die a natural death, yet it was possible that he might fulfil his term safely, and, having served his purpose as a potential lightning-

[3] *Revue d'Assyriologie*, vol. XL, nos. 3-4, pp. 131 f.

conductor, might return to private life, in which case his subsequent death would have no apotropaic value.

In addition to the method above described of meeting the threatened danger, the texts show that a substitute might be provided without, or in addition to, the selection of a regular *šar puḫi*. In the much-discussed letter of Mar-Ishtar (ABL 437), the passage occurs: 'Damqi and the lady of the palace have duly died as substitutes of the king (*dinani ša šarri*) and as a ransom (*pidišunu*) for Šamaš-šum-mukin.' The situation revealed by the letter seems to be that at a dangerous period of an eclipse the son of the governor of Akkad died unexpectedly. The astrologers seized upon the occurrence as a fulfilment of the death presaged by the eclipse, and assured the king that Damqi had 'met his destiny' as a substitute and ransom for the king and his eldest son. The funeral rites which the letter goes on to describe are of a royal character. The use of the word *pidu* in this connexion is of special interest in view of the Hebrew use of *padah* and its derivatives. Here we may illustrate our theme by a couple of illustrations from modern primitive ritual:

'During the purification ceremonies . . . the young king was present as a prince. One of his younger brothers was deceived by the chiefs into believing that he was the chosen king. Clad in royal robes, he was placed on the throne, where the death of the preceding king was formally announced to him. The real king and the chiefs handed over gifts and gave assurances of their respect. This boy-king was always chosen and killed during the ceremonies in order that death might be deceived and the real king secured from any evil that might attach itself to him during the rites or that might not be completely removed by the purification.' I. Torstam, *The King of Ganda: Studies in the Institutions of Sacral Kingship in Africa*, pp. 74 f.

'When I was head of a subdivision on the Upper Volta, I went on a tour in the first months of my stay, and landed unexpectedly in a distant village, little visited. The Chief gave me a good reception. I came back there two years later, at the end of my tour, and had a still better reception. The Chief, however, did not seem to be the same man. I had before me an old man, whereas it was a young man who had received me the first time, and I recognized him, standing behind the old man. I asked the two of them why the chieftainship of the village had passed from the one to the other without my being told of it. The old man said to me: "He whom you see behind me was in front of me", and he explained, "It is I who am the Chief to-day as the other time, and in front of this man, as behind him. But two years ago we did not know you, and he showed himself in my place." The author goes on to explain the existence of *straw*-chiefs, as they are called, whose function is to protect the person of the real chief from any affront or injury to his dignity.' R. Delavignette, *Freedom and Authority in French West Africa*, p. 71.

But the substitution-ritual was not confined to royal persons. In the everyday life of the Assyrian or Babylonian any form of sickness was regarded as due to supernatural causes, to the hostility of the underworld powers, and especially to the activities of evil spirits and ghosts. In the valuable collection of exorcism-texts contained in Ebeling's *Tod und Leben* we find numerous examples of the way in which the ritual of substitution might be used to deliver a sufferer from ills caused by the attacks of evil spirits or ghosts. The term *puḫi amēli*, substitute for a man, occurs frequently. The substitute might take various forms. In a number of texts it is the clay image of the patient for whom the ritual is performed, or even an image of the ghost (*ṣalam eṭimmi*) which is troubling the patient; in other cases the substitute is an animal, generally a kid or a lamb; the hair and nails of the patient may be used as his substitute, and there are examples of the use of inanimate objects, such as a staff or a small tree. The general character of such rituals may best be seen by an example. Here is a translation of KAR 245 as given in Ebeling, *Tod und Leben*:

As a substitute for the man (*puḫi amēli*) for Ereškigal
at sunset should the sick man an unmated kid
in the bed with him place.
Before nightfall, while it is still light, you should rise,

bow yourself . . . the sick man should take the kid to his bosom.

Into the house, where there is enmity, you should enter, the sick man and the kid

you should throw down on the earth, the throat of the sick man

you should strike with a dagger of Tamarisk-wood,

the throat of the kid you should cut with a copper dagger.

The insides of the dead kid you should wash with water and rub with oil,

with incense you should fill its inwards, clothe it,

put shoes on it, paint its eyes with kohl,

pour good oil on its head, the head-band from the head

of the sick man you should remove, and bind it on the head of the kid.

You should treat it as a dead person and mourn for it. The sick man should get up

and go out through the door. The *mašmašu* should the incantation 'When the stroke of the god has struck',

repeat three times; the sick man should remove his . . . and give it to the *mašmašu*,

then the *mašmašu* should raise the cry for the sick man, 'He has gone to his fate',

he should say, he should make the lament,

three times you should make the funeral offering to Ereškigal . . . place a pot of barley-beer,

give praise and honour, water, beer, parched corn, milk,

honey, cream, oil, you should pour out,

you should bring a funeral offering to your family ghost,

to the kid you should bring a funeral offering,

the incantation, 'The great brother is his brother' before Ereškigal you should recite,

you should treat the kid as a living person, you should bury it,

. . . to Ereškigal, to the ghost of his family you should pour out grain,

. . . you should make the funeral lament, you should bring the funeral offering.

The sick man will recover, . . . (lit. 'return').

The general outline of the ritual is clear. The sick man first identifies himself with the kid which is said to be a substitute for the man (*puḥi amēli*) for the underworld goddess Ereškigal. Then the priest strikes the sick man on the throat with

o

a wooden dagger and cuts the throat of his substitute with a copper dagger. Then the substitute is treated in every respect as the corpse of the sick man; it is embalmed, adorned, dressed and shod; the sick man's head-band is fastened round its head, and the death-cry is raised. The kid is buried, and funeral offerings are brought to it in the guise of the family ghost. The final incantation is interesting, taken in connexion with K. 2001, another exorcism text in Ebeling's collection; it suggests the possibility that the object of the substitution was to effect an identification of the patient with Tammuz. In the above-mentioned text, the priest is instructed to strike the patient seven times with a seven-knotted reed; the ritual then continues, 'as soon as you have struck him, he has changed himself (*ramanšu ušpil*), and you should speak thus, "May Ištar thy beloved go at thy side".' It is clear from various references that the animal substitutes, as well as other forms of substitute, may be regarded as symbolic of various divine figures, Tammuz, Ištar, and others. In the Tammuz liturgies the cedar, male and female, repeatedly appears as the symbol of Tammuz and Ištar respectively.

Another point that calls for note in connexion with these substitution-rituals is that we frequently hear of the substitute animals or objects being taken into the desert, or thrown into the river, both being symbols of the underworlds.

It would take too long to pursue the subject of substitution in all its various forms in Assyrian and Babylonian religion, but before passing on to the forms of substitution in Hebrew religion we may sum up the results of our enquiry under the three heads mentioned above.

First, with regard to the kind of situation which called for the ritual of substitution. Wheeler Robinson has said, 'Outside the world of life and light there was another world of death and darkness' and it was the constant threat of invasion by this world of death and darkness, of disease, disaster, and death, of demons and ghosts, that demanded the substitution of some symbolic form, animate or inanimate, for the threatened king or commoner.

Second, the forms of substitute were numerous. Animal

forms might be bull, kid, lamb, pig, rat, and in the highest form of substitute for the king, a human being, a man, noble or commoner. Inanimate objects might be the hair, nails, or articles of apparel belonging to the threatened person; we also find the clay image of the patient or of the unquiet ghost used as a substitute; a staff decked with red wool, and a cedar tree, no doubt a small one, cut from the forest, occur in some rituals.

Third, the main object of the ritual was, of course, the averting of the danger, the removal of the threat, and the recovery of the patient. But various conceptions of the way in which the substitution worked may be discerned. In the case of the *šar puḥi* it would appear that the gods were willing to accept a person who had been fully invested with the powers and attributes of kingship as a substitute for the king. In the case of the *puḥi amēli* some kind of exchange of personality seems to have been effected, and it is possible that the sick man was thought to have become identified in the ritual with the dying and rising god and thus to have been delivered from the attack of the demon or ghost which had caused his disease. But there is also the possibility that the underworld powers might be deceived into accepting the substitute for the human object of their attack.

When we turn to the practice of substitution in the Old Testament our first problem is to distinguish the traces of earlier conceptions and practices as they have survived in the midst of the transformation of the meaning and use of all ritual brought about in Hebrew religion by the prophetic exposition of the character of God and Israel's relation to him.

We may turn our attention first to the ritual of the scape-goat, as laid down in Lev. 16. Of this ritual Buchanan Gray has said, 'We must distinguish between the fundamental ritual element and the particular associations with which it appears. The one is certainly ancient enough, not to say primitive; the other of less certain age and probably enough late' (*Sacrifice in the Old Testament*, pp. 313 ff). The 'primitive' features in the ritual may be defined as the selection of a goat to serve as the substitute for the corporate personality of Israel, the binding of a fillet of crimson wool about its horns—a detail not found in Leviticus, but preserved in *Yoma*, and the sending away of the goat into the wilderness, for Azazel. Both in Babylonian and early Hebrew thought the desert was the abode of demons; in the exorcism texts the river and the desert are both symbols of the underworld. Another link with Babylonian ritual practice is the crimson wool, a feature which occurs in the similar substitution-ritual for the leper in Lev. 14. In one exorcism text the staff which is used as a substitution object is decked with crimson wool. On this ritual Pedersen remarks, 'The special removal of the sin of the people by transferring it to an animal which is turned out into the wilderness, again shows how much of their cult ceremonial the Israelites had learned from foreigners. Assyro-Babylonian exorcism was based on such methods, and both the Babylonians and the Hittites had rites reminiscent of the Israelitish ritual'.[4] In connexion with this statement it may be remarked that in the recently published *Hittite Ritual of Tunnawi* (p. 74) a distinction occurs between the respective efficacy of the living substitute and clay figures used for this purpose.

It may be suggested that in these two rituals of the scapegoat and the leper we can perceive the process of fusion at work whereby the earlier non-moral conception of substitution is combined with later prophetic conceptions of the relation between Jahveh and Israel. In both rituals there are two substitutes, in the Yoma ritual two goats, and in the leper ritual two birds. In the former one goat is for Jahveh and one for Azazel, the goat for Jahveh being also for the people (Lev. 5.15). The people's goat is killed and its blood sprinkled in the most holy place to cleanse it from the uncleannesses of the children of Israel. But, while in the Levitical form of the ritual the goat for Azazel is also associated with the sin of the people, the fact that it is devoted to the demon would seem to show that behind the moralized form of the ritual there lies an earlier, non-moral, stage in which the goat as the substitute for the corporate personality of Israel went away into the

[4] Pedersen, *Israel*, III—IV, p. 454.

underworld and thus averted the threat of evil from demonic powers, just as in the Babylonian ritual the kid was *puḫi amēli* for Ereškigal. It is not unreasonable to see in the leper ritual the same significance of the second bird which is released after the purification is effected. No explanation is offered for the presence of the cedar, the scarlet, and the hyssop in the ritual, nor are we told what was done with them after the release of the second bird, but the close parallel with a similar use of cedar and scarlet in an exorcism text, where these objects are also devoted symbolically to the underworld together with the substitute, suggests that these elements in the Hebrew ritual are survivals whose original meaning has been lost.

A second form of substitution of a somewhat different kind, also suggesting traces of earlier conceptions, may be found in the use of the staff and the mantle to represent the person of prophet or king. For the former we have the story of Elisha sending Gehazi with his staff with instructions to lay it on the body of the dead child[5]; for the latter, David's remorse at having mutilated Saul's mantle, a remorse which was caused by his sense that he had violated the person of the king.[6] The substitution of the royal mantle for the person of the king is frequently mentioned in the correspondence of the Assyrian kings.

A third example of substitution, where the part stands for the whole, involving also the principle of the psychical character of inanimate objects, is seen in the use of the hair and the nails to represent the person, a use which is of frequent occurrence in the exorcism texts. In Ezek. 5, the prophet as the representative of Israel is told to cut off his hair and divide it into three parts; the symbolic actions which he is told to perform upon each third of his severed hair constitute the active curse which will come upon his people; the hair represents the people.

One more example of the survival in Hebrew religion of an earlier conception of substitution may be offered, although the interpretation of the ritual here suggested is not that usually accepted. It is the ritual described in Deut. 21.1-9

[5] II Kings 4.29.   [6] I Sam. 24.5.

and is intended to deal with the case of the discovery in the
open field of the body of a slain man whose slayer is not
known. One of the commonest causes of fear among the
Babylonians was the visitation of an *eṭimmu*, or ghost, especially the ghost of one for whom the proper rituals of the dead
had not been performed. Exorcism texts dealing with the
threat from ghosts are numerous, and there are features in
the Deuteronomic ritual which recall certain common features
in Babylonian exorcism texts. For the heifer לֹא עֻבַּד בָּה,
we have the parallel of the unmated kid, *uniqa la pitita*; the
breaking of the heifer's neck corresponds to the cutting of the
kid's throat; the flowing stream and the desert nature of the
place where the ritual is performed are underworld symbols
in Babylonian usage. Hence I venture to suggest that originally the heifer was a true substitute for the corporate personality of the community, devoted to the underworld to
avert the threat of evil from a dangerous, unhouselled, ghost
let loose upon an innocent community. In its later transformation it has become a recognition of Jahveh's attitude
towards unavenged slaying. The relation of Israel to Jahveh
has become the determinant factor in the intention of the
ancient ritual.

Passing from these traces of an earlier, non-moral, conception of substitution, we may take for discussion the curious
case of substitution which is found in Num. 3. Here Jahveh
is represented as announcing to Moses that he will accept the
tribe of Levi as a collective substitute for all the firstborn
of the children of Israel. The substitution is still thought of
in such a materialistic way that since it is found that the
number of the firstborn males of Israel exceeds that of the
Levites, the excess must be ransomed by a money payment.
This transaction is bound up with the very ancient practice,
probably Canaanite or even pre-Canaanite, of the sacrifice of
the firstborn, human or animal. Whatever the origin of the
practice, the earliest Hebrew codes show that the dominant
conception of Israel's relation to Jahveh has begun to colour
and transform the ancient practices. This relation has been
established in the historic act of the redemption from Egypt,

and Jahveh's right to the firstborn rested upon this act. The custom of redeeming the firstborn was a compromise between the old *ad hoc* practice of substitution as a means of averting a threatened supernatural danger on the one hand, and the recognition of Israel's peculiar relation to Jahveh and his consequent right to the firstborn on the other. But in the development of the Hebrew sacrificial system a new factor emerged, the priestly class and their interests. The particular case of substitution now under consideration was probably a legal fiction intended to bring together the assertion of Jahveh's right to the firstborn and the claim of the priesthood to maintenance. Substitution is transformed into a temple tax. But it also foreshadows the morally important conception of the mediatorial function of the priesthood, a conception which appears in the narrative in Num. 16.48 where Aaron stands between the living and the dead and makes 'atonement' (וַיְכַפֵּר) for the people; the same conception is seen in Ex. 32.30-33, after the episode of the golden calf, where Moses offers himself as an atonement for the people. It is noteworthy however, that Moses' offer is met by Jahveh's assertion of individual responsibility, 'Whosoever hath sinned against me, him will I blot out of my book'.

The conception of corporate substitution, a whole class of persons acting as a permanent substitute, a ransom (פִּדְיוֹן) in respect of Jahveh's rights over Israel, raised problems which exercised the minds of the seventh century prophets with their growing sense of the direct and unmediated relation between Jahveh and the individual Israelite, but before we turn to the development which the idea of substitution undergoes in their treatment of this relation, something must be said about the nature of the transformation so far effected. It may be said that a mechanical conception of substitution has given place to a moral one. While the whole sacrificial system in the hands of the priesthood continued to provide both for the community and the individual a means of dealing with the sin which impaired the relation between Jahveh and his people, we find frequent expressions of a feeling that, in the words of a New Testament writer, 'It is impossible for the blood of bulls and goats to take away sins' (Heb. 10.4). It is perhaps not too fanciful to suggest that a dim sense persisted of a divine quality in these sacrificial victims; in earlier times as we have already seen, the bull, the goat, the lamb, the dove, were divine symbols, and as the sense grew that ransom and atonement involved cost, and that man had nothing of sufficient value to offer, we find in the later prophets the assertion that it is Jahveh who will himself pay the ransom and bear the cost. But here we are anticipating.

A foreshadowing of the moral element in the conception of the substitute appears in the function of the Levites previously mentioned. It is suggested (Deut. 33.9-10) that a moral reason underlay the choice of Levi as a permanent substitute for Israel. Levi had taken the side of Jahveh in the time of crisis at the cost or renunciation of all personal ties. The substitute represents both sides of the relationship; he is identified with Jahveh's character and purposes on the one hand, while he is bound up with the history and fortunes of the people on the other. This mediatorial element in the conception of the substitute become strikingly apparent in Ezek. 4. There the prophet as the divine representative is instructed by Jahveh to perform a symbolic act of the highest import. As the representative of the people he is to lie on his left side for 390 days and bear the sins of Israel, and on his right side for another forty days bearing the sins of Judah. During this period he is to share the experiences of the siege, rationing his food and water and undergoing the various hardships which were the consequences of the people's sins. While it seems clear that these experiences and symbolic actions of the prophet have a vicarious character, and that he is in a certain sense a substitute, yet what is missing from the picture is any indication that the prophet's substitutionary activity effects deliverance or redemption for the people. His function seems to be that of a witness, a demonstration to Israel by things which he suffers for their sins that Jahveh will without delay bring these same sufferings upon them. They say, 'The vision that he seeth is for many days to come, and he prophesieth of times that are far off'. But the prophet, in the urgency of his

[216]

own suffering for them, testifies, 'Thus saith the Lord, There shall none of my words be deferred any more'. So, by the beginning of the sixth century, the conception of the substitute has so far increased in depth as to require that he shall be identified both with Israel in their sins and sufferings and with Jahveh in what his holiness has caused him to suffer on account of their sins. Forgiveness glimmers in the future (Ezek. 16.63), but its connexion with the sufferings of the substitute is not yet made clear. Before we come to the culminating point of the development which we have been endeavouring to trace, there are two passages to be considered which show that after the exile the problem of substitution was exercising the minds of religious thinkers very deeply.

The first is the difficult passage in Ps. 49.7-9, part of a poetic *mašal* belonging clearly to the Wisdom literature. Accepting the emendations of אַךְ for אָח, יִפְדֶּה for יִפְדֶּה, and נַפְשׁוֹ for נַפְשָׁם: it may be read:

But no man may redeem himself, nor give to God his ransom-price;
Costly is the ransom (פִּדְיוֹן) of his soul, that it should go on existing
    for ever,
that he should live on still, and never see the Pit.

The general meaning is clear, even if the parenthetic clause is difficult to restore. The sage says that, speaking on the human level, there is no ransom for a soul or life; no wealth can pay the price. It is almost literally the counterpart of our Lord's words in Matt. 16.26, τί δώσει ἄνθρωπος ἀντάλλαγμα τῆς ψυχῆς αὐτοῦ; 'What shall a man give as an exchange for his life?' We have already seen that the thought of ancient times conceived of the possibility of a *puhu*, human or animal, acting as a פִּדְיוֹן, or ransom, for a man's life, and that the conception persisted through the various stages of development of Hebrew religion. Here the final conclusion of wisdom, considering realistically the limitations of human activity, is that it lies beyond the power of man to provide a ransom for his life. The question of what God can do in this respect is not raised here. Though the poet recognizes that God can do it in v.16.

The other passage is in Job 33.22-24, 'When his soul has drawn near to the Pit, and his life to the dead (לְמוֹ מֵתִים for לִמְמִיתִים); if there be over him (i.e. standing over his sick-bed) a messenger (i.e. from J.), an interpreter, one of thousands, to declare to man his right course of action, (i.e. towards J.); one who will be gracious to him and say, Redeem him (reading פְּדָהוּ for פְּדָעֵהוּ) from going down into the Pit, I have found the ransom-price' (possibly inserting נַפְשׁוֹ, 'of his soul'). It is perhaps permissible to suppose that the author of this had the utterance of the sage in mind; the contrast between Ps. 49.19, 'never more will he see the light', and Job 33.28, 'my life shall behold the light', seems almost deliberate. The situation depicted is that of a man at the point of death, lying on his sick-bed. The poet asks what hope there is for him and answers, 'What is impossible with man is possible with God'. He sees the divine messenger standing over the sick-bed, just as we may see on exorcism tablets the Babylonian priest standing over the sick-bed; the messenger is an interpreter, one among those 'thousands' who 'at his bidding stand'; his business is to show the patient the cause of his sickness, where he has gone wrong; then follows the announcement, 'I have found the ransom-price'. The poet goes on to describe the sick man's recovery, his songs of thankful praise, and concludes with the significant statement, 'Lo, all these things God does twice and even three times with a man'. This passage brings us near the end of our search. It is a clear recognition that God can do what man cannot do, he can provide a ransom, a substitute, he can pay the price. The whole thing has been lifted completely on to the moral plane; the cause of disease has been connected with sin, and the first step in the divine healing with the situation is the ἔλεγχος, the showing to man how he may get right with God. But something still remains to be shown. We have still to look for the revelation of how the divine activity announced in the passage from Job would manifest itself, and this brings us to the climax of the whole development of the idea of substitution, namely the figure of the Suffering Servant. So many eminent scholars have discussed the problems

[218]

of the Servant passages of Deutero-Isaiah, that it would be a work of superogation on my part to attempt a fresh discussion of them. All I wish to do here is to emphasize the relation of the substitutionary work of the Servant to the development of the idea and practice of substitution which we have been endeavouring to trace out. But before doing this, I wish to deal briefly with one point which I have intentionally passed by. In discussing the evidence of the Babylonian texts I did not include among the examples of the practice of substitution drawn from those sources the rôle of the king at the New Year Festival in Babylon. While it is clear that the king performed certain ritual acts during the festival as the representative of the people, notably his humiliation and confession, and again, that he performed other ritual acts as the representative of Marduk or Asshur, as the case might be, yet I am not sure that any of these activities were, in the true sense, substitutionary. I cannot, at least at present, feel that the king in the rituals of the Akitu Festival was a substitute for the people in the sense that the *šar puḫi* was a substitute for the king in certain critical situations. The three ideas of representation, substitution, and sacrifice are very closely connected, yet they are not equivalent. For instance, we find that in the *puḫi amēli* ritual already discussed the offerings made to Ereškigal are distinct from the kid which is devoted to her as the substitute for the sick man. This is why I have not included the figure of the king as a substitute, an element in the conception of the Servant which has been so strongly stressed by Engnell in his monograph on the Ebed-Jahveh Songs and the Suffering Servant.

The particular view taken of the figure of the Servant does not affect the validity of the points which I wish to emphasize, save in so far as the question may be involved of some prophetic experience underlying the description of the figure and function of the Servant. First of all we have the emphasis laid on the divine initiative, an initiative of which the Servant is fully conscious, 'Jahveh called me from the womb, from the bowels of my mother he made mention of my name', words which recall Jeremiah's similar expression of his sense of the

divine mission. Second, by this experience of the divine choice
he is marked out as Jahveh's agent and representative, his
function is to carry out the will of Jahveh. Third, he is seen
as voluntarily offering himself, 'Truly he gave himself as a
guilt offering'. Fourth, he carries the experience of Ezekiel,
the bearing of Israel's sins, to the ultimate limit of death and
descent into the underworld. Fifth, we have the declaration
put into the mouth of those for whom this divine activity of
substitution has been wrought, 'The chastisement leading to
our welfare was upon him, and by means of his stripes there
is healing for us'. Finally, whether in figure or reality, the
poet prophet sees in resurrection and return to light Jahveh's
acceptance of the Servant's substitutionary work and the
pledge of his success.

We may consider here the nature of the transformation
which has taken place. Instead of the vague, though none the
less very real, fear of threatened evil or disaster from hostile
gods or underworld powers, demanding the protection afforded by the substitute, we have a situation which has been
brought about by sin; not some unwitting breach of a taboo
or failure to fulfil some ritual detail, but a breach of the relationship between Israel and Jahveh, a burden of guilt, and
an ever-present sense of wrath impending. The situation is
the more desperate for the realization that sacrifice will not
avail, and that man cannot provide the substitute or the
ransom.

Then instead of the mechanical selection of the substitute
by the religious authorities, we have the divine initiative,
Jahveh himself chooses the substitute. Instead of the passive
rôle of the selected substitute, waiting for an unknown fate,
we are shown a substitute voluntarily offering himself, fully
conscious both of Jahveh's righteous requirements and of
Israel's need.

Lastly, instead of the uncertainty which must always have
shrouded the effect of the substitution-ritual, we are shown
the triumph of the divinely provided substitute; everything
has been lifted to the moral plane: sin is removed, Jahveh's
holiness vindicated, and the Servant-substitute emerges from

the dark destiny which he has willingly gone to meet, into the light of glory.

Thus the transformation of images is carried as far as it could be carried until the coming of the only perfect Servant, the Son, in whom all the images reached their complete transformation and fulfilment.

Finally a word may be said about the echoes in the Servant Songs of the circle of ideas connected with the Tammuz rites so strongly emphasized by Engnell in his monograph already referred to. North, in his remarks on the mythological interpretation of the Servant Songs, has said that 'the Servant is a soteriological figure, while nature gods of the Tammuz variety are not'.[7] I should like to qualify this by pointing out that in the substitution rituals from the Babylonian texts the kid is a symbol of Tammuz, and the intention of the ritual would clearly seem to be that the sufferer, by identifying himself with Tammuz is delivered from the evil power which threatens him with death; Tammuz in symbol is his substitute, Tammuz is slain and goes into the underworld instead of him, while he goes free. This is soteriological thinking. While I agree with North that the nature gods are not saviour gods in the true sense, yet I would urge that this primitive sense of the need of salvation, even if only on the material plane, laid hold of the myth of the passion and death of these gods and gave it in the substitution rituals a soteriological intention, so creating a pattern of images which passed into early Hebrew religion and underwent those transformations which we have tried to trace out. We are not committing ourselves to a mythological interpretation of the Servant Songs in recognizing that the Tammuz imagery and phraseology which Engnell finds in the Songs is being gathered up and transformed into spiritual terms in the great substitute figure of the Ebed-Jahveh. So we find, in the words with which this paper began, that 'since every image has its place in the revelation, *nothing is left behind* in the passage of thought'.

[7] C. R. North, *The Suffering Servant in Deutero-Isaiah*, p. 201.

CHAPTER SIXTEEN

The Sign of Immanuel[1]

THE well-known passage in Isa. 7 in which the oracle containing the sign of Immanuel occurs raises two issues which it is proposed to examine in this paper: first, the prophetic use of signs, and second, the function of prophetic activity in the pattern of revelation.

In general, the Hebrew word *'ōth*, which the LXX usually renders by *sēmeion*, is used to denote some activity or some object intended by God to indicate his purpose in some special situation; it may serve to point out to a man the right course of action, or it may serve as an indication that God is about to do something. It may also serve to attest a prophet's claim to speak or act with divine authority. But underlying its various uses may be found the thought of power, God's power, at work. The use of signs is of very ancient origin. In the Babylonian Epic of Creation, where the young god Marduk presents himself to the assembly of the gods as their champion against the chaos-dragon Tiamat, he gives a sign as a guarantee of his power by casting down a mantle and causing it to disappear and then to re-appear. This expectation of, and often request for, a sign is of constant occurrence in the Old Testament record of man's dealings with God. We have, so to speak, nuclear points in the history of Israel where signs cluster like stars. They throng about the exodus and the wilderness progress; the saga of Elijah and Elisha is thick with them; from the rise of the eighth century prophets they disappear or change their character until the coming of Christ, when once more acts of power abound and continue into the early period of the Church. But it must not be overlooked that Jesus did not regard his acts of power (*dunameis*) as 'signs', and always refused the request for a sign, 'there shall no sign be given to this generation' (Mark 8.12).

[1] Paper read at the Summer Conference of the Fellowship of St Alban and St Sergius, 1954. First published in *Sobornost*.

Moreover, the word 'sign' (*sēmeion*) acquires a new meaning in the Fourth Gospel. In II Kings 1.10f, as a sign that he is a man of God, Elijah calls down fire from heaven to consume those who have been sent to arrest him. In Luke 9.52-55, when a certain Samaritan village was unwilling to receive Jesus, James and John asked him if he wished them to call down fire from heaven as Elijah had done, to consume the inhospitable Samaritans; Jesus told them that they did not know what spirit they were of, for the Son of Man had not come to destroy men's lives but to save them. The incident shows that the old conception, or rather, misconception of God's use of power persisted in the minds of the disciples, and it also shows how uncompromisingly Jesus rejected it.

If we examine the first great cluster of signs that mark the beginning of the redemption of Israel from Egypt, we find first of all that a group of signs is offered to Moses intended in the first place to convince the Israelites that Moses is accredited by Jahveh to be their deliverer from the Egyptian bondage, and secondly to demonstrate to Pharaoh that Jahveh is intervening in power on behalf of his people. It is not suggested that the signs are intended to convince Moses of the reality of his own experience and of the authenticity of the divine communication; that had been sufficiently effected by the vision of the burning bush and the revelation of the Name, the Tetragrammaton. It is also to be observed that a different word is used for the signs addressed to the Israelites, and for those intended for Pharaoh: in the former case it is *'ōthōth*, 'signs' LXX *sēmeia*, and in the latter it is *mōphethim*, LXX, *terata*, 'wonders'. We find the same pair of words frequently used together in the Old Testament, e.g. Ps. 68.45 *et al.*, and in the New Testament, e.g. John 4.48. We also find that, in Deut. 13.1-3, with the growth of understanding of the character and ways of God, it has been discovered that 'signs and wonders' cannot be depended upon to guarantee that he who performs them is speaking with divine authority. This is also recognized in the Exodus story in that the Egyptian court magicians are able to duplicate the first three signs performed by Moses, although a point is reached when they are forced to acknowledge their own limitations and say, 'this is the finger of God' (Ex. 8.19). Speaking of the happenings recorded in the story of the Exodus, the late Principal Wheeler Robinson has said[2]: 'Interpretation is inseparable from miracles of the Old Testament pattern. We begin at the wrong end if we try first to rationalize them, and to reduce them to their smallest nucleus of historical event. We should begin rather with the faith of both prophet and people, by which the events of the physical world, normal or abnormal, were interpreted in a particular context of history.'

We have thus to do with three levels, each of which represents an aspect of reality: first the level of historical event; something happened at the Exodus; if we are writing history we are bound to try and discover the nucleus of historicity underlying the saga; second, there is the level of interpretation; those who participated in the events, and those who, later on, reflected on the traditions, oral or written, of the events, interpreted them in terms of the divine activity and purpose as it concerned themselves and their people. We have to recognize that, in the economy of revelation, the interpretation was bounded by the horizon or mental climate of the time, and might be modified or even contradicted in the light of a fuller knowledge of God. Third, there is the level of the divine activity itself, transcending and embracing in its eternal reality both the other levels. If it be asked how we may distinguish the characteristics of this level, the answer is that the full light of the revelation of God in Christ illuminates the past and shines through the images, so that we no longer see the revelation πολυμερῶς καὶ πολυτρόπως, but as a whole, from the first glory of creation to the final glory of redemption, summed up in the Son.

As the signs given to Moses illustrate the principles which we are about to discuss, something may be said about them at this point. In the first sign Moses was told to cast his rod, his shepherd's instrument of control, upon the ground; he did so and it turned into a terrifying serpent from which he fled. He

[2] *Inspiration and Revelation in the Old Testament*, pp. 43-4.

was then told to take it up by the tail; he obeyed and it turned into a rod again in his hand.

The rod is a very common symbol of power, especially in connexion with the display of redemptive power seen at the Exodus, while the serpent appears from the beginning of man's story as the symbol of evil in opposition to the purposes of God. Moses is about to be entrusted with power for the accomplishment of God's purpose, and in preparation for his task he has to learn that power in the hand of man uncontrolled by the will of God becomes evil; only when it is exercised in accordance with and at the direction of the divine command can it be the agent of the divine purpose. A poignant commentary on this lesson is found in Num. 20.1-15, where Moses, stung to anger by the people's rebellion and murmuring, forgets that the power entrusted to him may only be used in accordance with the divine direction; instructed only to speak to the rock, he takes the rod and strikes the rock twice with it, and says, 'Hear now, ye rebels, shall *we* bring you forth water out of this rock?' The consequence for Moses was disastrous; he was not allowed to finish the work entrusted to him and to enter the promised land.

The second sign develops the theme of the first, and like the first deals with the question of power, but from a different angle. The rod symbolizes power as an instrument, the hand power seen from the point of view of the agent. There is no more frequently used symbol of Jahveh's power in action than the hand and arm of Jahveh. The other symbols that come together in the action are the bosom and leprosy. The bosom, which is often a synonym for the heart, is a symbol of the secret workings of the mind, a man's inner consciousness, while leprosy is the regular symbol of uncleanness. Moses is told to put his hand, the rod-holding hand, into his bosom; when he draws it out it is all leprous. He is then told to thrust it again into his bosom, and when he withdraws it he finds it is clean. We may compare the effect upon Isaiah of the vision of the Lord in the Temple, high and lifted up; the prophet is forced to cry out: 'Woe is me, for I am undone; I am a man of unclean lips, and I dwell among a people of unclean lips, for mine eyes have seen the King, the Lord of Hosts' (Isa. 6.5). Moses, like Isaiah, has received and responded, though reluctantly, to the divine call, and he, like Isaiah, has to discover his own unworthiness to be the wielder of the rod, the agent of Jahveh's power, until he has been cleansed by divine grace. To use the striking phrase in Solomon's prayer of dedication in I Kings 8.38, he has to learn 'the plague of his own heart', where the word for 'plague' is the one regularly used for the 'stroke' of leprosy.

The third sign, although rich in apocalyptic symbolism, does not immediately concern the response of Moses to the call of God, and need not be discussed here.

From the study of the Old Testament signs a principle emerges which may be said to constitute one of the fundamental laws of revelation. It is this, that where we find the response of surrender to the divine will and call, out of the signs and activities which follow such an act of faith and obedience there arise images whose import looks beyond the immediate situation on to the fulfilment of all images in Christ. For example, Abraham's act of obedience in offering up Isaac gave birth to a constellation of images whose significance embraced the whole plan of redemption. This is why a narrow application of the *Sitz im Leben* principle to the interpretation of scripture has its dangers; for, while it is important to keep hold of the fact that God acts in history, yet it is even more important to remember that the significance of God's act is never exhausted by the immediate historical situation in which it takes place.

Coming now to the sign which is the subject of this paper, we have first to consider the historical situation which served as its occasion. With the death of King Uzziah of Judah in 745 B.C. the period of Israel's greatest material prosperity since the days of Solomon came to an end. The same year was for Isaiah the turning point of his life; it was the point of time when he had his overwhelming vision of God, and surrendered to the divine call. The result of this is that we read the history of the next forty-five years through the eyes of the prophet. For him, as for his predecessors, Amos and Hosea, history

was the scene where God was working out his purposes, and
for him Assyria and Egypt, no less than Israel and Syria,
were instruments in his hands to that end.

The immediate situation was that Assyria, now rising from
a period of depression, was beginning the third and most
brilliant period of her history. As she had already done in the
ninth century, she was threatening the small kingdoms to the
south of her, and they were resorting to the usual policy of
what Isaiah in Chapter 8 calls *qesher*, 'confederacy'. They
formed a league, led by the kings of Syria and northern
Israel (generally called Ephraim by Isaiah) to resist the advance of Assyria. Ahaz, the grandson of Uzziah, was now
reigning in Judah, and he was unwilling to join the northern
alliance against Assyria. Hence the kings of Syria and Ephraim
made an attack on Judah and besieged Jerusalem in an attempt
to force Ahaz to join the coalition. The narrative in II Kings
16 records that they were unable to take Jerusalem. But the
crisis caused considerable alarm in the city; in the vivid words
of the narrator of the account in Isa. 7.2, 'his heart (i.e. the
king's) was moved, and the heart of his people, as the trees
of the forest are moved with the wind'. At this point of time
the prophet was told to go and meet Ahaz at a significant
spot, the place where the 'softly-flowing waters of Shiloah'
brought the waters of the Virgin's Well, or Gihon, to a pool
in the Tyropoeon Valley. This was, of course, before Hezekiah had brought the same waters into the city by the Siloam
tunnel. The prophet was also told to take his eldest son,
Shear-jashub, with him to the meeting. Isaiah was no doubt
aware that the king was planning to deal with the crisis in a
way which he regarded as wholly contrary to God's purpose
for Judah, namely, to bring about the intervention of Assyria
by the offer of a heavy subsidy. Hence his first admonition to
the king emphasized the necessity of refraining from any
decisive move, and of committing himself in faith to the hands
of God. He spoke contemptuously of the two invading kings
as 'two tails of smoking firebrands', and promised in the
name of Jahveh that they would speedily be extinguished.
Then came the test of faith. The prophet urged the king to

lay hold of the power that controlled the universe to its utmost bounds, from the height of heaven to the depths of Sheol. God was ready to meet his faith with the full majesty of his power. We cannot tell what the prophet expected the king to ask, but he knew that such an act would commit the king irrevocably to God, and prevent him from carrying out his foolish and mad plan to call in the power of Assyria. But Ahaz realized this too, and fell back upon a pious evasion of the challenge by appealing to a word of scripture, 'Ye shall not put the Lord your God to the test as ye tested him at Massah'. The prophet saw that the challenge had failed; the king would persist in his suicidal folly. He has chosen Assyria and must abide the consequence of his choice. But God's patience is not exhausted, though the prophet's, as the Targum of Jonathan has it, might well be. 'What you will not ask for in faith God himself will give'. Then come the words of the given sign: 'Lo, a maiden is pregnant and is about to give birth to a child, and she (LXX has 'you') will call his name Immanuel. Curds and honey will be his food, that he may learn to refuse the evil and to choose the good. For before the child knows how to refuse the evil and choose the good, the land whose two kings thou dreadest shall be forsaken.' The prophet then goes on to tell the king what will be the consequences of his appeal to Assyria. The country will suffer the worst disaster since the fatal day when the great schism took place, when Ephraim departed from Judah. The land will be so ravaged that there will be a return to a pastoral economy. Those who are left after the desolation will have to live on curds and honey, probably wild honey. Such will be the condition under which the child of the sign will pass his early years.

Before considering the meaning of the sign we must turn our attention to certain features which appear in the course of the narrative and its connected oracles in Isa. 7-8. In Chapter 8, which belongs to the same situation as is described in Chapter 7, the prophet is represented as saying to his people, 'Behold I and the children whom Jahveh hath given me are for signs and for portents in Israel from Jahveh of hosts who dwelleth in Mount Zion.' Now it is clear that Isaiah and the

two sons who are mentioned in Chapters 7 and 8 bear significant names. The prophet's own name means 'the salvation of
Jah'. Many years ago the late Professor Margoliouth in his
book *Lines of Defence of the Biblical Revelation*, suggested that
Isaiah was not the original name of the prophet, but one
which he had assumed or been given by Jahveh as a sign. The
name of his eldest son Shear-jashub means 'a remnant shall
turn' (not 'return'), while the name of the child whose birth
is related in the opening verses of Chapter 8, is Maher-shalal-
hash-baz, a truly portentous name, meaning 'swift to spoil,
haste to prey'. All these names are evidently 'signs', indicating the divine character, and the divine purpose active in
Israel. Those who asked the prophet why he had given his
children such names would learn from him the message for
their time. In the light of these facts it is not unreasonable to
suggest that the sign given to the unbelieving king in Chapter
7 lies in the name of the child that is about to be born. It is
not easy for us to consider the great name Immanuel apart
from its New Testament significance, but it is necessary to
remember that for the eighth century prophets the presence
of God among his people meant judgment. Amos says, 'because I will do thus unto thee, prepare to meet thy God, O
Israel', and again, 'wailing shall be in all the vineyards, for I
will pass through the midst of thee'. For the king the sign
was a sign of doom: 'You have chosen Assyria rather than
God, but you will find that in getting Assyria you have got
God, whether you will or no.' Nothing is told us about the
mother, though I am inclined to think that she may have been
the prophet's wife, and that the name of the next child,
Maher-shalal-hash-baz, indicated the judgment which was
the inevitable consequence of Immanuel, of God's presence
with his guilty people. But I have no wish to press the point.
Yet it is clear that we have here a cluster of signs, a sequence
of significant names, whose meaning, taken together, embraces the whole pattern of divine activity in redemption.

But there is a further point of deep significance in what is
said about the early experience of the child Immanuel. He is
to experience the suffering and privation which God's judg-

ment by the agency of Assyria will bring upon his people. In
5.15 we are told that his food will be 'curds and honey', not
the food of plenty but of poverty, 'in order that he may know
how to refuse the evil and choose the good'. Both the LXX
and the Targum of Jonathan render the Hebrew *le da'to*,
'*before* the child knows', but the *le* is clearly a *lamedh* of purpose and should not be taken as an adverb of time. We should
compare here the saying in Deut. 8.3, 'He humbled thee, and
suffered thee to hunger, and fed thee with manna which thou
knewest not, neither did thy fathers know; that he might
make thee know that man doth not live by bread alone, but
by every word that proceedeth out of the mouth of the Lord
doth man live'. By his experience and his sharing in the
suffering of his people the child is to learn the true nature of
good and evil. In the Garden man learnt good and evil by
choosing evil. In desolation and hunger the child who is
Immanuel will learn good and evil by choosing good. So the
sign deepens. Immanuel may spell judgment for the unbelieving king and people, but in Immanuel God enters into the
suffering of his people for their salvation: 'In all their affliction he was afflicted, and the angel of his presence saved
them'. (Isa. 63.9). Dr A. M. Farrer, in a meditation on the
Trinity, has said: 'All the gifts of God judge us as fast as they
save us, . . . and yet God's gifts save us as fast as they judge
us, or they would not be gifts: his mercy prevails.' The sign
of Immanuel was God's gift: 'the Lord himself shall give you
a sign', it was a sign that judged, but it was also in the most
pregnant sense a sign that saved. In the fulness of time Immanuel was to come, born of a woman, and was to gather up
into himself all the experience of Israel and the prophets. He
was to learn obedience by his *pathēmata*; he too was to suffer
hunger and testing, and to take up into his own experience
the Deuteronomic word, 'not by bread only shall man live,
but by every word that proceedeth out of the mouth of the
Lord'. But the prophet's immediate concern was with the
crisis of his own time. By surrendering himself wholly to the
will of God, he became the vehicle of revelation; he and the
children whom God had given him became signs and portents

to Israel. But, while the illumination of the sign was directed
upon the situation in which Israel found itself in 735 B.C., that
leaves us only on the first level, the historical level. At a
certain definite date, a critical date in the history of Israel,
God acted through the prophet and gave to king and people
a sign which indicated to those who could read it what God
was about to do to them and for them at that juncture of
history.

On the second level, the level of interpretation, the
earliest and most important work of interpretation comes
from the prophet himself as he considers the nature of the
crisis and the implications of the sign. It is fairly certain that
the group of oracles in Chapters 7-9, with some possible
slight exceptions, arise out of the prophet's contemplation of
the actual state of things between 735 and 732 B.C., not only
the external shape of things, but also the moral condition of
king and people. As we have already seen, the oracles in
Chapter 7 describe the desolation of the land resulting from
the king's Assyrian policy and God's judgment on it, the
doom of Immanuel, the consequence of God's presence among
the sinful people; but they also describe Immanuel's sharing
in the suffering of his land and his people, and his learning
thereby to choose the good and refuse the evil. But after the
birth of Maher-shalal-hash-baz the situation seems to have
sharpened, the alarm caused by the *qesher*, or coalition is
intensified, and the prophet is instructed under strong pressure
from Jahveh ('with the grasp of his hand upon me'), to with-
draw completely from the unbelievers. They have refused the
quiet way of faith, the waters of God's sending, springing
from his depths, and in their panic and despair seek on behalf
of the living to the dead, as Saul had done in a similar access
of darkness and despair. For such, says the prophet, there is
no daybreak. It is probable that the oracle in 28.14 f belongs
to the same situation as 8, and the covenant with death and
the agreement with Sheol upon which the rulers of Jerusalem
are depending for protection from the overflowing scourge,
refers to the same resort to necromancy described in 8.19.
But the presence of God with us, in the sign of Immanuel,

brings about an expansion of the interpretation of the sign. Both in 8.14, and in the connected passage in 28.16, the prophet sees Jahveh placing in Zion something upon which faith can rest, a tried stone, a sure foundation, against which the gates of Sheol cannot prevail. On the one hand the stone is for judgment, a stone of stumbling and a rock of offence for the disobedient, but for faith it is Jahveh himself, God with us, a sanctuary; 'he that believeth shall not make haste': such a man will wait for Jahveh, and will not rush to take shelter in a refuge of lies. So the inner meaning of the sign expands and as the prophet waits for Jahveh, even while the divine face is hidden, images arise, the stone, the rock, the water of sending, the sure foundation, which could only yield up all their meaning on the third level of interpretation when Immanuel had come and God had spoken in a Son.

But a still further expansion of the interpretation of the sign takes place in the prophet's mind. He knew, for he said so in a later oracle, that judgment was God's strange work and could never be his last word. He saw the failure of the monarchy, the desolation of the land, only a very small remnant left, but the land was Immanuel's, God might have hidden his face from the nation, but Immanuel was there, God was with the remnant. So out of the darkness with which Chapter 8 closes light breaks. The prophet cries in triumph, 'Unto us a child is born, unto us a son is given'. The sign-bearing name of Immanuel expands into four mighty significant names: Pele-Yoez, El-Gibbor, Abi-Ad, Sar-Shalom. They may be rendered: Planning Wonders, Hero-God, Father of Eternity, Prince of Peace. They are great names for a child to bear, a great weight of government to rest upon a child's shoulders, a weight which not even the best of Israel's kings had been able to bear. But Isaiah knew that the zeal of the Lord of Hosts would perform it.

On the third level, the level of the divine activity seen in the Incarnation, the first transformation is found in the reference by the first evangelist of the sign of Immanuel to the birth of Christ. But here an element enters which is veiled on the first two levels. I have already pointed out that in Isa. 7.14, the mother of Immanuel is nameless, and no emphasis is laid upon her function as the vessel of the divine purpose. Not even her virginity is stressed in the Hebrew text which merely says that a young woman is about to bear a child. Perhaps it may be permitted to see an element of interpretation on the second level in well-known LXX translation of the Hebrew *'almah* by *parthenos*. Aquila's later and more literal version renders *'almah* by *neānis*, and quite correctly. But an examination of the LXX use of *parthenos* shows that in LXX usage the word was not limited to its classical sense and was used to render both *'almah* and *na'arah*, words which carry no implication of virginity. But there is more than one case in the New Testament where a mistranslation of a Hebrew word is used, we might say, with divine permission, to carry profound theological implications. A familiar example is the mistranslation of the Hebrew *shakhath*, the pit, as 'corruption' in Acts 2.27, 13.35, applied both by St Peter and St Paul to the resurrection of the Lord. So it may be that the virginity of Mary, veiled in the historical circumstances under which the sign of Immanuel was given, is hinted at on the level of interpretation in the LXX rendering of *'almah* by *parthenos*, and brought into the pattern of revelation by the emphasis laid on this element of the sign in Matt. 1.23. It can hardly be denied that the mystery of the Virgin Birth of the Lord remains to a large extent still veiled in the New Testament, but neither can it be denied that in the economy of revelation the Holy Spirit has magnified the importance and glory of the vehicle of the divine birth. As early as Ignatius we find a striking passage in his epistle to the Ephesians, 19.1, 'And the virginity of Mary, and her giving birth were hidden from the Prince of this world, as was also the death of the Lord, three mysteries of crying wrought in the silence of God'.

But other elements of transformation call for notice. We have already mentioned how Immanuel's sharing of the sufferings of his people and how he was to learn thereby how to refuse the evil and to choose the good, are taken up into the experience of Jesus. The *auctor ad Hebræos* sums it up in the words, 'yet though he were a son, he learned obedience by the things which he suffered'. The same writer puts into the mouth of the risen Lord the words of the prophet, 'Behold I and the children whom God hath given me'; but the children who were signs and portents are now 'sons brought to glory', Messiah's companions, and signs of his triumph and redemption. The stone of stumbling, the stone which the builders rejected, the tried and precious corner-stone, laid in Zion for a foundation, has become both the 'head of the corner' and the foundation of Messiah's new community, the Church. There is one word uttered by the angelic interpreter to the seer of Patmos, which may sum up what this paper has very inadequately endeavoured to say, 'The testimony of Jesus is the spirit of prophecy'.

CHAPTER SEVENTEEN

The Corner-Stone of Scripture[1]

'BEHOLD I lay in Zion for a foundation a stone, a tried stone, a precious corner *stone*, of sure foundation: he that believeth shall not make haste.' This is the English Revisers' rendering of Isa. 28.16. The passage has for centuries taxed the ingenuity of commentators, and the early Christian use of it as a favourite Messianic proof-text has obscured the original meaning by detaching it from the historical situation in which it was uttered. This paper is an attempt to examine the passage afresh in connexion with a number of other passages in the Old Testament which mention the 'stone' with a symbolic meaning. The passages in question are Gen. 49.24; Isa. 8.14; Ps. 118.22; Dan. 2.34-35 and 45; Zech. 3.9, 4.7 and 9, 12.3.

It may be as well to take the passages in their chronological order, so far as that is ascertainable. The earliest is probably the difficult oracle in Gen. 49.24, described by Eduard Meyer as 'hopelessly corrupt'[2]; but it clearly refers to some period in the history of the tribe of Joseph, when that tribe successfully played the part of the champion (so Gunkel interprets the epithet *nazir* in verse 26)[3] of its brother tribes against the attacks of the 'archers'. The period to which the oracle refers is most probably the early settlement in the time of the Judges, when the newly settled tribes were constantly harried by the raids of the nomadic peoples always hovering on the border of the fertile lands. In the struggle Joseph is said to be strengthened:

> By the hands of the Bull of Jacob,
> By the name of the Stone of Israel,

a translation which restores what was probably the original

---

[1] Paper read at the Summer Meeting of the Society for Old Testament Studies, Cambridge, 1953.
[2] *Die Israeliten und ihre Nachbarstämme*, p. 282.   [3] *Genesis*, p. 487.

pointing of *'abir* and *shām*, and omits as an explanatory gloss the 'shepherd' of the M.T.

In later prophetic usage these two epithets are frequently applied to Jahveh, although it is the word 'Rock' that is commonly used, poetic parallelism showing that 'rock' and 'stone' are interchangeable. But it is possible that at this early stage of Hebrew religion the expression was not merely a metaphor, but, as Eduard Meyer says, 'can hardly be other than the sacred Stone of Bethel'.[4] The term could also be applied to the gods of other nations; 'their rock is not as our Rock' (Deut. 32.31, 37); also of Assyria, 'his rock shall pass away by reason of terror' (Isa. 31.9). Whether Meyer's suggestion is correct or not, the context shows that strength and reliability are the divine qualities symbolized by 'stone' or 'rock' as epithets of Jahveh.

Next in chronological order come the two closely connected passages from Isa. 8.14, and 28.16. The historical setting of the first text is clear. It belongs to the troubled period in 735-4 B.C., when Tiglath-pileser III was threatening Palestine, and the northern confederation, headed by Damascus and Israel, were trying to force Ahaz, who was Assyria's vassal, to join the confederation. The prophet had already, in Chapter 7, warned Ahaz against panic, and given him the highly ambiguous sign of Immanuel; here, in the same crisis, he warns his own disciples not to be disturbed by the prevailing state of alarm: 'Do not fear what they fear, nor be in dread; but let Jahveh be the holy object of your fear, and the object of your dread'; then follows our passage which is rendered by the Revisers: 'And he shall be for a sanctuary; but for a stone of stumbling and for a rock of offence to both the houses of Israel, for a gin and a snare to the inhabitants of Jerusalem'. The first difficulty arises over the words וְהָיָה לְמִקְדָּשׁ *wehāyah lemiqdāš*, and both the LXX and the Targ. Onk. show indications of uncertainty in their readings. The LXX rendering of verse 14 is: καὶ ἐὰν ἐπ᾽ αὐτῷ πεποιθὼς ᾖς, ἔσται σοι εἰς ἁγίασμα, καὶ οὐχ ὡς λίθου προσκόμματι συναντήσεσθε αὐτῷ οὐδὲ ὡς πέτρας πτώματι: 'And if thou hast put thy trust in him,

---

[4] *Op. cit.*, pp. 283-4.

he will be to thee as a sanctuary, and you (pl.) will not meet (him) as the stumbling-block of the stone nor as the falling (on account) of the rock.' The Targ. Jon. reads: 'And if ye will not hearken, his Memra shall be amongst you for vengeance and for a stone of smiting, and for a rock of offence to the two houses of the princes of Israel.'

Both the LXX and the Targum suggest the possibility that the protasis of a conditional clause has fallen out before $w^e h\bar{a}yah$, but the LXX reading ἁγίασμα would point to the M.T. reading $l^e miqd\bar{a}\check{s}$, while the Targum seems to have read $l^e moqe\check{s}$ or some other form.

This uncertainty concerning the original form of the oracle makes it difficult to be certain of the prophet's original meaning. Verse 11 shows that the oracle was uttered under extreme pressure of spirit. The prophet felt 'the grasp of Jahveh's hand' upon him. He felt compelled to dissociate himself and his disciples completely from the 'way of this people' which was leading them to disaster, described in verse 11 as 'stumbling', 'falling', 'being broken', 'snared' and 'taken'. In the companion passage in 28.13 the prophet's message, 'the word of Jahveh', causes the same people 'to go', i.e. to continue on their course of rebellion, and consequently to 'stumble backward', 'to be broken, snared, and taken'.

In an earlier oracle relating to the same crisis, the prophet had said to the king and people, 'If ye will not believe, surely ye shall not be established'. For the prophet the 'Word' of Jahveh was a living and powerful thing; once it had gone forth from Jahveh's mouth it could not return to him void. To the believer it imparted its own character of rock-like stedfastness, it established him; the same thought recurs in 28.16, הַמַּאֲמִין לֹא יָחִישׁ, the believer remains firm as a rock. But the 'Word' has another face for the unbeliever; as he pursues his course of opposition to Jahveh's word by the mouth of his prophet he discovers its rock-like quality, its abiding reality; he cannot evade it, and stumbles upon it, falls, and is shattered. Hence, whether we assume a missing protasis or not, and whether we read $miqd\bar{a}\check{s}$ or $m\bar{o}qe\check{s}$, it seems clear that the subject of *weháyah* is, as the Targum has rightly seen, the all-potent 'Word' of Jahveh. Before passing on to the third passage in Isa. 28.16 it may be remarked that the two New Testament citations of Isa. 8.14 in Rom. 9.33 I Pet. 2.8, are not taken from the LXX, but agree in substituting σκανδάλου for the LXX reading πτώματι. Rendel Harris is probably right in suggesting that the Old Testament passages concerning the Stone, so often quoted in the New Testament and in early Christian writings, are not taken from the LXX, but from a Testimony Book in a translation which often corrects the LXX rendering.[5]

The opening verses of Isa. 28 show that at least part of the oracles comprising that chapter may have been uttered before the fall of Samaria, and it is possible that oracles originally referring to the northern kingdom may have been recast later and applied to Judah in the critical years between 705 and 701. The later situation was similar to that in the time of Ahaz but graver. The attitude of the religious leaders also seems to have been similar. The address to the 'scornful men, that rule this people which is in Jerusalem' would suggest that Hezekiah's piety was not able to bring about in Judah the faith in Jahveh and acceptance of his purpose which the prophet never ceased to urge. It is also possible that the allusion to the practice of necromancy in 8.19 may explain the 'covenant with death' and the 'agreement with Sheol' denounced by Isaiah in 28.14. If we may assign the oracles in 10.5-34 to this crisis, it is apparent that the prophet was expecting the consummation, 'the end', Jahveh's *kālah*, as the final issue of this crisis, and the fixed point of his hope lay in the 'turning' of the remnant. The fulfilment of Jahveh's purpose and the future of Zion lay in the remnant, consisting no doubt of Isaiah's disciples and those whom he calls 'the meek', who believed the prophet's word and were waiting for Jahveh to act. This is the context in which we must set the oracle in 28.16. In a scene which is about to be devastated by the Assyrian flood, and where the hail of Jahveh's wrath is about to sweep away the refuge of lies, some resting-place must be

[5] *Testimonies* I, p. 28.

found for faith, and this, the prophet declares, Jahveh will provide. The M.T. of verse 16 runs:

הִנְנִי יִסַּד בְּצִיּוֹן אָבֶן אֶבֶן בֹּחַן

⁶פִּנַּת יִקְרַת מוּסָד מוּסָד הַמַּאֲמִין לֹא יָחִישׁ׃

The LXX rendering of this is: ἰδοὺ ἐγὼ ἐμβάλλω εἰς τὰ θεμέλια Σειὼν λίθον πολυτελῆ ἐκλεκτὸν ἀκρογωνιαῖον ἔντιμον, εἰς τὰ θεμέλια αὐτῆς, καὶ ὁ πιστεύων οὐ μὴ καταισχυνθῇ.

The version given in I Pet. 2.6 varies considerably from the LXX, and probably comes from a Testimony Book. It runs: ἰδοὺ τίθημι ἐν Σιὼν λίθον ἀκρογωνιαῖον, ἐκλεκτόν, ἔντιμον· καὶ ὁ πιστεύων ἐπ᾽ αὐτῷ οὐ μὴ καταισχυνθῇ.

Finally the Targum of Jonathan has: הָאֲנָא מְמַנֵּי בְּצִיּוֹן מֶלֶךְ מֶלֶךְ תַּקִּיף גִּיבַּר וְאֵימְתָן אַתְקְפִנֵּיהּ וְאַחְסְנִינֵּיהּ אָמַר נְבִיָּא וְצַדִּיקַיָּא דְּהֵימִנוּ בְּאִלֵּין בְּמֵיתֵי עָקָא לָא יִזְדַּעְזְעוּן׃

The rendering of the Targum runs: 'Behold, I will appoint in Zion a king, a strong king, saith the prophet, but the righteous who have believed in these things shall not be dismayed when distress cometh' (Stenning, *The Targum of Isaiah*, p. 88).

Considering first the details of the M.T., the perfect Pi'el of *yāsad* with *hineni* is very awkward, and we should probably read *yōsēd*, or with the Dead Sea Scroll of Isaiah, *meyassēd*, 'I am placing' or 'fixing'. The Targ. J. evidently had the duplicated *'eben*, as against the LXX, and the New Testament, but paraphrased it as 'king', with Messianic significance. The root meaning of *yāsad* seems to be 'to make firm', 'to fix', and the connexion with 'founding' or 'foundation' is secondary. The LXX emphasizes the latter idea, but the New Testament rendering does not, while the Targum paraphrase avoids the architectural association altogether. The next point is the meaning of *bōḥēn*.

The meaning of the root presents no difficulty: it is 'to try' or 'test'; but the question is whether the form is active or

---

⁶ For a recent discussion of this text see J. Lindblom, 'Der Eckstein in Jes. 28.16' in the Mowinckel *Festshrift* (Oslo, 1955).

passive. The same form occurs in the very difficult verse—
Ezek. 21.13 (18), where *BDB* gives it as third person sin-
gular Pu'al perfect and renders 'the trial has been made'; but the
same authority gives the form in Isa. 28.16 as a noun, only
found here, and renders it as 'testing', although it goes on to
render *'eben bōḥēn* as 'a tested, tried stone, i.e. approved for
use as a foundation-stone'. It is quite permissible to understand 'stone of testing' as meaning a stone which has survived the process of testing, and not necessarily as meaning a
stone which is used for the purpose of testing; this would
justify the rendering of *BDB*. Here reference may be made to
an interpretation of *'eben bōḥēn* which has been put forward in
The Quarterly Statement of the Palestine Exploration Fund,
1946. In an article entitled 'Was the Corner-Stone of Scripture a Pyramidion?', the author, Mr E. E. LeBas, taking
bōḥēn as active, maintained that the prophet had in mind a
pyramidal apex-stone used to test the accuracy of a pyramid
or pyramidion by applying it to the summit of such a building.
In two subsequent articles he went on to connect Isa. 28.16
with Zech. 3.9, 4.7 and 9; and Ps. 118.22, taking Isaiah's
stone in a Messianic sense. This Messianic testing-stone was
rejected by the builders, i.e. Israel, because it revealed the
imperfection of their building, but it was hidden by Jahveh
in the foundations of Zion, and was destined to be brought out
of its hiding-place and placed on the summit of Jahveh's new
building as the 'head of the Corner'.

With regard to this theory the following remarks may be
made. First, as to the point that all three passages refer to the
same stone, and present its history in dramatic symbolism,
it seems necessary to say that such an interpretation depends
on the New Testament reference of all the Old Testament
passages now under discussion to Christ, and it is doubtful,
to say the least, whether the passages will bear such an interpretation for the circumstances under which they were
uttered. The original meaning of each passage can only be
determined in relation to its historical setting. Second, it is
equally doubtful whether, in any of our passages, the shape
and architectural function of the stone were predominant in

the prophet's mind as he uttered his message. It is not to be denied that in the New Testament interpretation of these favourite passages an architectural reference is to be found, especially in the Petrine quotation, where the building of a spiritual temple is in the author's mind; nor is it absent from the Synoptic use of the passage from Ps. 118, as quoted by Jesus. But the historical setting of the passage which we are now considering does not seem to favour the view that the prophet had a somewhat elaborate piece of architectural symbolism in mind. Third, the suggestion that the stone had the shape of a pyramidion would seem to require a pyramid or obelisk as its architectural complement, in order that its function as a testing implement might come into play, and even if it were admitted that some kind of divine building operation might have been in the prophet's mind, it is improbable that it would have taken the form of a pyramid.

Returning, then, to the question of what kind of divine action was envisaged by Isaiah in this enigmatic oracle, it is clear that he believed that, in the eschatological crisis indicated by the word *kālah*, 'consummation' (verse 22), when the whole established order was threatened by destruction, Jahveh was providing in Zion a refuge and sure support for faith, symbolized by the Stone. It seems that the quality of the stone which is uppermost in the prophet's mind is neither its use for building, nor its function of testing, but that which is characteristic of Jahveh himself as the Rock of Israel, namely, stedfastness and immutability. Jahveh is placing in Zion something that will survive the coming judgment, the fiery ordeal, something upon which the fulfilment of his purpose depends. I should like to suggest that Isaiah here expresses in vivid symbolism his belief that Jahveh intends to bring out from the fires of purgation and establish in Zion a godly and righteous remnant to be the basis and nucleus of the restored order and the coming kingdom of Jahveh. It is interesting to observe that Zephaniah, speaking some three-quarters of a century later, and using the same range of ideas as his great predecessor, says to Zion, 'I will leave in the midst of thee an afflicted and poor people, and they shall trust

in the name of the Lord. The remnant of Israel shall not do
iniquity, nor speak lies; neither shall a deceitful tongue be
found in their mouth, for they shall feed and lie down, and
none shall make them afraid' (Zeph. 3.13-14).

Taking the epithets used in the description of the stone in
their order: first, *bōḥēn*, 'testing'. The context seems rather
to require the meaning of something that has been tested or
will be tested by the coming of Jahveh in judgment; it will
surely survive that fiery test. There is a sense in which the
stone will be a testing stone, and that was given in Isa. 8.14;
it was to be the cause of stumbling and disaster to those who
pursued their own rebellious way in defiance of Jahveh; but
here the testing is not carried out by the stone, but, as indicated in verse 17, by the measuring-line of *mishpāṭ* and the
plummet of *ṣedāqah*. Next we have *pinnath yiqrath* in the con-
struct state dependent on *mūsād*. The root of *pinnah* is possibly
a strengthened form of *pānah*, and the root meaning of *pānah*
is 'turning'. While its architectural use as the corner of the
building is common, yet it has other uses, and where it is
used of persons, I would suggest that it has the sense of
'pivotal', a central point round which things or events turn.
An example of its use which, I think, throws light on its use
here is found in Zech. 10.4, 'From him goes forth the corner,
from him the tent-peg'. Here comparison with Isa. 22, where
yāthēd is used as a symbol of something sure and fixed, and
applied to a person, suggests that the *pinnah* and the *yāthēd*
provided by Jahveh symbolize fixed rallying-centres for the
restored community. Hence it may be permitted to interpret
pinnah in Isa. 18.16 in a similar sense. For the adjective
yiqrath attached to *pinnah* we may compare Isa. 43.4, where
Jahveh tells ransomed Israel, chosen (or perhaps 'tested') in
the furnace of affliction, that she is 'precious' (*yaqarta*) in his
sight. Similarly, in Mal. 3.17 the same godly remnant is
declared by Jahveh to be his *segullah*, his most valued possession. Lastly, with regard to *mūsād*, it is the primary meaning
of *yāsad* which is uppermost in the prophet's mind, namely,
that which is fixed and firm. The stone is to be, or is being,
placed by Jahveh as the precious centre of the securely-founded

redeemed community which will emerge from the eschatological tribulations of the consummation envisaged by the
prophet. Hence, while the idea of building is not absent from
the symbols used by the prophet, it is not uppermost in his
mind, and he would probably have regarded the shape and
position of the stone as irrelevant details.

In selecting the next passage for discussion, it is not easy
to determine the relative dates of Ps. 118 and the early
visions of Zechariah. The latter can be dated with comparative
certainty between 520-16 B.C., but the psalm is not so easy to
date. It is almost certainly post-exilic, and the fully developed
liturgical order of processions, antiphonal choirs, and sacrifices, which it presupposes, suggest, as Professor Oesterley
holds, a late post-exilic date. Hence we shall take the Zechariah passages first. They are 3.9 and 4.7 and 10.

The English Revisers' rendering of the passages runs: 3.9,
'For behold the stone that I have set before Joshua; upon one
stone are seven eyes: behold, I will engrave the graving
thereof, saith the Lord of hosts, and I will remove the iniquity
of that land in one day'. 4.7, 'Who art thou, O great mountain? before Zerubbabel thou shalt become a plain: and he
shall bring forth the head stone with shoutings of Grace,
grace, unto it'. 4.10, 'For who hath despised the day of small
things? for they shall rejoice, and shall see the plummet
(*'eben habdīl*) in the hand of Zerubbabel'.

The most notable LXX variant in 3.9 is ἰδοὺ ἐγὼ ὀρύσσω
βόθρου which is its rendering of the puzzling הִנְנִי מְפַתֵּחַ
פִּתֻּחָהּ. In 4.7 the LXX has: καὶ ἐξοίσω τὸν λίθον τῆς
κληρονομίας ἰσότητα χάριτος χάριτα αὐτῆς. The verse has evidently proved too much for them; it can only be rendered, I
suppose, as, 'And I will bring out the stone of the inheritance
(with) equality of grace as its grace.' In verse 10 the LXX
has rendered *'eben habdīl* by τὸν λίθον τὸν κασσιτέρινον. The
adjective only occurs here, and the noun κασσίτερος occurs in
three passages for 'tin' as the rendering of *bᵉdīl*. But the word
for 'plummet' elsewhere, as in Amos 7.7 is *'anākh*, and the
translation 'plummet' here is very dubious. But before we
deal with the difficulties of these passages, and attempt to

arrive at their meaning, something must be said about the general historical setting of the series of visions in which they are found. The situation is the same as that described in Haggai. Both prophets were seeking to rekindle the first enthusiasm of the returned exiles, and to induce them to resume work on the rebuilding of the Temple. The revolts which broke out during the early years of Darius raised Messianic hopes among the returned exiles, and in the oracles of both prophets Zerubbabel is clearly the centre of these hopes. To this background the interpretation of the symbolic stone in the visions of Zechariah must be related. The passage in 3.8-10 in which the stone is introduced contains a series of statements whose bearing on the meaning of the stone will have to be considered:

(*a*) Joshua the high-priest and his companions are declared by Jahveh to be 'men of portent' (*'anshē mōphēth*). It may be recalled that Isaiah, in an earlier crisis, had claimed that he and his children were appointed by Jahveh to be signs and portents for Israel, implying that their names and the things done to them or by them were symbolic indications of what Jahveh intended to do. So here, the prophet declares that Joshua and his companions are set in a similar position for the present crisis. The first portent is shown in the preceding vision. Joshua is seen defiled, standing before Jahveh, and confronted by the Satan. Jahveh rebukes the accuser, causes Joshua to be cleansed and restored, and declares that he, as the representative of Jerusalem, is a brand saved from the fire. What has happened to Joshua is a portent of what Jahveh will do for Israel.

(*b*) Jahveh then declares that he is about to bring in (*mēbī'*) his servant *ṣemaḥ*. The anarthrous state of the term 'Branch' or 'Shoot' suggests that it had now become a prophetic commonplace, an appellative like *māshiaḥ*. The previous use of the term in Isa. 11 and Jer. 23 shows that it was associated with the restoration of the Davidic kingdom in the person of a Messianic figure.

(*c*) The stone is then placed (*nāthati*) by Jahveh before Joshua, and his attention is directed to a certain feature of the stone. Literally translated the Hebrew would seem to mean: 'Upon one stone (are) seven eyes.' A whole library has been written about this enigmatic phrase, and I have no intention of discussing all the possible interpretations that have been put forward, but would only offer the following tentative suggestions arising from the context of this and the following visions. I would also suggest that the prophet's mind is moving in the frame of the symbolic tradition of his prophetic predecessors. He is setting forth in symbolic form his belief that Jahveh is now about to establish a new order, with a purified priesthood, a pure worship, a people cleansed from iniquity and emerging from the fires of purgation, under the leadership of a Messianic king, a shoot from David's line, in the person of Zerubbabel. The stone, still retaining its significance of the fixed and immutable character of Jahveh, has now become a Messianic symbol, the prophet's mind having switched from the 'shoot' (*ṣemaḥ*) to the 'stone'. Hence, if we may take the stone as a symbol of Messiah, then, in keeping with the symbolism of the vision as interpreted by the angelic messenger, the seven eyes should surely be the seven spirits of Jahveh, already connected with the figure of the Messianic king in Isa. 11. The seven spirits rest upon (*'al*), or are in attendance upon, the stone as a symbol of the Messiah. The suggestion of some commentators that *'aynayim* may be 'springs' or 'fountains', is attractive in view of the subsequent reference to the cleansing from sin, but with this meaning the word has always a feminine plural, which puts this suggestion out of the question.

(*d*) Then comes the announcement of another divine action הִנְנִי מְפַתֵּחַ פִּתֻּחָהּ 'I will open its (i.e. the stone's) opening.' The primary meaning of *pāthaḥ* is 'to open', and the Pi'el form frequently found with the meaning 'to engrave' is only a secondary form of *pāthaḥ*. Most translators and commentators prefer the meaning 'to engrave' here. Goodspeed's American version renders the verse: 'Upon a single stone with seven facets I will engrave its inscription.' Mr Le Bas, following the LXX rendering, ἰδοὺ ἐγὼ ὀρύσσω βόθρον, 'I will dig a pit', finds in the verse, to quote his own words,

'God's intention to tunnel a channel to the cache in the heart of Mount Zion in which this corner-stone lies buried'. I would rather suggest a connexion with (*niphtāḥ*) the saying in Zech. 13.1, 'And in that day a fountain shall be opened for the house of David and for the inhabitants of Jerusalem for sin and for uncleanness.' One of the characteristic features of the later development of Jewish eschatological symbolism was the idea of a purifying stream or fountain flowing out from the Temple and cleansing the land from defilement. The declaration which follows the opening of the stone says, 'I will remove the iniquity of that *land* in one day'. Hence, though we may not take *'aynayim* to mean 'fountains' or 'springs', it may be permissible to think of Jahveh's opening of the stone as the source of the fountain in 13.1, which was to remove sin an uncleanness. This would explain the puzzling connexion of the removal of guilt with what Jahveh does to the stone.

So much for the first Zechariah passage. I cannot find any suggestion there of the architectural significance of the stone. But this is not so with the second passage, 4.6-10. The R.V. rendering runs: 'This is the word of the Lord unto Zerubbabel, saying, not by an army (mg.), nor by power, but by my spirit, saith the Lord of hosts. Who art thou, O great mountain? before Zerubbabel (thou shalt become) a plain: and he shall bring forth the head-stone with shoutings of Grace, grace, unto it. Moreover the word of the Lord came unto me, saying, The hands of Zerubbabel have laid the foundation of this house; his hands shall also finish it; and thou shalt know that the Lord of hosts hath sent me unto you. For who hath despised the day of small things? for they shall rejoice, and shall see the plummet in the hands of Zerubbabel.' Here, in an address to Zerubbabel, the prophet's horizon is still that of eschatological expectation. Jahveh's purpose will not be accomplished by armed force, but by his mighty spirit. The great mountain of Persian power will be levelled before his chosen instrument, and the head-stone will be brought out with shouts of triumph. Zerubbabel is assured that since it was he who laid the foundations of the Temple, it is he who

will be privileged to finish it, as the vindication of the prophet's mission. Two questions arise here: first, what is meant
by *hā'eben hār'ōshah*, and second, is this *'eben hār'ōshah* the
same stone as that which was placed before Joshua in 3.9?
The promise to Zerubbabel which immediately follows the
bringing out of the stone suggests that the stone is to complete the building of the Temple. It is clearly the topmost
stone of the building. But nothing suggests that it was a
corner-stone, nor do the versions so designate it. The LXX
κληρονομίας evidently arises from a confusion with a deriva-
tive of *yārash*, and the odd blunder ἰσότητα is due to a similar
confusion between *shāvah* and *shū'a*. The significance of the
stone lies, not in its shape, but in its position as the crown of
the edifice. With regard to the second question, it is very
doubtful whether the prophet thought of the two stones as
identical. The situation and symbolism of the stone placed
before Joshua, presumably in the heavenly Temple of the
former vision, differ entirely from the scene in which Zerubbabel is envisaged as completing the building of the earthly
Temple in Jerusalem. Belonging to the same situation is the
prediction that those who had doubted whether Jahveh was
able to carry out his purpose, would rejoice when they saw
Zerubbabel standing with a stone which the M.T. describes
as *hā'eben habdīl*, and the LXX as λίθον κασσιτέρινον, 'a tin
stone', while most English versions render it as 'plummet'.
Whatever the stone may be, it is hardly to be identified with
the head-stone, nor is it appropriate to the situation to think
of Zerubbabel with a plumb-line in his hand. It is tempting
to emend *habdīl* to some participial form of *bādal*, 'to divide',
'separate', which would permit the conjecture that Zerubbabel
held a stone possessing some distinguishing quality, a mark
of rank or office, such as a signet. We might then connect it
with Hag. 2.23, where Jahveh promises to make his servant
Zerubbabel, 'in that day', as a signet. But such fancies are
only a confession of ignorance.

We come now to the much quoted passage in Ps. 118.22.
The M.T. is:

אֶבֶן מָאֲסוּ הַבּוֹנִים   הָיְתָה לְרֹאשׁ פִּנָּה:

The LXX has: λίθον ὃν ἀπεδοκίμασαν οἱ οἰκοδομοῦντες, οὗτος ἐγενήθη εἰς κεφαλὴν γωνίας.

The R.V. renders, 'The stone which the builders rejected is become the head of the corner'. The text presents no difficulty, nor does the translation; the only problem concerns the situation in which the words were uttered. It is generally recognized that the psalm is a processional liturgy sung at the Feast of Tabernacles, but its date is hard to determine. It has been placed as late as Maccabaean times, and as early as the Feast of Tabernacles described in Neh. 8.14 ff. Hence it is difficult to assign the allusions it contains to any specific triumph over enemies. Although most of the psalm is in the first person, yet its liturgical character and its antiphonal responses suggest that the leader of the procession is expressing the collective thanksgiving of the worshipping community as it approaches and enters the Temple. If we divest ourselves, as we must, of the New Testament Messianic interpretation of this and other passages relating to the stone, it seems clear that the stone is a symbol of Israel, chastened and humiliated but not delivered over to death, and now exalted by Jahveh to the key position in his purposes. The architectural reference here is unmistakable, and the position indicated by the expression *r'ōsh pinnah* is almost certainly the same as that of the *hā'eben hār'ōshah* in Zech. 4.7, the crown of the building. But nothing suggests the shape of the stone, nor is it probable that the author of this liturgy had the stone of Isa. 28 in mind.

The last two passages may be dealt with briefly. In Zech. 12.3 Jahveh declares that he will make Jerusalem a 'burdensome stone', *'eben m'amōsah* in the day of his intervention on behalf of his people. Here the stone has something of the quality of the 'stone of stumbling' in Isa. 8.14; it becomes an instrument of Jahveh's judgment upon the nations. But there is no Messianic significance here.

The last passage in Dan. 2.34–36 brings us entirely into the realm of apocalyptic. In the king's dream as interpreted by the seer, a stone appears, cut out of a mountain without human agency. It is launched against the proud symbol of earthly empire, utterly destroys it, and itself becomes a great mountain which fills the whole earth. The stone is interpreted by the seer to be the kingdom which the God of heaven is about to set up, which shall never be destroyed. The situation in which the activity of the stone takes place lies on the visionary horizon of apocalyptic, on the twilight verge of history, but it is still not Messianic.

Hence, of all the passages we have examined, only those in Zech. 3 and 4, owing to the special circumstances in which a revival of the Messianic idea had taken place, have a definite Messianic significance. Nor have we found any justification for the view which links up the references to the stone in Ps. 118, Isa. 28, and Zech. 3 and 4 to compose a dramatic history of the fortunes of a Messianic symbol. When we enter the realm of the events in the New Testament and discover the extraordinary transformation of images which centres in Christ, we are in another world altogether, and one which lies beyond the scope of this paper. Here we have only been concerned with the more limited aim of attempting to discover what these various references to the stone meant to those who uttered them in certain definite historical circumstances.

CHAPTER EIGHTEEN

The Mixture of Cults in Canaan[1]

THE heresy of one generation is the orthodoxy of the next. Half a century ago the Graf-Wellhausen theory of the origin of Hebrew religion seemed a daring innovation, and the evolutionary conception of a gradual ascent from a pre-animistic stage through animism, polydæmonism, polytheism, henotheism to a monotheism, which in a pure form never was on sea or land, was a most dangerous and subversive belief.

Now the inevitable onward movement of discovery makes ancient good uncouth. It is no longer possible to think of the Canaan of early Hebrew settlement as inhabited by barbarous tribes in the backward stages of animism. Everybody knows to-day that Canaan in the time of Abraham, was, like the place where Paul's ship ran aground, the meeting-place of the great waters of the nations of the ancient East. It was permeated by the cultures of Egypt, Babylon, the Ægean, and the Hittites. It was full of small city-states such as the early history of Sumer has familiarized us with. The tangled history of the relations between Canaan and her more powerful neighbours during the pre-Israelite period is gradually falling into order as fresh material from Hittite sources comes to light.[2] Excavation in Canaan, which had lagged behind and been thrown into the shade by the brilliant results of discovery in Egypt and Mesopotamia, has lately yielded results of the most startling nature. We are now waiting to see what fresh and surprising material may be revealed by Virolleaud's translation of the new documents from Ras Shamra.

Nothing has been more striking than the emergence of the picture of the strange mixture of cults in Canaan in the period

[1] Paper read to the Oriental Society of the University of Manchester, 1931. First published in *The Journal of the Manchester Egyptian and Oriental Society*.

[2] See P. Dhorme, 'Les Amorrhéens', in *La Revue Biblique*, 1929-30.

conveniently called the Tell el-Amarna period. Years ago, in his great book *Adonis und Eshmun*, Baudissin made a statement about the religion of Canaan which the subsequent progress of discovery has abundantly confirmed: 'It is not possible to speak of a religion of the West-Semites as an independent and homogeneous thing, since the Aramaic peoples who are comprised under this designation show in their religion as far back as we can trace them not only the influence of the Babylonians . . . but also an almost complete identity with the Babylonian conceptions about the gods, a fact which goes to prove how much the Aramæans borrowed from the Babylonians, and how much the latter borrowed from the former.'[3] To this we now have to add extensive borrowings from Egypt, from the Ægean, and from Hittite sources.

But it is not the object of this paper to prove what is already generally recognized, nor to describe the results of recent discoveries. It has the more limited purpose of directing attention to the relation between the general religious pattern disclosed by these discoveries and certain features of Hebrew religion. In a previous paper I discussed the central religious pattern of Babylonian religion, a pattern which can be traced from the earliest period of Sumerian religion. It takes the form of a dramatic ritual, an annual ritual, as far as Akkadian religious practices are concerned, in which the central part is played by the king-god whose death, resurrection and sacred marriage re-enacted at each New Year Festival, form the outline of the pattern. The way in which this central ritual serves as a pattern and source for all kinds of less important rituals is illustrated by the recurrence of the Enuma Elish as an incantation in rites of exorcism, restoration of sacred buildings and even in the curing of a toothache.[4]

That a similar pattern existed in Egypt from the earliest times needs no proof, but I might refer in passing to the recently edited Ramesseum Papyrus which contains a large fragment of a coronation ritual of the twelfth dynasty, but whose contents in the judgment of its learned editor, K. Sethe, go back to the Old Kingdom. This ritual consists of a series

[3] *Op. cit.*, p. 2.   [4] See *J.M.E.O.S.*, XIII, 1927, pp. 29-38.

of scenes in which the principal episodes of the Osiris myth are enacted at the coronation of the new king. The dead king is Osiris; his son and successor takes the part of Horus, who conquers Set and restores his scattered limbs to Osiris. In one interesting scene two carpenters appear and make the ladder by which Osiris ascends to heaven. The extent to which this ritual pattern coloured the whole of Egyptian life is too well known to need description.

Hence, when we find from every fresh discovery in Palestine fresh proofs of the way in which Egyptian and Babylonian religious and cultural features mingle in the strangest medley, we are justified in assuming that in one form or another the central pattern of which we have spoken must have been familiar to the inhabitants of Canaan in the Tell el-Amarna period. In a series of ritual fragments from Ras Shamra, deciphered and translated by Père Dhorme,[5] one ritual included the introduction of Horus by Astarte into the royal palace. The Gezer material is of course well known by now, but Macalister's words may be quoted in passing: 'Relics of Egyptian influence came to light almost daily in the course of the excavations. Traces of the domination of Egypt in the fields of politics, art, trade and religion were found in every stratum of the first Semitic, wherever a pit was dug.'[6]

In the same chapter we have a list of 397 scarabs from the twelfth dynasty and Hyksos period down to Roman and Byzantine times. Illustrating the presence of Egyptian religious ideas and ritual is an interesting fragment of a funerary statue with an inscription whose translation by Dr F. Ll. Griffith runs as follows: 'May the king give an offering to Osiris, the living lord; he gives sepulchral feasts, clothing, divine incense wax . . . to the citizen Dudu-Amen, son of . . . having been made for him by his beloved brother. He gives sepulchral feasts, an offering, divine food, to the double of the Dudu-Amen.'[7]

Turning now to an aspect of the subject which may seem at first sight to be somewhat irrelevant, but whose relevance

[5] *Revue Biblique*, Jan. 1931.
[6] *The Excavation of Gezer*, vol. II, ch. 8, p. 307.   [7] Ibid., p. 313.

will appear later, I should like to draw attention to a study of ancient oriental law by Dr Jirku, entitled *Das Weltliche Recht im Alten Testament*. Starting from the observation of the fact that the Code of Hammurabi, the ancient Assyrian laws, and the fragments of Sumerian law-books extant, all present the feature of a uniform introductory formula, with which each law begins, he examines the Hebrew codes in the light of this fact.

As a result of this examination he finds that the body of Hebrew law preserved in the Pentateuch falls into ten classes, each characterized by a different introductory formula. Dr Jirku goes on to draw the conclusion that behind the various editorial stages into which the Pentateuch has been divided on literary-historical grounds, there lie older collections of laws, each characterized by a distinctive introductory formula. Hence the problem of dating the legal material of the Pentateuch can no longer be decided on the ground of whether a particular law happens to be found in one or other of the accepted divisions J, E, D, or P, but is thrown back on an analysis of the nature and contents of these older collections. One of the most striking results of this analysis and the comparison of the Hebrew material with the parallels in the code of Hammurabi and the old Assyrian laws, is the discovery that the Israelite laws in every case represent the earlier stage of development.

This is particularly noticeable in the case of the group of laws which Jirku calls '*d. religiöse Staatsrecht*', dealing with such aspects of religion as affect the life of the State. It is outside the purpose of this paper to criticize the very interesting suggestions of Dr Jirku's book. The point which I wish to draw attention to is that these findings throw the general picture of Hebrew religious organization back into a much earlier stage of settled life in Canaan than the orthodox Wellhausen view of the nomadic origin of Hebrew religion allows.

Hence, we find so far that several currently accepted positions come up for revision in the light of fresh advances in our knowledge. In the first place, we have an entirely different picture of the cultural conditions of Canaan in the period of Israelite settlement. Whatever movements of Semitic people may be represented by the biblical stories of the patriarchs, the results of Palestinian excavation give us a picture of cultural and religious conditions of which the biblical narratives give hardly the faintest hint. Moreover, the orthodox evolutionary view of the development of Hebrew religion, based mainly on the theory that the religious customs of the pagan Arabs, so brilliantly described by Robertson Smith, represent a primitive stage of religious development, fails to solve the new problems raised by the advance of discovery in Palestine. It is becoming increasingly clear that in the study of Hebrew religion we have to deal with processes of culture mixture and degradation, rather than with a process of evolution. The Arab religious customs, the sacred nature of stones, trees, wells, mountains, the sacred communal meal, must be regarded rather as the *membra disjecta*, the relics of a pattern with which the nomad peoples were once in contact but have now lost.

A further change of orientation appears in the matter of the literary criticism of the Pentateuch. It is clear that we shall be obliged to go behind the sources into which the critical studies of the last generation of scholars have divided the Hebrew codes.

Lastly, the attention which has recently been focussed on the importance of ritual in the ancient civilizations of the Near East has made it clear that the prevailing ritual pattern must have had a larger place in Hebrew religion than has been hitherto supposed. This brings us to the main point of this paper.

In the '*religiöse Staatsrecht*' of which Dr Jirku speaks, there occurs a group of prohibitions to which some may be added from the body of ritual enactments which he has left out of consideration. These prohibitions appear to deal with very diverse subjects, but on closer examination a common element is observable. They are the prohibition to make steps up to the altar, to seethe a kid in its mother's milk, to use leaven or honey in the sacrifices; the prohibition of necromancy, of various forms of incest, of ritual prostitution, and of the interchange of apparel between the sexes.

The reason given in the Code of the Covenant for the

prohibition of steps up to the altar is clearly a later rationalizing one, much as the reasons assigned for other ritual precepts or prohibitions. In a series of valuable studies by Miss M. Levin on the Brahman ritual of Prajapati, recently published in *Man*, the place of the altar in early ritual is apparent. The fire-altar represents the sky-world, the place where the making of the king into a god is consummated. The altar-steps, like the ladder of the coronation ritual in the Ramesseum Papyrus, are the means of ascent to heaven, to the sky-world. Hence I would suggest that the real underlying reason for the prohibition is the knowledge, lost perhaps later, that the steps of the altar were connected with the ritual of the deification of a king. We can see in Ezekiel's famous description of the king-god of Tyre the attitude of the later Hebrew religious legislators towards the central idea of the religious pattern of the ancient East, the idea of the king-god.

The next prohibition, that crux of commentators, 'Thou shalt not seethe a kid in its mother's milk', is connected by its introductory formula with Jirku's *'Du sollst'* group in which most of these prohibitions occur. The various attempts at an explanation from an anthropological standpoint are generally felt to be unsatisfactory. I am indebted to an article by Dr Max Radin in the *American Journal of Semitic Languages*, Vol. XL, for an interesting suggestion which connects the prohibition with an early Orphic ritual text. In this the neophyte says: 'I a kid have fallen into my mother's milk.' The context shows that some kind of initiatory rite is in question. The general pattern of the later mystery rites is well known. They all exhibit the central idea of the dying and rising god, with whom the initiate is identified by sacramental rites. The Orphic and Dionysiac rites, with their dismemberment myth, to say nothing of other elements, go back clearly to the original Osirian myth and ritual. Hence, the most probable solution of this extremely perplexing prohibition is that it represents some early Canaanite ritual element whose connexion with the deification ceremonies against which we can trace a growing protest in Hebrew religious legislation was well known to the author of this prohibition.

We know that honey was very early discovered to possess preservative properties and was used in embalming. It is a constant element in the offerings prescribed in Babylonian ritual texts. The peculiar properties of leaven may have led to its being regarded like blood as a life-giver, and so to its ritual taboo.

The ancient name *elohim*, given to the spirits of the dead who were consulted by necromancers, leads us back along the same line to that original underlying pattern of ritual which made dead people into gods. The long persistence of the practice of 'seeking to the dead' among the Hebrew people shows how deeply it was rooted in early ritual.

The question of the origin of incest prohibitions is too intricate a subject to deal with here, but it will suffice to point out that the trail leads in the same direction. It is well known that the early Egyptian ruling houses practised incest as a consequence of their beliefs concerning the divine nature of the kingship. Incestuous unions were therefore a part of that general pattern of which we have spoken.

Ritual prostitution, again, was a practice arising out of the vitally important element of the sacred marriage, a rite which generally formed the consummation of such a ritual complex as the Babylonian New Year Festival, a rite upon which the prosperity and fertility of the state depended, and one which had grim associations with the rite of human sacrifice. Mr Sidney Smith's valuable and learned paper in the *Journal of the Royal Asiatic Society*,[8] on the meaning and use of the Babylonian *gigunu*, with the light which it throws on the recent discoveries at Ur, may be referred to in this connexion.

This list of examples might be considerably enlarged, but I think it is clear that behind these widely differing prohibitions the presence of that ritual pattern already described is evident. Hence at the beginning of the growth of Hebrew religion we have to deal with two factors. One is the presence of this pervading type of religious belief and practice in Canaan at the time of the Israelite settlement; the other is the rise, earlier than the age of Moses, of an attitude of opposition

[8] *J.R.A.S.*, 1928.

to the central idea of the divinity of the kingship. In the Hebrew Psalter occur several passages which contain the conception of the divine sonship of the king. These passages, together with those elements in the Psalter upon which Mowinckel has based his theory of an annual New Year feast in which Jahveh's enthronement was celebrated, point to a period in the development of Hebrew religion when the conception of a divine king and the ritual elements which accompany it were dominant. The transference of the idea to the Messianic king is, so to speak, the sublimation of these older elements which were too deeply rooted in the ancient soil to be entirely obliterated. But the recognition of the influence of the strange mixture of culture in Canaan upon Hebrew religion in its formative stages also raises in a new form the problem of the source of the protest against this influence. For the poet the traffic of Jacob's ladder may still shine between heaven and Charing Cross, but for the student of the history of civilization Jacob's ladder points to a time when the strange traffic between men and gods, embodied in the old ritual practices of which we have spoken, was still familiar to the ancestors of the Hebrew people.[9]

[9] Note: This paper represents a very early stage of the 'myth and ritual pattern' thesis, and by no means represents the author's present position.

CHAPTER NINETEEN

What is Christianity?[1]

CHRISTIANITY may be regarded as a movement which has appeared in the course of human history, upon which it has exercised a profound influence; but any account of it which is based merely upon its historical character must fail to represent its true significance. Gibbon's famous description of Christianity during the early centuries of its development is an example of how completely a historian of the greatest eminence, dealing with Christianity purely as a historical phenomenon, may remain blind to its essential nature.

The name by which this religious movement has come to be known is not to be found in the New Testament. Its earliest adherents would have described themselves as Jews. Paul, in his defence before the Roman governor Felix, is represented as affirming 'that after the Way which they call a sect, so serve I the God of our Fathers, believing all things which are according to the law, and which are written in the prophets' (Acts 24.14). We are also told, in the same historical work, that it was in Syrian Antioch that the followers of this new Way received the gibing name of *Christians* (Acts 11.26). But the gibe tells us what its authors saw in the people whom they thus contemptuously designated; they saw that the followers of the new Way were, as they would say, 'possessed' by a person who bore the strange and apparently meaningless name of Christ. The early confusion between 'Christos' and 'Chrestos' shows how unintelligible to Greco-Roman ears was this name, so full of meaning to both Jews and those who were of the Way. Paul sums up the matter with his characteristic vividness in the words, 'we preach a crucified Christ, to the Jews an offence, and to the Gentiles folly, but to those who are called, both Jews and

---

[1] First published by the Modern Churchmen's Union in 'Modern Statements of Christian Belief' Series, 1948.

Greeks, a Christ who is God's power and God's wisdom'.

Christianity as a continuing movement has a history, as a religion it has a body of beliefs, as an institution it has a ritual pattern, but its history, its beliefs, and its ritual, all spring from the central fact of Christ, Jesus of Nazareth, Messiah and Son of God, Risen Lord of the Church.

Those who looked back on the course of events wrote the history to the best of their ability, and it still rolls on to its appointed end; those who tried to interpret the meaning of Christ and the living movement that streamed from him, shaped the doctrines, also to the best of their ability; and those who sought to guide the supply of sustaining grace in ordered channels, created the pattern of the ritual which has remained unchanged in essentials through nearly two thousand years of change. But, even if it were possible in the brief space available to give a comprehensive account of the history, the doctrines, and the ritual pattern, of what we call the Christian Church, the question: what is Christianity? would still remain unanswered. For the essence of Christianity is the Spirit which has informed the history, the doctrines, and the ritual, and here again Paul has the ultimate vital word, 'now the Lord is the Spirit'. That means that we cannot know what Christianity is without knowing what the Spirit is; and we cannot know what the Spirit is without getting back to the focal point of all, to Christ, what he is, and what God has done in and by him.

This essential character of Christianity has been finely expressed by Baron von Hügel in a sentence, 'Certainly Christianity is irreducibly *incarnational*'.[2] The implication of that epithet is that Christianity presents itself as being something that no other religion has claimed to be, the living expression of God's complete entry into human life. It does not merely mean that God entered into human flesh at the birth of Jesus, but that the whole story of God's relations with man from the beginning is one of the unresting movement of divine love towards a union in which both God and man might find complete satisfaction. As an incarnational religion Christianity

[2] von Hügel, *Thoughts on the Essentials of Catholicism* (1913), p. 6.

offers as the divine end and purpose, not the absorption of the human into the divine, not the extinction of human personality, not an eternity of bliss after death as the reward of a virtuous life on earth, but a living union with God here and now, a life already belonging to the timeless realm, in which the human spirit, freed from the bondage of sin, enriched by the knowledge of God, will develop to the utmost in communion with all the other spirits moving towards the same goal, the full potentialities with which grace has endowed it.

The account of how God has made this possible is a description of Christianity. In giving this account, Christianity, speaking through those who have had experience of it, makes certain basic assumptions apart from which no religion, however excellent it may be, can claim to be Christian. The first of these is that God, at some timeless moment of divine activity, of which biological time can give no account, made the experiment of creating human spirits capable of choice, capable of choosing to find their fullest life in knowing and loving him, and in being known and loved by him. All the creation myths scattered throughout the earth are but the faint and distorted image of this original truth. The second fundamental fact which Christianity recognizes as unescapable is the fact that, also at some timeless moment, a breach occurred in the relationship which God had set up between himself and man. The act of choice was made by man; he chose to be independent of God, and, cut off from the source of his true freedom, he became a slave, evil became his good. God's making and man's breaking are the two initial acceptances of Christianity.

The corollary of the second of these facts, continually reaffirmed by experience, is that man is incapable of re-making what he has broken. He is in the tragic position of knowing, because of the divine image in him, what is his true good, but is incapable of realizing it. *Video meliora proboque, deteriora sequor*; 'the good that I would, I do not, and the evil that I would not, that I do'. It is an experience in which the philosopher and the pharisee agree. The third fundamental affirmation of Christianity concerns God's age-long search for a way by which the breach may be healed. Christianity holds that God has never recalled his gift of free choice, and that no plan which involves any violation of man's freedom of choice is possible for God, since in grace he has so limited himself. The Christian interpretation of human history finds the traces of God's search in all the broken lights, the dim gropings, the nostalgia for a lost Eden, the myths of a dying god, the awful rituals of human sacrifice. All such things bear witness, not merely to man's search for the country from which he is self-exiled, but still more to God's activity of grace seeking for the response which may serve as a starting-point for the work of recovery. This is the appropriate point of entry for the great witness of an early Christian writer, 'God, who in many parts and in many ways spake in time past unto the fathers by the prophets, has in these last days spoken unto us in a Son'. Not in Egypt nor in Babylon, but among that insignificant people who called themselves the children of Israel, so the record runs, did God find the response he was seeking. He found it in the people called the prophets. Other nations possessed the phenomenon of prophecy, but only in Israel was the link established by the divine encounter which made it possible for the work of recovery, of re-making, to begin.

When the author of that remarkable book which we call Deuteronomy wrote the words, 'What great nation is there, that hath a god so nigh unto them, as the Lord our God is whensoever we call upon him?', he was only stating what was coming to be recognized by the whole of the ancient world. This little people had found God; in Judah was God known; in Zion he laid the sure foundation, the corner-stone upon which he could build something against which all the power of sin and death should not prevail. From that point the activity of incarnation moves steadily on to its climax. The many parts and the many ways converge on the central point of glory—'hath in these last days spoken unto us in a Son', and it is the Son who is 'the effulgence of his glory, the very image of his substance'.

Here we reach the great central affirmation of Christianity. 'God was in Christ.' It affirms that, at a definite point of

[261]

historical time, the Timeless entered into Time. We are shown in the Gospels how God found in a man such a complete and perfect response of a human will to his own will that he was able to carry through to its triumphant consummation the work of recovery, the work that is called redemption; he was able to span the abyss of separation that man's disobedience had opened between himself and God. In the Gospels we are shown Jesus, as a Son, learning obedience through the things which he suffered. We see him at the outset experiencing, but in a far profounder way, the divine encounter which the prophets of Israel had experienced before him; we see him tested in the matter of obedience, and, through the experience of testing, laying down for himself the fundamental principles of action, from which he never swerved. He is shown employing the powers of the Kingdom as one under authority, not as signs and wonders to compel belief, but as pledges of good will, of the activity of grace to meet human need; he lays down the standards of the righteousness of the Kingdom, nothing less than the character of the Father. We see him reaching the crucial moment when it is borne in upon him that the Messiah must die, and are finally confronted by the Cross where he is seen enduring an eternity of spiritual suffering infinitely greater than any physical anguish; in Paul's words, he was 'made sin'; that is, he underwent the experience of the ultimate effect of sin, the separation of the spirit from God.

The central affirmation of Christianity, then, is that the Cross is the focal point of God's activity of grace. Here God, in Christ, passed over to the human side of the abyss, 'reconciling a world to himself'. But in this affirmation the Cross is never separated from the Resurrection. While the Resurrection may be regarded as the most signal act of divine power, as in the deepest sense it is; it was, and is, for in essence it is timeless, primarily the triumphant experience of Jesus, as he passed from the darkness of that experience of abandonment into the full light of God's delight in him, into the new Creation where forgiveness was to be known, and of which he, as the Firstborn from the dead, had become the Head. By whatever means the knowledge of this supreme reality was conveyed to the minds of the first witnesses, the fundamental significance of the fact was that a new thing had come into existence; Jesus had carried over beyond death all the experience of his earthly life; all the love, the faith, the obedience, the stedfast will, liberated from the limitations of flesh, had become the content and character of the life of the Spirit, and, as Paul says, 'the Lord is the Spirit'. So the Christian affirmation of belief in the Spirit cannot be separated from its belief in the reality of the nature and character of that Lord who is the Spirit, and by whom that Spirit is imparted to those who accept by faith the consequence for themselves of God's great act of restoration. The corn of wheat, falling into the ground and dying, has produced much fruit. The risen Christ does not remain alone in splendid isolation; many sons are to be brought to glory; he is the Firstborn among many brethren. So the affirmation of the Spirit is followed by the affirmation of the result of the Spirit's coming, the creation of a new community, possessing the new life of the Spirit, carrying on through weakness and failure God's incarnational activities in the world. The Spirit who spake by the prophets, in the first stages of the process of incarnation, now speaks by the witness of the Ecclesia, that one Catholic, Apostolic, Church, which still, in spite of divisions and rendings of the unity, remains the living embodiment of that divine fact which is Christianity.

So, to return to the point from which we started, the essence of Christianity is not to be found in its history, its doctrines, its ethics, or its ritual; these things, of profound importance, are nevertheless only the outcome of what is essentially, from its inception in the mind of God to its still unrevealed consummation, God's ultimate act. We often hear it said that if we could only purge the Church of its superstitions, of its unintelligible metaphysics, of its overgrown officialdom, we might recover the simple Christianity of the Sermon on the Mount. But this is an unfortunate delusion. The affirmation 'God was in Christ' may appear a simple statement, and indeed is a simple fact presented for the acceptance of faith, nevertheless it is infinitely complex, comprising circle beyond circle of glory, beyond the spirit's farthest soaring. The Sermon on the Mount is not, and never can be, Christianity. It is the authoritative statement of the standard of character demanded of the sons of the Kingdom; but by itself it only exposes still more disastrously the total incapacity of man to attain such a standard. Not until, by the death and resurrection of Christ, the new creation had come into being, did it become possible for God to send forth the Spirit of his Son into the hearts of lost and helpless men; and with the Spirit came life, freedom and power. Those who live by the Spirit, as Paul says, produce the fruits of the Spirit. A vine does not produce grapes by Act of Parliament; they are the fruit of the vine's own life; so the conduct which conforms to the standard of the Kingdom is not produced by any demand, not even God's, but it is the fruit of that divine nature which God gives as the result of what he has done in and by Christ.

Hence any account of the relations between man and God which does not affirm the total act of God in Christ, meeting man's need, triumphing over the power of evil, and bringing eternal life in the knowledge of the only true God and Jesus Christ whom he has sent, falls short of Christianity. There is no such thing as a reduced Christianity. In the infinite richness of the reality which is Christianity there must be degrees of apprehension, but nothing short of that all-embracing richness of grace may rightly be called Christianity.